Real Estate
Tax Delinquency

Real Estate Tax Delinquency

Private Disinvestment & Public Response

Robert W. Lake

With the Assistance of
Thomas E. Fitzgerald, Jr.

The Center for Urban Policy Research
Rutgers—The State University of New Jersey
New Brunswick, New Jersey

Robert W. Lake is an Assistant Research Professor at the
Center for Urban Policy Research, Rutgers University, and a
Ph.D. candidate in geography at the University of Chicago.
He is currently directing a two-year study of institutional
influences on black suburban homeownership. His published
articles have appeared in the National Tax Journal, Annals of
the American Academy of Political and Social Science, the
American Journal of Sociology, and elsewhere.

Cover Design by Francis G. Mullen

Published in the United States of America
by the Center for Urban Policy Research
Building 4051—Kilmer Campus
New Brunswick, New Jersey 08903

Library of Congress Cataloging in Publication Data
Main entry under title:
Lake, Robert W 1946—
Real Estate Tax Delinquency.

Bibliography: p.
Includes bibliographical references   1. Real property tax—
United States. 2. Tax collection—United States. 3. Real property tax—
Pennsylvania—Pittsburgh. 4. Tax collection—Pennsylvania—Pittsburgh.
I. Title.

HJ4182.A25L34   336.2'2   79-12207
ISBN 0-88285-046-6

Contents

Exhibits

Chapter 8   **THE CYCLE OF TAX DELINQUENCY: PROPERTY MAINTENANCE, PROPERTY VALUE, AND VACANCY RATES**

ACKNOWLEDGEMENTS

As with most of the work emanating from the Center for Urban Policy Research, this book is a product of the combined efforts of many individuals. George Sternlieb was instrumental in suggesting the focus on tax delinquency as an important urban policy issue, and provided an unflagging source of encouragement and support. Initial funding for analysis of the Pittsburgh case study in 1973-74 was provided by the City of Pittsburgh through Arthur Young and Company, management consultants. This segment of the study could not have been completed without the enthusiastic cooperation of all parties involved. Stephen Reichstein, Deputy Director of the Pittsburgh Department of City Planning, and Marilyn Cosetti, Assistant Executive Secretary, Office of the Mayor, facilitated access to necessary data sources and provided invaluable comments and criticism on early drafts of the study. At Arthur Young and Company, Pittsburgh, John Madden and Rick Wyand provided helpful coordination of various aspects of the study. Rick Wyand efficiently supervised field operations in the delinquent owners survey; the job of locating and interviewing survey respondents was conducted by Arthur Young and Company personnel. A special debt is owed to Franklin J. James who, as Research Associate at the Center for Urban Policy Research during 1973-74, forged the groundwork for the Pittsburgh case study. Mr. James performed the statistical analysis of the magnitude of delinquency in Pittsburgh reported in Chapter 6, prepared the survey instrument used to interview delinquent owners, and supervised the sampling procedure followed in selecting survey respondents.

Both the national analysis of delinquency and the Pittsburgh case study have been substantially revised and expanded in the preparation of the present volume. Thomas E. Fitzgerald contributed to the historical review of the delinquency literature and provided substantial assistance in reanalyzing the statistical data. William Dolphin contributed invaluable computer programming services in all phases of the project, and prepared the computer maps in Chapters 5 and 6.

Warmest appreciation is due the Center staff who contributed to the seemingly unending task of project completion and manuscript preparation. Mary Picarella provided administrative coordination that could not be matched in competence and efficiency. Joan Frantz, Lydia Lombardi, and Anne Hummel, unheralded mainstays of the Center, typed and retyped the manuscript in all of its various drafts. Deirdre M. English and Evelyn Kuhlman edited the manuscript, and Daniel Sohmer, publications director, skillfully guided the book through publication. All errors of interpretation or analysis remain solely the responsibility of the author.

R.W.L.

Real Estate
Tax Delinquency

Part 1

Theoretical & National
Perspectives

Chapter 1

Introduction

Real estate tax delinquency — the non-payment of municipal property taxes — is a serious, deep-rooted, and growing problem in American cities. In 1974, for example, New York City lost $191.3 million in revenues from uncollected taxes; corresponding figures are $67.3 million in Chicago, $29.4 million in Boston; $14.5 million in Newark, New Jersey, $13.7 million in Houston, $7.3 million in St. Louis, $7.2 million in Baltimore, $5.1 million in Los Angeles, and $4.6 million in Pittsburgh, to list only a few of the cities affected.[1] The ramifications of these figures are played out in three closely related dimensions. First, a large and growing ratio of uncollected taxes wreaks havoc with any city's budgetary and planning process. Increasing administrative firmness is required in a setting where falling revenues leave less and less room to maneuver. Second, any attempt at more than token implementation of municipal title acquisition for non-payment of taxes raises difficult and fundamental questions of private property rights, public sector efficacy in the role of landlord, and the de facto socialization of large segments of urban real estate. These are more properly questions of ideology and political doctrine than of one or another administrative response. Finally, an increasing rate of tax delinquency, as but one component of the urban fiscal crisis of the 1970s, is symptomatic of fundamental changes in the role of the city in American society and political economy.

3

THE CONTEXT OF CRISIS

The fiscal crisis confronting the nation's largest cities in the mid-1970s has generated considerable alarm but yielded few solutions. Where solutions have been sought, they have been typically short-range measures focusing on symptoms rather than causes. Budgetary shortfalls have been met on the cost side with cuts in municipal services and on the income side with requests for state and federal loan guarantees. In all cases (e.g., New York, Philadelphia, Chicago), even these meager steps, though long overdue, have been implemented only after enormous effort and have been adopted in the midst of a crisis atmosphere. At best, however, they can be seen as only stopgap devices directed at immediate crisis intervention.

In contrast, the so-called fiscal crisis is but a surface manifestation of deep-rooted underlying trends affecting the nation's older and larger cities. Demographic changes attendant on thirty years of massive postwar decentralization and the inevitable aging and increasing obsolescence of the urban infrastructure have wrought substantial changes in both the supply and demand sides of all sectors of the city's economy, of which housing, labor, capital investment, and services are perhaps the most salient. Yet, while these trends have been extensively documented, little attention has been focused on examining the direct links between these underlying processes and the current fiscal plight of the American city. *The issue of tax delinquency represents exactly such a link: its roots are embedded in the ferment of urban change; its impact is focused at the heart of the municipal fisc.*

What social, demographic, and economic factors appear to be associated with a high tax delinquency rate? What is behind the individual owner's delinquency decision? How do the relationships revealed by the answers to these questions fit into the overall context of urban development and decline? What are the implications of these questions for the molding of urban policy? These are the issues that we attempt to address in the following analysis.

At the root of our approach in this study is the proposition that the non-payment of real estate taxes is only one component of a broad trend in which private capital and resources are being drawn out of the nation's older central cities. It is the link between an individual property owner's decision to discontinue real estate payments to the city and the overall aging and decline of the city as an institution that we examine in this book.

A further key to our approach is the proposition that while the problem of tax delinquency is most *manifest* in the central city, the *origins* of the problem reside in the broader social and economic system of which the city is but a single element. As Michael Aiken and Manuel Castells point out: "If one accepts the premise that many, if not most urban problems do not necessarily have their origins in the local community, then it would follow that an adequate understanding of urban problems in a given locality would of necessity have to include an analysis of the larger social forces which produce them."[2] This suggests to us the need to look beyond the local scene if more than rudimentary solutions are to be found. The focus on processes broader than the city not only should yield a deeper understanding of the problem but also should have significant implications for policy. If the fundamental locus of causation is external to the city, then ameliorative programs limited to internal administrative remedies are bound to be insufficient. Jurisdictional realities limit city administrators to manipulating *internal* administrative and programmatic machinery. But, while every step must of course be taken to ensure that this machinery does not *exacerbate* the problem, attempts at *solution* will be ultimately unsuccessful unless it is realized that central city tax delinquency has its roots in *national*, not merely local, trends.

TAX DELINQUENCY AS A PROBLEM

On one level, the implications of real estate tax delinquency bear directly on the immediate fiscal and administrative concerns of municipal officials. On a second level, the problem can be viewed in terms of the broader theoretical question of the evolving nature of urbanism as a societal form. Thus we preface our analysis with a brief summary of the impact of tax delinquency as manifested on each of these equally important levels, the immediate and the abstract.

PRACTICAL IMPLICATIONS

The immediate implications of delinquency for municipal budget-making and administration are numerous and substantial. A survey of the more significant implications indicates the magnitude of the problem:

1. Nonpayment of real estate taxes in effect reduces the tax base without allowing for an increase in the tax rate to make up for decreased yield. A high level of nonpayment further indicates that a tax rate increase in subsequent years would not necessarily reduce the deficit but might instead generate further delinquency.

2. Widescale nonpayment of property taxes causes severe budgetary problems for municipal government since actual revenues cannot be adequately projected. This is clearly even more of a problem when payment rates fluctuate over time and anticipated shortfalls cannot be estimated accurately. Many municipalities employ no equivalent to a "bad debt" fund as a buffer for uncollected billings.

3. The retirement of short-term revenue anticipation bonds sold to ensure an adequate cash flow for operating expenses assumes timely receipt of tax

revenues. A rising delinquency rate diminishes anticipated revenues, requiring renegotiation of additional short-term notes to repay previous borrowings, a by now familiar tale leading to fiscal insolvency.

4. In addition to contributing directly to annual budget deficits, a high delinquency rate has a negative impact on municipal bond ratings: municipalities with a high rate of noncollection are unlikely to be awarded the high bond ratings required for easy marketing of note issues at favorable interest rates.

5. In a related area, the revenue sharing formula by which federal funds are distributed to local municipalities explicity considers the scale of locally raised revenues in determining the magnitude of federal monies to be allocated to the municipality. A locality with a high delinquency rate loses doubly since it is deprived not only of uncollected local revenues but also of federal and state transfers foregone in anticipation of higher local yield.

6. Property tax nonpayment generates substantial administrative and managerial problems for local government. Additional billings, collections, record keeping, accounting procedures, and legal action are required, multiplying the personnel and administrative resources that must be committed to the collection process. As the rate of nonpayment increases, a larger and costlier effort is required to extract a dwindling flow of revenue.

7. The facet of collection and delinquency administration that constitutes the potentially greatest commitment of municipal resources is the acquisition and management of delinquent parcels. As local governments more stringently enforce statutes through which the city takes title for nonpayment of taxes, officials must be both financially and managerially prepared to administer difficult programs of property acquisition, management, and dispersal, undertakings that few municipal governments are currently equipped to handle.

THEORETICAL CONCERNS

The current fiscal instability of the older central cities represents a threat to the continued life of these cities on a par in severity with the financial panics of the late nineteenth century and the Depression of the 1930s. The nonpayment of property taxes in those cities constitutes a serious breakdown in the basic circulation of resources that makes urbanism, and the continued existence of the city, possible. The inextricable link between current trends and the very essence of urbanism can be appreciated with reference to the work of such diverse writers as Jane Jacobs and David Harvey.[3]

Basic to these authors' discussions is the concept of *surplus product*: the amount of output produced by one worker in excess of the subsistence needs of that worker. Aggregation of such excess yields a social surplus product. In turn, cities are formed through the geographic concentration of the social surplus product.[4] In order for the surplus product to be reinvested and the benefits of such investment realized, production of the social surplus must be accompanied by *circulation*: exchange of goods and services, movement of people, and flows of investment, money, and credit. Inherent in the social and economic systems of production and exchange, however, are first, the tendency for failure of the mechanisms that ensure creation of the surplus and, second, the tendency of this failure to undermine circulation. Harvey illustrates this point with reference to the commercial and banking crises of the nineteenth century, the "near-cataclysm" of the Depression, and the balance of payments and monetary crises of today.[5] The tendency for failure of the mechanisms of surplus creation is termed by Harvey a "structural weakness. . .potentially able to inflict a severe and perhaps total disruption in the circulation of the surplus upon which urbanism relies."[6]

The current flight of private capital from the older cities, of which the nonpayment of real estate taxes is a major symptom, can thus be seen as exactly such a "structural weakness." The failure of the housing market as a profit generator in these cities constitutes a fundamental breakdown in the mechanism for creation of a social surplus. In turn, disinvestment and tax delinquency represent the resultant dislocations in the circulation of the surplus. The magnitude of private abandonment of the older central cities constitutes a vital threat to the continued life of these cities — a threat that the use of governmental transfer payments to replace private capital as a means of maintaining circulation of the surplus will not overcome.

A CRISIS OF INSTITUTIONS

The problem of widespread nonpayment of property taxes is at a fundamental level an *institutional crisis,* manifest at two organizational scales. At the broadest scale, as we have seen, is the crisis of the continued viability of the city itself as an institution. At a finer scale is the crisis of the institutions available within the city which city administrators might utilize to counter the problem at the local municipal level.

THE CITY AS AN INSTITUTION

At the broad scale, tax delinquency is a symptom of the private sector's abdication of responsibility for property ownership in the central city. This shift can be seen as part of both cause and effect of the changes taking place in the nature of the city as an institution.

As always, American cities continue to function as ports of entry for the poor and the immigrant. But, with the departure to the suburbs of industry and capital and with the development of corporate and institutional forms that have largely eliminated the pushcart and the mom and pop corner grocery store, the cities no longer contain the avenues for upward mobility once available to those on the bottom. This, coupled with the suburban migration of those who *can* afford the move, has left the city with few functions other than to contain the poor and the racial minorities for whom housing opportunities outside the cities are limited through income or racial restrictions, or both.

In the view of at least one analyst, then, the city has been reduced to a "sandbox" for the idle rich and the luckless poor,[7] control of which sociologist H. Paul Friesema has termed a "hollow prize."[8] It must be reiterated, however, that this loss of function is not so much a problem *of the city* as one that is most manifest and visible *in the city*. Cities do not *have* functions; rather, they represent locations in which certain economic functions have traditionally been carried out *by actors* on the economic stage. If certain cities are losing their functions, this means that entrepreneurs and investors are choosing to carry out their activities elsewhere. With the decline of the city as a viable institution, private capital is less likely to view the city as a profitable locus of investment, property owners are likely to limit their (financial) commitment to the city by minimizing both capital investment and operating expenses, and tax delinquency is likely to increase. To the extent that delinquency represents an investor's or property owner's decision to withhold funds from the city and invest elsewhere (or simply increase present consumption), the problem can be seen to be rooted in those national and regional systemic changes that make other locations relatively more attractive investment locales and thus contribute to the decline of the city as an institution.

The Census Bureau indicates that since 1970 more people reside in the suburban portions of metropolitan areas than in the central cities. The very trends that constitute the root of the cities' problem have also caused a shift in political power and a reorientation of national commitment away from the cities. The growth of an anticity, suburban oriented, national electorate has given the traditional antiurban ideology in America a political voice:[9] the widespread popular opposition to extensive federal intervention in New York City's near bankruptcy in the early months of 1976 can be seen as only the latest expression of this phenomenon. In a paradox inherent in the current urban fiscal crisis, the broad-scale national trends that, to a large extent, are responsible for the decline of the city as an institution also serve to militate against an effective national response.

INSTITUTIONS WITHIN THE CITY

At a finer scale, a serious question arises regarding the adequacy of the institutional mechanisms available to the city for administering and disposing of large numbers of delinquent parcels. *If one dimension of the problem is the private sector's abdication of responsibility for ownership of private property in the central city, a second dimension resides in the inability of the public sector to fill in the gap.*

Left largely to their own devices, city officials are faced with the realization that the very steps necessary to generate adequate municipal finances carry the seeds of the city's continuing travail. Thus, for example, faced with ballooning budget deficits, both Philadelphia and Detroit enacted record increases in municipal and school district taxes for fiscal year 1976. With even greater tax increases projected for fiscal year 1977, however, officials in both cities have become concerned that continued tax increases, required to yield sufficient municipal revenues, would in fact have such deleterious long-term effects on income and investment in the city that the ultimate impact would be destructive of the city's continued economic viability.[10]

Focusing on the specific case of tax delinquency, we can trace a similar chain of reasoning through a series of newspaper reports that appeared in the *New York Times* in 1975-1976, during the height of New York City's flirtation with bankruptcy. Page one for January 16, 1975 reported an estimate by the City Controller that the cost of debt service in fiscal year 1975-76 would require a 14.8 percent increase in the city's real estate tax. The report engendered a storm of protest from both tenants and realtors: one spokesman predicted that ". . .the only thing that will happen with the raise will be to accelerate nonpaid real estate taxes and abandonment of buildings."[11]

By the end of March 1975, the *Times* warned editorially that "if the trend early in this fiscal year is maintained, real estate tax arrears. . .are likely to jump by one-third over the 1973-74 level." But the editorial also commented, somewhat plaintively, on the untenable nature of the city's position, caught in a stranglehold between the need for higher real estate tax revenues and the threat of increased tax delinquency.[12]

The realization that the City was losing substantial revenues through nonpayment of taxes[13] caused renewed interest in the procedures for administering delinquent properties. By early 1976, the City Council's Charter and Governmental Operations Committee was considering legislation designed to accelerate collection of delinquent taxes and increase the penalties that could be charged on delinquent accounts.[14] A week later, under the heading "Taxing Delinquents," the *Times* editorialized in favor of such changes and, in fact, castigated the City Council for its tardiness in enacting more stringent measures to counter delinquency.[15] Finally, on October 6, 1976, Mayor Beame signed into law legislation that increased the interest rate on unpaid taxes and reduced by two-thirds, from three years to one, the time the city must wait before it can foreclose on a delinquent property.[16]

Increased stringency in collections and acceleration of the foreclosure procedure are likely to result in at least some improvement in the City's collection rate. At the same time, however, these procedures suggest that *acquisition of delinquent parcels by the city is likely to increase substantially.* If this is the case, serious questions must be raised concerning first, the advisability of the City becoming a large-scale landlord, and secondly, the City's ability to administer and dispose of large numbers of acquired parcels.

A glimpse of the scale of this dilemma is revealed in what may be the capstone of the sequence of *Times* articles on the tax delinquency question, this one titled "Harlem Tenants Join in Assailing Slumlord: The City of New York."[17] The article details citywide tenant complaints of substandard conditions in city-owned buildings, including "lack of heat and hot water, broken windows, faulty wiring, the lead poisoning of children from chipped paint, poorly plastered walls and unsatisfactory security."[18] A spokesman for the Department of Real Estate is quoted as saying that "the agency was 'aware that conditions are bad' but that it was 'doing the best' it could . . . that the Department of Real Estate was 'generally maintaining essential services,' and that they were 'adequate, considering the circumstances.'"[19]

The "circumstances" in this case ultimately refer to the inadequacy of public sector institutions involved in the ownership and administration of residential real estate. The city is increasingly being called upon to provide the property ownership, maintenance, and administrative functions repudiated by the private sector. But it is in precisely these functions that public sector involvement has traditionally been most restricted. The "circumstances" alluded to involve attempting to administer the provision of decent rental housing in a society in which *the public sector is not "supposed" to be involved in such activity.* Housing in the United States is a private, not a public, good. With the single exception of public housing, in which the stigma attached to residence is so strong that the anomalous character of the endeavor is clearly identified, the public sector has been actively enjoined from developing the institutional mechanisms and expertise necessary for efficient and cost-effective provision of housing.

While private sector withdrawal is thus a *fait accompli,* it is still to be seen whether the traditional barriers to public sector involvement in central city housing and property management will be relaxed. For the present, the legacy of tradition is the absence of workable institutional mechanisms *within* city administrations to adequately manage the central city housing stock that is no longer of economic interest to private ownership.

A NONDETERMINISTIC APPROACH

A final important factor that guided our approach to this study was the realization that real estate tax delinquency is a *property of individuals,* not of parcels, neighborhoods, areas, or cities. Several of the following chapters are indeed devoted to identifying the characteristics of high delinquency areas, and such identification has important implications for targeting public policy. The presence of such characteristics, however, must be viewed as a necessary but not of itself sufficient criterion for the occurrence of tax delinquency. For any given parcel, there is an equal possibility that an individual property owner may either discontinue tax payments (and other expenditures on the property) or reinvest in upgrading or renovation. The ultimate decision is derived largely from the flexible and arbitrary structure of urban property ownership. It is not an inevitable decision flowing unavoidably from "natural" conditions.

The question that must be addressed is one of ascertaining why — for a given parcel, neighborhood, area, etc., with a given set of objective characteristics — delinquency, rather than reinvestment, occurs. Again, the answer must lie within a broad consideration of not only parcel and neighborhood characteristics but also the contextual social and economic processes at work. With this perspective, we avoid the ecological fallacy of examining the characteristics of areas and imputing behavior to the residents of those areas, and we avoid the pitfalls of neighborhood typologies and stage theories of decline with their inherent oversimplification, deterministic bias, and too facile prediction of the direction of change.

PLAN OF THE BOOK

Our analysis of the problem of property tax delinquency is cast within a framework of the basic premises introduced here and expanded in Chapters 2 and 3. In Chapter 2, building from the basic postulates presented in this Introduction, we explore a theoretical framework for the analysis of tax delinquency as an element of the fiscal crisis of American cities. Rounding out the introductory discussion, Chapter 3 provides a brief survey of the available literature on tax delinquency, focusing on the change in emphasis over time from a concern with administrative remedies to a search for systemic solutions.

The next three chapters present the results of our analysis, conducted at both the city-wide and neighborhood scales, of the environmental correlates of high tax delinquency areas. The national context is discussed in Chapter 4, where we examine comparative data on tax collection rates in forty-eight cities over a twenty-five year period. Chapter 5, the first of several chapters devoted to an in depth case study of the City of Pittsburgh, presents an overview of housing and demographic trends affecting that city in recent years and an analysis of neighborhood structure in Pittsburgh. The link between neighborhood structure and the distribution of delinquency in Pittsburgh is discussed in Chapter 6, providing an overview of the "ecology" of tax delinquency at the neighborhood level.

We turn in Chapters 7 and 8 to the perspective of the individual property owner. Having established the *context* of delinquency in the previous chapters, we here utilize a unique store of interview data, derived from a survey of 158 delinquent property owners in Pittsburgh, to delve into the *behavior* of delinquent owners. The question addressed in these chapters is one of determining *who* responds to the environment of delinquency by becoming delinquent.

Finally, the city's role and implications for policy are discussed in Chapter 9. Ameliorative steps are considered in terms of the twofold objective of (1) avoiding the conditions that lead to delinquency, and (2) improving the city's institutional capability of administering parcels acquired through tax taking mechanisms.

NOTES

1. Moody's Investors Services, Inc., *Moody's Municipal and Government Manual* (New York: Moody's Investors Services, Inc., 1975).

2. Michael Aiken and Manuel Castells, "New Trends in Urban Studies — Introduction," *Comparative Urban Research,* 4 (1977): 8.

3. Jane Jacobs, *The Economy of Cities* (New York: Random House, 1969); David Harvey, *Social Justice and the City* (Baltimore: Johns Hopkins University Press, 1973).

4. Harvey, p. 216.

5. Harvey, p. 249.

6. Harvey, p. 249.

7. George Sternlieb, "The City as Sandbox," *The Public Interest* 25 (Fall 1971: 14-21.

8. H. Paul Friesema, "Black Control of Central Cities: A Hollow Prize," *Journal of the American Institute of Planners* 35 (March 1969): 75-79.

9. See, for instance, Morton and Lucia White, *The Intellectual Versus the City* (Cambridge, Mass.: Harvard University Press, 1962).

10. Press release issued by the Director of Finance, City of Philadelphia, August 1976.

11. "Record Rise Seen in City Realty Tax," *New York Times,* 16 January 1975, p. 1.

12. "Expiring Goose," *New York Times,* 28 March 1975, p. 26.

13. Outstanding real estate taxes as of June 30, 1975, the end of the fiscal year, were estimated at approximately $220 million. See City Council of New York, Committee on Charter and Governmental Operations, *"Report on Real Estate Tax Delinquency,"* mimeographed, April 14, 1976.

14. "Bills to Help New York City Improve its Tax Collections Gaining in Council," *New York Times,* 11 August 1976, p. 70.

15. "Taxing Delinquents," *New York Times,* 18 August 1976, p. 36.

16. "Tax-Seizure Time Cut to a Year," *New York Times,* 7 October 1976, p. 30.

17. "Harlem Tenants Join in Assailing Slumlord: The City of New York," *New York Times,* 17 February 1977.

18. Ibid.

19. Ibid.

Chapter 2

Tax Delinquency in Theoretical Perspective

INTRODUCTION

Property tax payments represent one of the principal mechanisms linking the private and public sectors of the American social and economic system. As Dick Netzer has concluded, "Property taxation has been the major fiscal resource of American local governments since seventeenth century colonial days."[1]

In this light, the *nonpayment* of real estate taxes[2] is evidence of a breakdown in the relationship between the public and private sector in the American city. As we have seen, not only is tax delinquency a symptom of fundamental change in the institutional structure of the city but also, to the extent that municipal revenues are adversely affected, it directly inhibits the ability of the city to constructively counteract the negative effects of such change.

Both analysis of real estate tax delinquency, and an adequate municipal response, must be based on an understanding of: (1) the changing relationship between public and private sectors over the recent course of American urban evolution; and (2) the manner in which this changing relationship has affected the respective roles assumed by the public and private sectors in meeting the needs of the urban residential population. Only after these crucial relationships have been confronted can we address adequately the question of whether, and to what extent, municipalities should become involved in the acquisition and administration of tax delinquent properties.

This chapter examines the rough outlines of these changing trends in order to provide a general framework for the analysis of tax delinquency. A full investigation of the nature and ramifications of the institutional structure of the American city might itself be the subject of many volumes, and is well beyond the scope of this book. We do, however, attempt to identify the significant dimensions of what we consider to be a fundamental change, unique in American urban history, that has recently emerged in the institutional composition of the older industrial city. This view provides us with a basis for developing a model of tax delinquency that serves as a framework for the analysis presented in the following chapters. In this model, the nonpayment of real estate taxes represents one end product of structural changes taking place in the nation's older and larger industrial cities in the late 1970s and, through a feedback loop, contributes to further structural change.

INSTITUTIONAL CHANGE IN THE AMERICAN CITY

In a dynamic world, new forms of urbanism continually evolve from within the crucible of previous forms. The nineteenth century industrial city was built by private entrepreneurs who saw the city as a locus of profitable investment. The development of "postindustrial America," however, has left the older industrial city a less profitable locale for private investment. Accordingly, investors and entrepreneurs are pulling their capital out of the older cities to reinvest it elsewhere. Evidence of this trend is substantial as seen, for example, in the wave of corporate relocations from the older cities to the suburbs and the "Sunbelt," and in the pattern of inner city financing encapsulated in the term "redlining"

The decline of private sector activity in the older city is not confined to the commitment of investment capital. As will be discussed below, the extent of private sector abandonment of the older central city is reflected in the substantial post-1970 decreases in almost all categories of nongovernmental employment in the older cities. The data on net population losses are indicative of repudiation of the city even as a place of residence by a significant proportion of those who can afford to move.

The withdrawal of the private sector from the central city, however, while substantial in terms of absolute magnitude, is highly selective and firmly rooted in the class structure of American cities. The population and employment declines registered in the older industrial cities represent not general depopulation but selective outmigration of the middle-and upper-class population. While capital has thus abandoned the city, a large resident population certainly remains. A small fraction of those who stay behind do so by choice; the vast majority remain because of financial restrictions, lack of alternatives, and/or an anachronistic dependence on the city as a port of entry and avenue to upward mobility.

The persistent residence in the city of a large and disproportionately dependent population produces a major dilemma in the face of declining private sector provision of jobs, goods, and services in the city. *The dilemma arises from the need for replacement of withdrawn private sector resources with new resources from within the public sector.* The need on the part of the urban working-class population for housing, for employment, and for goods and services certainly remains. But with private capital no longer economically interested in the central city either as a labor market or as a market for goods and services, responsibility for meeting persistent central city demand falls, by default, to the public sector.

While demand is constant, built-in societal constraints dictate and severely limit the nature of the mechanisms through which the public sector can provide goods and services to a resident population. As a result of these constraints, the requisite transition from private to public delivery has not been, and will not be, an easy one to make. The root of the difficulty resides in two principal areas.

First, societal norms, steeped in traditionally accepted ideology, specify the terms of the appropriate rhetoric that must be employed in legitimating both the private and public sector's activity in the economic arena. Access to the competitive economic marketplace is not unobstructed; it must be justified through a claim of performance of some legitimate function. The shift from private to public provision of access to the means (jobs) and the output (goods and services) of production thus requires a shift in the legitimating rhetoric and the motivating force for such activity. The private sector's aggressive profit motive is replaced by the reluctant, self-conscious, and publicly suspect fulfillment of government's social welfare function. This switch in motivation is more than a simple substitution of rhetoric, however. It is in turn accompanied by a downward change in the performance standards (i.e., lower productivity) applied to the providers and in the social acceptability (i.e., stigmatization) granted to the accepters of the fruits of the public "dole."

Secondly, the socially accepted institutional mechanisms presently available within the public and private sectors for meeting the needs of the resident urban population are fundamentally not comparable. Employment in private industry and commerce is replaced by a swollen municipal bureaucracy, unemployment compensation, and burgeoning welfare rolls. In the field of housing, private ownership and management in return for market rents is replaced by public subsidy and management in return for (at best) break-even "shelter costs" which provide no explicit incentive for maintenance of quality. As in the general case, these changes in the mode of delivery do not represent a simple substitution at par. Rather, substantial differences in multiplier and neighborhood effects generated by the two sets of institutions carry with them severe repercussions for the continued economic growth and viability of the municipalities in which these shifts are occurring.

In sum, the result of private capital's abandonment of the nation's older industrial urban cores is a growing demand for local government to fill in the gap. As presently constituted, however, local government is seriously hampered in assuming this role because (1) the necessary rhetoric of legitimation has not been developed — government is not *supposed* to substitute for private enterprise, and (2) the requisite mechanisms and procedures are not available — government is *unable* to substitute for private enterprise.

The dilemma imposed by the nonpayment of real estate taxes spans these two concerns. To the extent that tax delinquency and housing abandonment are related, these phenomena are indicative of the forfeiture by private ownership of the provision of housing as a commodity. In the face of the restrictions outlined above, however, neither the mechanisms nor the legitimating rhetoric have been developed to allow (and to justify) efficient public response to persistent central city housing demand. Property acquisition programs are hampered by limited funds and inadequately developed administrative procedures, and most municipal officials, imbued with the traditionally accepted ideology, are reluctant to push for aggressive acquisition programs. The result is increasing deterioration of a substantial housing stock and abandonment of large segments of our central cities as these areas become caught between private disinterest and public inadequacy. The form of this pincer movement derives from the terms of the traditional relationship that has historically existed between the public and private sectors in the American city. Any program of widespread municipal acquisition of delinquent real estate must be grounded on a full understanding of the nature of this relationship.

TRADITIONAL SECTOR RELATIONSHIPS

The public and private sectors in the American city are linked in a traditionally well-defined relationship. A focus on the terms of this relationship provides a context for identification of public policy options in response to high private sector tax delinquency.

(1) *Private enterprise dominates in economic activity.* The dominant role of American private enterprise has been documented by Andrew Shonfield in an insightful comparative analysis of public and private power in Western Europe and the United States.[3] As Shonfield concludes: "Among the Americans there is a general commitment to the view, shared by both

political parties, of the natural predominance of private enterprise in the economic sphere and the subordinate role of public initiative in any situation other than a manifest national emergency."[4] This view is hardly controversial, but all other aspects of public and private sector interaction stem from this basic precept.

(2) *Not only does private enterprise predominate, it actively engages in minimizing government involvement in competitive activity.* In his seminal analysis of the structure of the American political economy, James O'Connor examines the interactions between (1) the private sector, composed of a monopoly sector (large high-productivity enterprises) and a competitive sector (small business), and (2) the state sector — government at all levels.[5] Within this framework, O'Connor concludes that "it is in the interest and within the reach of monopoly capital to seize all profit-making opportunities for itself and to resist the encroachment of state capital on its own 'natural territory'."[6]

Especially in the case of state and local governments, the private sector exerts control over governmental activities through the provision or withholding of finance capital. First, capital is withheld from activities that would compete with private interests: "finance capital does not make funds available for any economic activity that competes with private capital." Second, the investment that does occur is directed toward those activities that will serve the interests of the private sector: "private bankers normally do not underwrite local and state bond issues unless they are reasonably certain that the borrowed funds will be used to finance. . .projects that expand the tax base by encouraging private investment and economic activity."[7]

(3) *Traditionally, the role of government at all levels has been to stimulate and support the activities of the private sector.* Historically, governmental action has ranged along a continuum from passive compliance with a doctrine of laissez faire to active underwriting and support of private sector activity. In O'Connor's words, "the purpose and effect of state enterprise is to underwrite private profit."[8]

(4) *Influenced by the dominant ideology, government actively disengages itself from the possibility of competing with the private sector.* Restrictions on the development and use of government-owned facilities are spelled out in federal directives. These restrictions apply to direct governmental involvement as well as to private operation of government-owned facilities. A policy directive issued in the 1960s by the Bureau of the Budget rules that "even the operation of a government-owned facility by a private organization through contractual arrangement does not automatically assume that the government is not competing with private enterprise. This type of arrangement could act as a barrier to the development and growth of com-

petitive commercial sources and procurement through ordinary business channels."[9] There is little to suggest that the Office of Management and Budget (OMB) has initiated significant changes in this policy. As Shonfield concludes: "All the evidence suggests that these regulations are very strictly obeyed. The hostility to public initiative has deep roots in American traditional mythology."[10]

(5) *Government enacts its role by fulfilling the dual functions of support and legitimation.* David Harvey indicates that the two "broad aims" of governmental activity in capitalist countries are (1) "to keep market exchange functioning properly" and (2) "to ameliorate the destructive consequences stemming from the self-regulating market."[11] The first of these may be termed the supportive function and the second the legitimation function.[12]

O'Connor provides a typology of governmental expenditures tied to each of these two basic functions. At this point in our discussion, this typology serves to classify public sector activities; later it will provide a useful framework for examining available policy options. State expenditures keyed to the *legitimation function* take the form of *social expenses*: "projects and services which are required to maintain social harmony" and which do not contribute directly to the accumulation of private profit. Examples of social expenses are welfare payments, fire and police protection, and the court system. Also included in this category would be the maintenance and administration of housing facilities abandoned by private ownership. In the other category, state expenditures keyed to the supportive function take the form of *social capital*: expenditures that directly contribute to profitable private accumulation. Private profit arises when productivity increases as the cost of labor decreases. Social capital is, accordingly, divided between *social investment* and *social consumption*: the former involves projects and services that increase the productivity of labor (e.g., capital expenditures) and the latter comprises projects and services that reduce the reproduction costs of labor (e.g., medicaid and medicare, workmen's compensation). Further subdividing the category of social investment, O'Connor distinguishes between *physical capital* expenditures (e.g., physical infrastructure development) and *human capital* expenditures (education, research, and development).[13]

(6) The growth of private industry is increasingly dependent on the support of the state. O'Connor argues that "monopoly sector growth depends on the continuous expansion of social investment and social consumption projects that in part or in whole indirectly increase productivity." Similarly, Miliband concludes that private enterprise ". . . depends to an ever greater extent on the bounties and direct support of the state, and can only preserve its 'private' character on the basis of such public help."[14]

The increasing complexity and interdependence of production generate a need for more and larger physical social capital expenditures. Several reasons can be cited for this increased dependence. First, such facilities are required on a permanent basis but are actually used only sporadically by any particular firm. Second, infrastructure projects are increasingly large in absolute terms. Third, the costs of such projects often exceed the resources available to individual firms. Fourth, the financial risks involved are often unacceptable to the private companies concerned.[15] Although private capital both requires and profits from public sector supportive expenditures, the *costs* of these expenditures are absorbed by the public. In O'Connor's words, "although the state has socialized more and more capital costs, the social surplus (including profits) is appropriated privately . . . The costs of social investment are not borne by monopoly capital but rather are socialized and fall on the state."[16]

The implications of these traditional relationships have direct bearing on the development of public policy. First, it is becoming evident — and the evidence is discernable first at the local municipal level — that the public sector is increasingly unable to carry on *both* the supportive and the legitimation functions. As more and more costs of private accumulation are publicly absorbed, government has proportionately fewer resources for social expenses. Second, it appears that the legitimation function — the maintenance of social harmony — constitutes an acceptable ideological rationale for public sector activity only when it *complements* the supportive function. The maintenance of social harmony is necessary, and is granted the requisite justification, only when its disruption would interfere with private accumulation. As witnessed by the intense stigmatization ascribed to the "dole," the public provision of social welfare (i.e., the commitment of social expenses) is unacceptable solely as an end in itself. In the terms presented above, social expenses are justified only when they complement social investment.

Given these terms of social and political reality, the question confronting the cities becomes one of identifying appropriate responses in a situation in which private investment interest is minimal. Like falling dominoes, the disappearance of private sector investment removes the justification for social investment by the public sector — there is no longer any private accumulation to support. In turn, the negation of social investment to support private accumulation undermines the justification for social expenses — there is no longer any "need" to maintain social harmony.

For the older cities, then, the loss of private investment interest signals the parallel loss of the only traditionally acceptable justification for the expenditure of resources for social welfare. This is of fundamental importance for the identification of viable policy options available to the city in its attempt to counter the effects of private disinvestment. The loss of private sector interest in the city not only detracts directly from the city's viability but also, as we have seen, places severe limits on the city's options by vitiating any justification for social welfare expenditures. Put somewhat crudely, if the function of public expenditures is to support returns to private investment and if private investment has abandoned the city, then the city will find it increasingly difficult to marshall the requisite political justification for first obtaining and then expending large sums for the maintenance of social welfare.

This interpretation provides a perspective for proposals — termed "planned shrinkage" — to limit municipal expenditures in cities abandoned by private enterprise.[17] Recent proposals for curtailing municipal services in large sections of the New York City boroughs of Brooklyn and the Bronx are simply examples of limiting *social expenses* for the maintenance of social welfare (legitimation) in those areas of the city where the demand for *social investment* in support of private accumulation has disappeared through the termination of private investment interest. The criterion for the allocation of social expenses in the areas planned for "shrinkage" is not the demand or need for social welfare but rather the demand for support of private accumulation. As the pace of private disinvestment quickens in the older central cities, it can be expected that the pressure for shrinkage of allocations for social expenses will proceed proportionately.

PRIVATE INVESTMENT AND PUBLIC SUPPORT IN THE OLDER CITY

The vicissitudes of private investment and public support can best be documented in a brief account focusing on three principal phases in the development of the older industrial city. The current plight of the older industrial city can be understood as the end product of these successive stages of U.S. urbanization. Each phase is marked by a pronounced shift both in the nature of private interest in the city as an investment locale and in the associated public support of this investment. The three phases coincide with the periods of industrialization, suburbanization, and regional decentralization. It is not our intent to document the nature of each of these historic periods: an already voluminous literature on these processes would benefit little from yet another superficial sketch. Rather, our concern is with the shifting roles of the public and private sectors at each of these key periods and with the impact of these roles on the equally shifting fortunes of the central cities.

THE INDUSTRIAL CITY

Nineteenth century American urban history is a history of the rise of the industrial city. A rich literature, beginning with Weber's classic work on "The Growth of Cities in the Nineteenth Century," documents the development of industrial urbanization.[18] As Brian Berry concludes: "A new kind of city emerged during the nineteenth century, built on productive power, massed population and industrial technology."[19]

The industrial city was built by private entrepreneurial capital under the aegis of an ideology of "privatism." As Sam Bass Warner, Jr. has developed the term, the doctrine of privatism held that "the individual should seek happiness in personal independence and in the search for wealth" and that the community should "help to create an open and thriving setting where each citizen would have some substantial opportunity to prosper."[20] The city, in other words, was the locus of private investment supported and encouraged by local government. This relationship was basic, pervasive, and of fundamental long-term importance in the development of American cities. "Under the American tradition," Warner writes, "the first purpose of the citizen is the private search for wealth; the goal of a city is to be a community of private money makers."[21] The explosion of industrial activity in the American cities of the late nineteenth century and the accompanying burst of population growth were eloquent testimony to the magnitude of investment in the cities during the period. The attractions of the city as an investment locale have been extensively documented in the literature linking industrialization and urban growth: cheap and diversified labor in large amounts, a readily accessible market, well developed transportation facilities, and intermediate goods and services made available through "agglomeration" and "localization" economies.

That this investment was *private* investment, however, is crucial for an understanding of subsequent (and most recent) trends. As Warner has expressed it:

> From that first moment of bigness, from about the mid-nineteenth century onward, the successes and failures of American cities have depended upon the unplanned outcomes of the private market. The private market's demand for workers, its capacities for dividing land, building houses, stores and factories, and its needs for public services have determined the shape and quality of big cities. What the private market could do well American cities have done well. What the private market did badly or neglected, our cities have been unable to overcome.[22]

The basic relationships between the public and private sectors thus were firmly set by the time of the Civil War. The private sector was dominant and government served to facilitate returns on private investment: "the city was ᴌo be an environment for private money-making, and its government was to encourage private business."[23]

The means by which government saw fit to exercise its supportive role underwent an important change during this period. In the early decades of the nineteenth century, local and state governments took on an active role in the creation of supportive facilities. As expressed in the legislative address of the Whig Party of New York State in 1838, the role of government was ". . . to apply the means of the state boldly and liberally to aid those great public works of railroads and canals which are beyond the means of unassisted private enterprise."[24] According to Shonfield's analysis, however, this high level of public activism gradually gave way in the third quarter of the nineteenth century with the ascendency of extreme *laissez-faire*. If the emphasis in the earlier period was on maximizing active support through the provision of large-scale infrastructural elements, by the end of the period the reigning ideology focused on minimizing potential competititon. Among the reasons cited by Shonfield for this switch, perhaps the most significant was that government involvement was simply no longer needed and, in fact, was viewed as increasingly competitive. After a half century of rapid industrialization, "there was no longer any lack of private risk capital on a sufficient scale to finance large enterprises, particularly in the field of public transport. Private investors were now eager to engage in this lucrative business."[25] Enterprises that a supportive government had sought to provide to aid private industry in its infancy were gradually seen as sources of potential private profit as industry matured. As a consequence, government involvement in such activities was minimized, and the requisite change in legitimating ideology was affected through the courts:

> The courts gradually introduced a restrictive set of criteria which made it unconstitutional to use tax money for anything other than an essential 'public purpose.' The decision on what constituted a proper 'public purpose' depended in the last resort on the judge's view of the relationship between public and private responsibilities. And in the late nineteenth century fashionable judicial doctrine in the United States squeezed the former almost to the vanishing point."[26]

That the courts functioned in this respect to usher in the change from active government support to passive nonintervention should not be surprising. Judges were hardly immune from the reigning ideology of privatism and could be expected to base their decisions on the dictates of that philosophy. This is especially likely to be the case given the close class affinity between members of the judiciary and the business community.

The calamity of the Great Depression and the national emergency of the Second World War constituted massive shocks that required almost instantaneous and far-reaching shifts in the institutional structure of the economic and political system. The failure of the market required large-scale government intervention, primarily in the areas of capital funding and employment, in order to maintain the circulation necessary for continued extraction of a social surplus, that is, in order to maintain and reproduce the social order. Only the massive production effort of the war years allowed the private sector to repair its capability to generate investment capital and to provide employment, and it was only during and after the war that the private sector regained its preeminent position. What was clearly needed following the war was an investment frontier on a scale equal to (or greater than) the investment opportunity represented by the industrial city of an earlier generation. This new investment sink was located in the suburbs of those older cities.

SUBURBANIZATION

Suburban development did not begin in the postwar period — its history extends back at least to the mid-nineteenth century — but the period following the Second World War witnessed the onset of suburbanization on a massive scale. As such, the postwar years represent the first significant shift in the locational focus of private investment from the traditional industrial cities to the suburban communities beyond the central city boundaries.

The signs of suburban growth and central city stagnation were indisputable. Between 1930 and 1970, the population of the suburban portions of the nation's metropolitan areas (as defined in 1970) increased by 210.8 percent. In 1930, 34.8 percent of the nation's metropolitan area population lived in these suburbs; by 1970, the suburban share of metropolitan area population had risen to 54.3 percent.[27] In absolute terms, the greatest growth of suburbs in the history of urban America occurred during the decade of the fifties: over 75 percent of metropolitan area population growth between 1950 and 1960 was in the suburbs.[28] During the same decade, the number of housing units in the suburbs increased at twice the rate (59.6 percent) of that in the central cities (29.8 percent).[29] Nearly 60 percent of the housing units added to the metropolitan inventory during the fifties were located in the suburbs.

The explosive boom in new suburban housing construction during the 1950s was indicative of the magnitude of new private capital being committed to the postwar investment mecca of the suburbs. The suburban attraction of new private investment, however, was clearly not limited to residential construction. Data on employment growth, commercial development, highway construction, automobile ownership, and related items indicate the windfall that accrued to private enterprise with the growth of the suburbs. The wealth of information marshalled by Tobin in his discussion of suburbanization and motor transportation illustrates the trends.

Between 1948 and 1963, manufacturing employment in the suburban portions of the twenty-five largest metropolitan areas increased by 61 percent; during the same period, the central cities of these SMSAs registered a 7 percent drop in manufacturing employment. For these same years, while central city trade employment decreased by 7 percent and service employment increased by only 32 percent, trade employment in the suburbs increased by 122 percent and employment in services increased by 135 percent.[30]

The rise of planned shopping centers is almost synonymous with the postwar growth of the suburbs: between 1946 and 1960, the number of privately developed planned shopping centers jumped from eight to an estimated 3,800.[31]

The extensive development of low-density housing and commercial facilities was made possible by, and itself occasioned, large-scale expansion of automobile production. As Tobin reports, 2 million cars were produced in 1946. By 1953, annual production exceeded 6 million cars and stayed at this level through the early sixties when production increased still further to the 9 million range. The trucking industry reflected similar gains during this period, also occasioned by the rapid expansion of low-density commercial and industrial development. The years between 1945 and 1955 witnessed a doubling in the number of registered trucks, from 5 million to over 10 million vehicles.

In short, the growth of the suburbs engendered direct private investment in land development, homebuilding, the finance industry, highway construction, automobile production, the fuel industry, the building products industry, and a broad range of steel and other primary products industries. Expansion of these industries in turn led to second-round investment in an incalculable array of intermediary and ancillary industries and services for all of which the source of stimulation could be traced to the investment boom occurring in the suburban areas outside the nation's older central cities.

That the suburban growth of population, housing, employment, retailing, and transportation was stimulated and supported by explicit governmental policy (largely, but certainly not only, at the federal level) has been extensively documented by commentators on both the left and the right.[33] With the return to quietism in the wake of World War II (and with the ascendancy of the Republican Party), the 1950s saw the reemergence of a traditional and conservative ideology that placed government passively at the service of private capital. The postwar period marked the differentiation and legitimation of the various categories of social expenditures defined by O'Connor and described briefly above.

As noted above, social capital expenditures contributing directly to the private accumulation of profit are divided between social investment and social comsumption. Social investment is designed to increase productivity while social consumption is aimed at reducing the reproduction costs of labor; profit accrues by maximizing the productivity of labor while minimizing the cost of reproduction of labor. The most significant public programs that contributed to the growth of private investment in the suburbs were federal and state highway construction, federal mortgage insurance, and changes in federal income tax provisions in favor of homeownership. Within the categories of social capital expenditure, the first of these programs — highway construction — constitutes social investment that contributed to large increases in productivity. The latter two programs — mortage insurance and tax credits — constitute social consumption that greatly reduced the reproduction costs of labor. Federal and state investment in extensive road and highway construction provided the basic infrastructure that made low-density development possible and contributed directly to the growth of the automotive and fuel industries. FHA mortgage insurance and Veterans Administration mortgage guarantees drastically lowered the cost of housing by virtually eliminating down payment requirements and heavily subsidizing the cost of mortgage interest payments. These programs made available extraordinarily large sources of funds to which the nation's financial institutions would not otherwise have had access. Income tax provisions favoring homeownership had the effect of increasing the real income of homeowners as well as providing a powerful stimulus to the demand for single-family suburban housing.

Socialization of the costs of these programs made possible the private accumulation of profit on a massive scale. The dominant ideology of privatism continued to reign as public subsidies made mortgage funds available for the purchase of homes built by private enterprise, and public highway construction stimulated private investment in the automotive, construction, and fuel industries. *Of utmost importance, however, for the fate of the older central cities, was that the locus of private investment, and thus the beneficiary of public support, was the suburban ring of each of these central cities and no longer the city itself.* The years since 1960 have seen yet a further displacement of the locus of private investment, this time not simply from the city to neighboring suburb but rather entirely out of the region.

REGIONAL SHIFT

The postwar shift in the locus of private investment from the city to the suburbs was motivated largely by considerations of "easy money." Utilization of the large available expanses of inexpensive developable land in the suburbs was far easier, faster, and less costly than in-filling of small vacant areas or redevelopment of older sections in the central cities. The regional shift in investment patterns that has emerged most noticeably since 1960 can be understood in the same terms. With the "urbanization of the suburbs" following thirty years of extensive development of the Northeast and North Central heartland, private enterprise has found an easier and more fertile locus of new investment in the relatively undeveloped areas of the South and the West. The third phase of modern American urbanization, marked by identification of a new geographic target for private investment, thus encompasses the set of processes that have collectively contributed to the rise of the "Sunbelt." As Brian Berry and Donald Dahmann indicate in their overview of post-1970 population trends: "The South has now emerged as the region experiencing the largest population gains and the center of population has begun to move southward."[34]

The pattern of regional shift encompassing the decline of the Northeast/North Central regions and the growth of the South and the West has been extensively documented in a series of studies by Sternlieb and Hughes.[35] Their analyses of recent Census data indicate that between 1970 and 1975 population growth in the South and the West exceeded that in the Northeast by a factor of ten. Virtual stagnation in the Northeast (a 0.8 percent increase between 1970 and 1975) and a slight increase of 1.9 percent in the North Central region were far outdistanced by 1970-1975 population growth rates of 8.4 and 8.7 percent in the South and West, respectively. Further, the South's gain was clearly the Northeast and North Central regions' loss. From 1970 to 1975, the Northeast and North Central regions experienced net migration losses of 686,000 and 878,000, respectively, while the South tallied a net migration gain of 2.6 million.[36] Of the 2.4 million people who left the Northeast for another region of the country between 1970 and 1975, fully 63 percent moved to the South while 16.0 percent moved to the North Central states and 21 percent went West.[37] During the first half of the 1970s, the South was the only region to experience net migration gains from all other regions of the country.

As in the earlier movement of population from the industrial city to the suburbs, this latest trend of population redistribution is indicative of a regional reorientation of private investment. Evidence for such reorientation is found in data on employment trends as well as in patterns of new private capital investment by region.

Total employment in the South mushroomed by 3.3 million workers during the 1970-75 period, while the Northeast experienced a drop in total employment of 35,700. As a result of this boom, the South accounted for fully 56 percent of total national employment growth for the first half of the decade. While manufacturing employment in the South increased by 23,900 workers, employment in this category in the Northeast dropped by close to a million — 936,200. Similarly, while private nonmanufacturing employment in the Northeast increased by 506,300 in this "postindustrial" era, employment in this category in the South increased by 2.4 million.[38] The astonishing rate of employment growth in the South since 1970 is clear in-dication of a massive commitment of private investment capital in the newly developing Sunbelt. Available data on the distribution of new capital expen-ditures in manufacturing offer additional support for this conclusion.

Data on capital expenditures for new plant and equipment in manufactur-ing industries are reported by the Census Bureau's *Annual Survey of Manufacturers* for regions, states, metropolitan areas, counties, and selected cities. To the extent that population follows jobs and jobs follow the development of new production facilities, regional shifts in the distribution of capital expenditures can be expected to generate important second-round impacts on employment and population patterns.

The changing regional share of total capital expenditures for new plant and equipment in manufacturing for 1960 to 1973 is summarized in Exhibit 2-1. As can easily be seen, both the Northeast and North Central regions captured declining shares of total expenditures at each succeeding time in-terval. With the Western states maintaining a relatively stable share of the total, the investment that was lost to the Northeast and North Central states was captured by the South. Whereas the North Central region at-tracted the highest regional share of capital expenditures throughout the 1960s, by the 1970-73 period the South, with 32.9 percent of the nation's total, had outdistanced the other regions and reported a level of capital ex-penditures that was 46 percent higher than that of the Northeast.

EXHIBIT 2-1

REGIONAL SHARES OF TOTAL CAPITAL EXPENDITURES FOR NEW PLANT AND EQUIPMENT IN MANUFACTURING INDUSTRIES, 1960-1973
(percents)

	1960-64	*1965-69*	*1970-73*
Northeast	25.4	23.4	22.6
North Central	33.7	33.6	31.8
South	28.0	30.6	32.9
West	12.9	12.4	12.7
U.S. Total: %	100.0	100.0	100.0
Dollars (in millions)	53,980.3	100,043.9	92,739.1

Note: Excludes Minnesota for which data were not available for 1970-73, and Alaska and Hawaii.

Source: U.S. Bureau of the Census, *Annual Survey of Manufacturers, 1973.* Statistics for States, Standard Metropolitan Statistical Areas, Large Industrial Counties, and Selected Cities. M73 (AS)-6. U.S. Government Printing Office, Washington, D.C. 1976.

A further indication of the regional shift in the locus of private manufacturing investment is provided in Exhibit 2-2. The changing pattern of capital expenditures for new plant and equipment is indicated by viewing average annual expenditures within successive periods during the sixties and early seventies. The fluctuating scale of national investment is indicated at the top of Exhibit 2-2 with annual expenditures in the first half of the sixties virtually doubling in the latter half of the decade and continuing to increase in the first few years of the 1970s. This pattern resulted in an 85.3 percent increase in average annual expenditures for new plant and equipment for the country as a whole between 1960-64 and 1965-69 and a further 15.9 percent increase between 1965-69 and 1970-73.

Regional differences within this overall national picture are significant, however. From the first to the second half of the sixties, new capital expenditures in the Northeast increased by 70.7 percent, well below the national average. In contrast, average annual capital expenditures in the South more than doubled during the sixties, increasing by 102.3 percent from 1960-64 to 1965-69. The shift to the South is even more pronounced from the late sixties to the early seventies. Between 1965-69 and 1970-73, average annual

EXHIBIT 2-2

CHANGE IN AVERAGE ANNUAL CAPITAL EXPENDITURES FOR NEW PLANT AND EQUIPMENT IN MANUFACTURING INDUSTRIES, BY REGION 1960-1973

	U.S. Total	North- east	North Central	South	West
Average Annual Expenditure (millions of dollars)					
1960-1964	10,796.1	2,736.9	3,635.7	3,027.1	1,396.3
1965-1969	20,008.8	4,672.7	6,728.4	6,123.4	2,484.2
1970-1973	23,184.8	5,234.7	7,375.1	7,627.6	2,947.4
Absolute Change (millions of dollars)					
1960-64 to 1965-69	9,212.7	1,935.8	3,092.7	3,096.3	1,087.9
1965-69 to 1970-73	3,176.0	562.0	646.7	1,504.2	463.2
Percent Change					
1960-64 to 1965-69	85.3	70.7	85.1	102.3	77.9
1965-69 to 1970-73	15.9	12.0	9.6	24.6	18.6
Regional Change as a Percent of National					
1960-64 to 1965-69	100.0	21.0	33.6	33.6	11.8
1965-69 to 1970-73	100.0	17.7	20.4	47.4	14.6

Note: Excludes Minnesota, for which data were not available for 1970-73, and Alaska and Hawaii.

Source: U.S. Bureau of the Census, *Annual Survey of Manufacturers, 1973*. Statistics for States, Standard Metropolitan Statistical Areas, Large Industrial Counties, and Selected Cities, M73 (AS)-6, U.S. Government Printing Office, Washington, D.C. 1976.

capital expenditures increased by 15.9 percent nationwide. The Northeast lagged behind this national average with a 12 percent increase, and new capital expenditures in the North Central states — the industrial heartland — sagged badly, increasing by only 9.6 percent on an annual basis. Again in striking contrast to these patterns, capital investment in the South increased by a full 24.6 percent, more than double the rate of increase for the Northeast. Finally, the last set of data in Exhibit 2-2 indicates the proportion of the nationwide increase in new capital expenditures accruing to each region. The South captured about a third (33.6 percent) of the national increase from the first half to the second half of the sixties, the same proportion that accrued to the North Central region. Disaggregating the increase in average annual capital expenditures from the late sixties to the early seventies, however, the South accounted for nearly half — 47.4 percent — of the nationwide increase. Both the South and the West increased their share of the national growth in capital expenditures in the later period at the expense of the Northeast and North Central regions.

The public sector role in support of this regional shift in private investment is less clear-cut than in the case of suburbanization but is still discernable. The initial impetus appears to have been provided by the massive federal outlays for military facilities, arms production, and the space program, all largeley concentrated in the South and West. Employment data indicate the burgeoning role of governmental expenditures at all levels — federal, state, and local — in these regions: between 1960 and 1975, total government employment increased by 87.7 percent in the South but only by 66.6 percent in the Northeast. On a nationwide basis, the South captured a third (33.3 percent) of the national increase in total government employment between 1960 and 1975 while only a fifth (21.8 percent) accrued to the North East. The public sector contribution to the Southern boom is even more striking if one focuses solely on the federal level: between 1960 and 1975, federal civilian employment increased by 3.3 percent in the Northeast and by 31.9 percent in the South.[39] Focusing on the 1970-75 period, Sternlieb and Hughes conclude:

> On a regional basis, it is apparent that federal government contraction in the Northeast from 1970 to 1975 must aggravate the readjustments fostered by the faltering of the private sector. In contrast, federal expansion in the South continually added to the overall matrix of growth. . . .[In] the aggregate the governmental trends.. .appear to emphasize the favorable southern climate for development and investment.[40]

The new generation of federal funding mechanisms have also favored the South and West at the expense of the urbanized Northeast. A recent Brookings Institution study of the Community Development Block Grant program concludes that "projected CDBG allocations to 1980 show a general pattern of reducing the advantages of certain regions and types of communities. . . . On a regional basis, the most important shift is from the New England and Middle Atlantic regions to three southern regions — South Atlantic, East South Central, and West South Central."[41] In a related vein, Beaton and Cox examine the extent to which the Rural Development Act of 1972, the Federal Water Pollution Control Act of 1972, and the Housing and Community Development Act of 1974 are "subsidizing" the "shift to the Sunbelt" under the aegis of what they term an "accidental national urbanization policy."[42] Finally, John Mollenkopf has noted that local municipalities, granted free reign to use federal revenue sharing funds as they wish, are allocating Community Development funds to precisely those uses most conducive to stimulating private investment — capital improvements, urban renewal, and lowering tax rates — rather than to innovative social programs.[43] A federal policy which supports the development of the "Sunbelt" in general is thus augmented by local government policy which funnels those federal funds into particular uses which most benefit private capital. The supremacy of privatism appears to be undiminished with the passage of time and the expansion of geographic scale.

THE CITY LEFT BEHIND

David Harvey has suggested that "the history of particular cities can. . .be understood only in terms of the circulation of surplus value at a moment of history within a system of cities."[44] Successive waves of capital development have made the industrial city of the nineteenth century a by-passed institution.

As a result of first suburbanization, and second the regional shift, the circulation of surplus has increasingly tended to by-pass the older industrial cities of the Northeast and North Central regions. Both private investment and the public sector expenditures that support it have been reoriented away from these older cities over the course of urban and corporate development in the United States. The economist David Gordon develops a useful distinction between "Old Cities" and "New Cities," the former being those that achieved "maturity" during the industrial era (pre-World War I) and the latter being those cities that reached maturity after the end of World War I. ("Maturity" is defined as the historical period during and after which a given city's population growth rate reaches a peak and begins to slow.) Gordon uses this distinction to explain the apparent selectivity of the urban crisis:

> . . .[The] urban crisis is not universal. It has not spread to New Cities. The current crisis is a general crisis of Old Cities in the corporate stage of capital accumulation. Capitalism has decreed that those cities are archaic as sites for capitalist production. The process of capital accumulation is leaving them behind.[45]

The preceding discussion has documented in brief the historical process through which the initial development and subsequent abandonment of the older industrial city progressed. Each successive stage of the relocation of private investment was accompanied by an accelerating loss of population, jobs, corporate headquarters, and retail establishments from the older cities of the Northeast and North Central regions. The pace of reorientation and change is ample evidence that private enterprise no longer views the "Older Cities" as profitable investment locales.

The result of private disinvestment in the older cities has been the emergence of serious dislocations in key market mechanisms. The normal operation of the housing market has been interrupted in large sections of many cities, in an example of what Harvey terms a "structural failure" in the mechanisms for creation and circulation of the surplus. In these areas, decreasing demand has undermined housing values, destroyed stored equity, increased vacancy rates, made maintenance problematic, and increased tax delinquency and ultimate abandonment. As will be discussed in greater detail below, between 1960 and 1970 total housing units in the City of Pittsburgh, for example, *decreased* by 3.2 percent while the vacancy rate climbed from 3.9 to 6.2 percent.

Private disinvestment in the older cities has an impact on the housing market both directly and indirectly. The flight of private capital directly diminishes demand for the city's realty, thus altering property values and undermining the market. As an indirect result, those owners who, through restrictions related to age, ethnic identity, low income, or other factors, cannot easily withdraw their capital from the market are faced with vanishing equity, low liquidity, and a negative investment climate. Operating and maintenance problems increase as a result of deteriorating neighborhood conditions, adding further to the problem.

From the standpoint of municipal government, the flight of the private sector means an ever increasing demand for public sector provision of jobs, welfare, and housing. Public provision of these services is hampered, however, by both economic (fiscal) and political (ideological) factors. Economically, the demand for public provision of traditionally private services is occurring at the very same time that private flight results in erosion of the tax base required by the public sector to sustain its activity. Politically, the demand for public substitution of private services is occurring at the very same time that private flight results in erosion of the requisite ideological justification for public sector activity, i.e., support of private enterprise.

Our analysis of real estate tax delinquency in the central city indicates that the delinquency problem arises as a result of both direct and indirect consequences of private capital disinvestment. The terms of this relationship are spelled out by means of the descriptive model of tax delinquency discussed below.

A MODEL OF TAX DELINQUENCY

Our descriptive model views the nonpayment of real estate taxes as an element of the behavior of individual property owners. Owners' behavior takes place within the context of housing market processes which themselves are set within a structural system of metropolitan and regional relationships. Thus, the model is comprised of three interlocking sectors in which *structure* give rise to *market processes* which in turn influence *individual owner behavior*. The aggregate effect of each property owner's behavior is then to feed back and alter the initial structural configuration and thus begin the interaction anew. The model of tax delinquency is outlined in Exhibit 2-3.

Based on the preceding discussion, we view the flight of capital from the older city as the initial premise defining metropolitan and regional structure. This aggregate flight of capital is directly indicative of a reduced commitment to central city property ownership on the part of individual property owners. This direct relationship is expressed by the continuous line across the top of the Exhibit and leads in turn directly to the individual owner's decision to discontinue tax payments to the city, i.e., tax delinquency. In parallel with this direct effect, the withdrawal of private investment from the city has equally important indirect effects that contribute to the tax delinquency problem through the mediation of housing market processes and the behavior of individual property owners.

The movement out of the central city of jobs, production facilities, offices, and retail facilities carries with it a citywide loss of population. The outflow of population is not generalized, however, but rather represents the selective out-migration of middle - and upper-income population and an associated concentration of lower-income population in the city.[46] An additional result of middle-class out-migration is the increasing concentration of elderly population in the city, since the elderly are relatively less mobile, more dependent on services (e.g., public transportation) not available in suburban or nonmetropolitan locations, and more subject to restrictions imposed by low income.

The structural implications of these regional and metropolitan trends are indicated in the left-hand segment of Exhibit 2-3. A citywide loss of population contributes to an overall decline in demand for (private sector) goods and services. Selective out-migration is conducive to the loss of facilities and institutions (e.g., financial institutions) that catered to the departing group.[47] The concentration of lower-income population in the city leads, as we have seen, to a drop in aggregate purchasing power. Finally, the concentration of elderly population in the city creates a setting marked by low mobility and

EXHIBIT 2-3

DESCRIPTIVE MODEL OF TAX DELINQUENCY

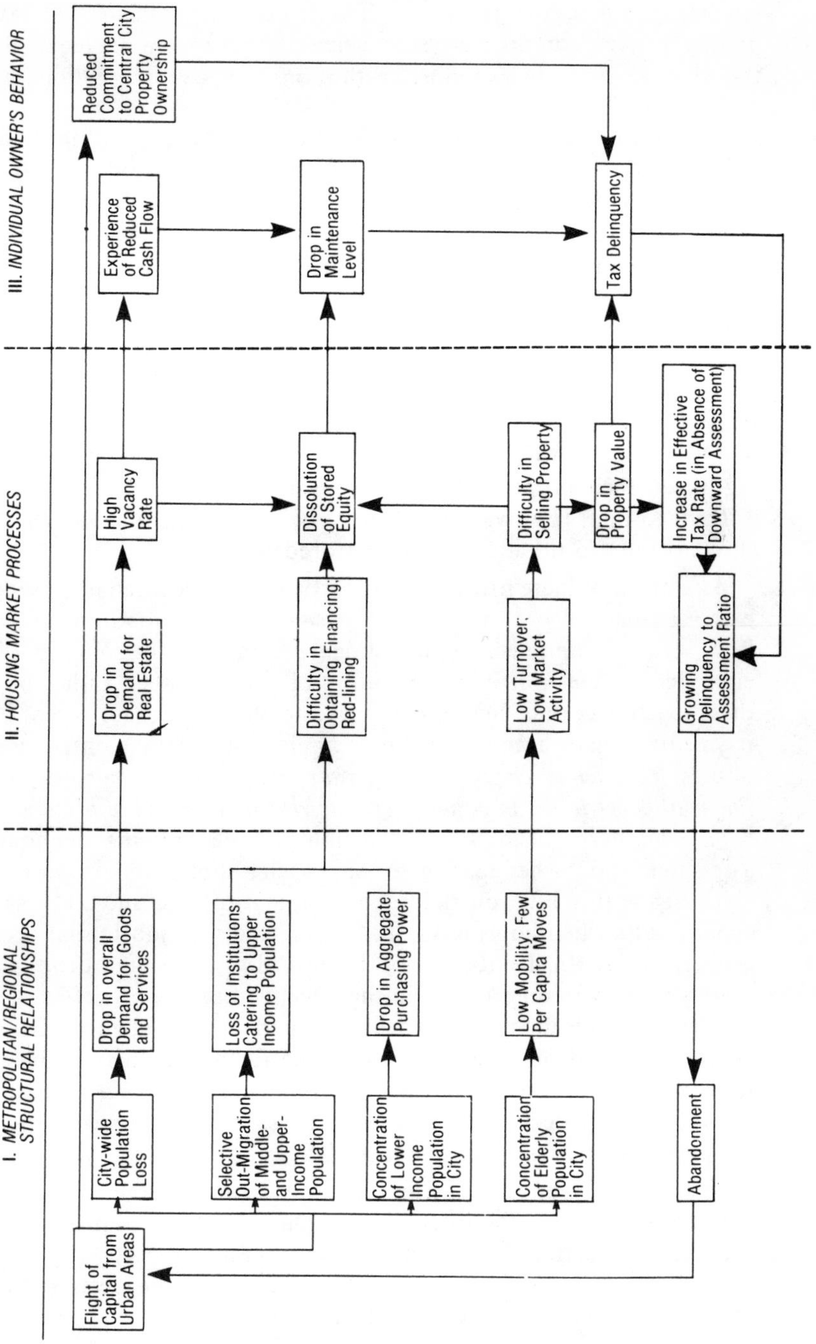

few per capita residential moves. The structural parameters of tax delinquency, in sum, comprise a system characterized by low aggregate demand,
the absence of viable support institutions, relative stagnation, and low
mobility.

The housing market in the older central city operates within these structural bounds. The drop in overall demand for goods and services encompasses a drop in demand for housing. Both the demise of financial institutions and the decline in income and assets make it increasingly difficult to
obtain mortgage financing: institutional demise limits the sources of financing while the decreasing asset base leads to deteriorating borrower qualifica-
tions. Low residential mobility rates generate little housing turnover and
promote stagnation of housing market activity.

Continuing through the links within the housing market, a drop in demand for housing contributes to an increase in the housing vacancy rate.
Similarly, low turnover in the market generates difficulties for owners seek-
ing to sell their properties: suitable buyers or renters become increasingly
difficult to find. High vacancy, lack of financing, and a shortage of buyers
all contribute to the dissolution of stored equity.

As a result of these processes, property owners are faced increasingly with
extreme financial pressure. A high vacancy rate results in a reduced cash
flow seriously diminishing operating revenue. The dissolution of stored
equity constitutes outright diminution of capital assets. Either or both of
these experiences are highly conducive to the decision to discontinue tax
payments, usually accompanied by a similar cutback in maintenance expenditures. *Tax delinquency thus results directly from an owner's experience of
financial constriction in either operating revenues or capital accumulation, or
both.* Long-term delinquency contributes to a growing delinquency-to-
assessment ratio; when taxes owed approach a substantial proportion of the
value of the property, outright abandonment often ensues. The same outcome results when housing market forces lead to a substantial decrease in
property value. In the absence of downward assessment, a drop in value is
synonymous with an increase in the effective tax rate; the effect again is a
growing delinquency-to-assessment ratio and ultimate abandonment. Finally, continued abandonment promotes the further flight of private capital
from the city and spurs yet another round of structural reorganization,
housing market decline, and owners' decisions to renounce responsibility
for property ownership in the central city.

This descriptive model informs our analysis of real estate tax delinquency.
The major thrust of the discussion which follows seeks to document the
hypothesized relationships between metropolitan structural change and individual owner behavior. The final chapter considers options for
ameliorative public policy, explicitly recognizing the burden of the

traditional public-private sector relationship oulined above. Before proceeding with this analysis, however, it is instructive to examine the thrust of available literature on the question of tax delinquency.

NOTES

1. Dick Netzer, *Economics of the Property Tax* (Washington, D.C.: The Brookings Institution, 1966), p. 3.

2. Strictly speaking, of course, real estate taxation and property taxation are not synonymous, the former constituting a subset of the latter. As Netzer indicates, however, real property and personal property yield 80 percent and 20 percent of total property tax revenues, respectively. Netzer, *Economics of the Property Tax*. Chapter II.

3. Andrew Shonfield, *Modern Capitalism: The Changing Balance of Public and Private Power* (London: Oxford University Press, 1965).

4. Shonfield, p. 298.

5. James O'Connor, *The Fiscal Crisis of the State* (New York: St. Martin's Press, 1973); see especially pp. 13-18.

6. O'Connor, p. 180.

7. O'Connor, p. 193.

8. O'Connor, p. 179. See also Ralph Miliband, *The State in Capitalist Society* (N.Y.: Basic Books, 1969), especially Chapter 4, "The Purpose and Role of Governments."

9. Quoted in Shonfield, p. 299.

10. Shonfield, p. 299.

11. David Harvey, *Social Justice and the City* (Baltimore: Johns Hopkins University Press, 1973), p. 274.

12. O'Connor, p. 6.

13. O'Connor, p. 102.

14. O'Connor, p. 24; Miliband, p. 78. Miliband continues: "State intervention in economic life in fact largely *means* intervention for the purpose of helping capitalist enterprise. In no field has the notion of the 'welfare state' had a more precise and opposite meaning than here: there are no more persistent and successful applicants for public assistance than the proud giants of the private enterprise system."

15. O'Connor, pp. 101-110.

16. O'Connor, p. 9, 24.

17. See for instance: Roger Starr, "Making New York Smaller" *New York Times Magazine,* 14 November 1976.

18. Adna Ferrin Weber, *The Growth of Cities in the Nineteenth Century* (New York: The Macmillan Co., 1899).

19. Brian J.L. Berry, *The Human Consequences of Urbanization* (New York: St. Martin's Press, 1973), p. 1.

20. Sam Bass Warner, Jr. *The Private City: Philadelphia in Three Periods of Its Growth* (Philadelphia: University of Pennsylvania Press, 1968), pp. 3-4.

21. Warner, p. x.

22. Warner, p. x.

23. Warner, p. 99.

24. Quoted in Shonfield, p. 302.

25. Shonfield, p. 305.

26. Shonfield, p. 306.

27. Advisory Commission on Intergovernmental Relations, *Trends in Metropolitan America,* (Washington, D.C.: Advisory Commission on Intergovernmental Relations, 1977), Table 1.

28. Gary A. Tobin, "Suburbanization and the Development of Motor Transportation," in *The Changing Face of the Suburbs,* ed. Barry Schwartz (Chicago: University of Chicago Press, 1976), p. 106.

29. U.S. Bureau of the Census, *Census of Housing: 1970.* General Housing Characteristics. Final Report HC (1)-A1. U.S. Summary.

30. Alexander Ganz, *Emerging Patterns of Urban Growth and Travel* (Cambridge: MIT Department of City and Regional Planning, 1968), cited in Tobin, p. 107.

31. Tobin, p. 107. See also: Yehoshua Cohen, *Diffusion of an Innovation in an Urban System: The Spread of Planned Regional Shopping Centers in the United States, 1949-1968.* (Chicago: University of Chicago Department of Geography, 1972). Research Paper No. 140.

32. Tobin, p. 107.

33. See, for example, both Edward C. Banfield, *The Unheavenly City* (Boston: Little, Brown and Co., 1968), pp. 14-17; and David Harvey, "Government Policies, Financial Institutions, and Neighborhood Change in United States Cities," in *Captive Cities,* ed. Michael Harloe (New York, John Wiley, 1977), pp. 123-140. For a more dispassionate view of government policy stimulating suburbanization, see Marion Clawson, *Suburban Land Conversion in the United States: An Economic and Governmental Process* (Baltimore: Johns Hopkins University Press, 1971).

34. Brian J.L. Berry and Donald C. Dahmann, *Population Redistribution in the United States in the 1970's* (Washington, D.C.: National Academy of Sciences, 1972), p. 2. (Throughout our discussion of regional shifts, definitions of geographic regions and divisions are those established and used by the Bureau of the Census.)

35. George Sternlieb and James W. Hughes, eds., *Revitalizing the Northeast: Prelude to an Agenda,* (New Brunswick, N.J.: Center for Urban Policy Research, 1977); idem, "Regional Market Variations: The Northeast versus the South," *Journal of the American Real Estate and Urban Economics Association,* 5 (Spring 1977): 44-67; idem, "New Regional and Metropolitan Realities of America," *Journal of the American Institute of Planners* 43 (July 1977): 227-241; idem, *Post-Industrial America: Metropolitan Decline and Inter-Regional Job Shifts* (New Brunswick, N.J.: Center for Urban Policy Research, 1975).

36. Sternlieb and Hughes, "New Regional and Metropolitan Realities," p. 233.

37. Adapted from Berry and Dahmann, pp. 19-20.

38. Sternlieb and Hughes, "Regional Market Variations," p. 48.

39. Ibid., pp. 59-66.

40. Ibid., pp. 65-66.

41. Richard P. Nathan et al., *Block Grants for Community Development* (Washington, D.C.: U.S. Department of Housing and Urban Development, 1977), p. 179.

42. W. Patrick Beaton and James L. Cox, "Toward an Accidental National Urbanization Policy," *Journal of the American Institute of Planners* 43 (January 1977): 54-61.

43. John H. Mollenkopf, "The Crisis of the Public Sector in America's Cities," *The Fiscal Crisis of American Cities,* eds. Roger Alcay and David Mermelstein (New York: Random House, 1977), pp. 113-131.

44. Harvey, *Social Justice and the City,* p. 250.

45. David M. Gordon, "Capitalism and the Roots of Urban Crisis," *The Fiscal Crisis of American Cities,* eds. Alcaly and Mermelstein, pp. 82-112.

46. Berry's and Dahmann's report concludes that "During this 4-year period [1970-1974] alone, central cities experienced a net loss of $29.6 billion in the aggregate personal incomes of their residents, due to the differential income levels between in-migrants and out-migrants and the greater number of out-migrants than in-migrants." The implications of this aggregate income loss for rent-paying capacity, residential valuation, housing demand, food purchasing, and retail support are explored by Sternlieb and Hughes, "New Regional and Metropolitan Realities," pp. 239-240.

47. David Harvey has dealt extensively with the changing involvement of financial institutions during the course of neighborhood change and urban evolution in Baltimore. See, for instance, "Government Policies, Financial Institutions and Neighborhood Change in United States Cities," *Captive Cities,* ed. Michael Harloe (New York: John Wiley, 1977), pp. 123-140.

Chapter 3

An Overview
of the Literature

INTRODUCTION

In contrast to the voluminous literature on the property tax in general, the problem of municipal tax delinquency has been examined infrequently in the United States. The overreaching questions of property taxation and municipal finance command a mountain of descriptive, analytical, and polemical literature. By restricting our focus specifically to tax delinquency, we have placed much of this literature beyond our purview: our review of the literature is limited to a narrow focus on the question of tax delinquency *per se*. Thus, we do not consider here the indisputably important questions of equity, incidence, assessment practices, or municipal revenue. In so doing, we have accepted the possible risks of myopia in the hope of benefitting from a narrower and more finely honed perspective.

HISTORICAL SKETCH

Modern analysis of municipalities significantly impacted by the decline in tax revenues resulting from delinquency begins with the Depression of the 1930s. The extent of tax delinquency pervading the nation at that time was closely parallel to the well-documented frequency of mortgage foreclosures, business failures, and other measures of financial illiquidity. Prompted by increasingly ailing fiscal postures brought on by other aspects of the Depression, municipalities recognized the need for effective methods of dealing with the loss of revenues from tax delinquency.

The focus of solutions proposed during this period was concentrated on the administrative process. With few exceptions, primary concern centered on methods of collecting taxes more efficiently rather than delving into the root causes of delinquency. Delinquency was viewed largely as temporary and attributable to the unstable economic conditions of the times. As the effects of the Depression began to subside, however, chronic tax delinquency emerged as a greater problem.

Some of the studies performed during the early 1940s began to differentiate between cyclical tax delinquency, brought on by the temporary *macroeconomic* conditions of an unhealthy economy, and the more serious (from the long-run perspective of the tax collector) problem of chronic tax delinquency, brought on by the realities of *microeconomics*. Tax delinquency came to be recognized by some as a symptom of the underlying socioeconomic ill health of a neighborhood, rather than as the disease itself. Later programs initiated by the federal government to spur urban renewal and the like were in part aimed at curing these underlying realities of urban blight.

The more recent history of tax delinquency research reveals a further shifting of interest to the causes of tax delinquency, abandonment, and related problems. As a result, more realistic solutions are being proposed aimed at attacking the causes rather than the effects of chronic tax delinquency.

DEPRESSION-ERA LITERATURE

In 1936, as the country was recovering from the peak Depression years of the eary 1930s, a number of articles appeared on the problem of tax delinquency. Despite extremely high rates of delinquency in major cities during

EXHIBIT 3-1

TREND OF TAX DELINQUENCY, 1930-1935
MEDIAN YEAR-END DELINQUENCY OF 150 CITIES WITH POPULATION OF
OVER 50,000

Year	Delinquency Rate (percent)
1930	10.15
1931	14.60
1932	19.95
1933	26.35
1934	23.05
1935	18.00

Source: Frederick L. Bird, "Extent and Distribution of Urban Tax Delinquency," *Law and Contemporary Problems* 3 (1936): 343.

the period (see Exhibit 3-1), the major emphasis in both the analytic literature and in legislation could be summed up by the phrase "relief for real estate." Extreme leniency in collections was instituted in order to avoid the spectacle of wide-scale public taking of private land. As one county official put it, "The only way this county can keep going is to keep all the land in private ownership, and if the owners are not able to pay the taxes every year, they may at least pay them some years, and if they cannot pay the full tax, we should accept a partial payment."[1]

One of the problems of such a method of tax relief is the failure of public policy to differentiate between those who cannot afford to pay their taxes and those who find it more profitable not to do so. In the aftermath of this type of tax relief legislation, one critic commented that:

> the spectacle accompanying the past few years' high property tax delinquency has been that of a wild legislative scramble to remove compulsion [for payment] in fact, if not in the letter of the law. There has been a mass of indulgence undermining the morale of the taxpayer who pays promptly while extending to delinquents, *without distinction as to their real needs*, every opportunity to continue delinquent under the pleasantest circumstances which can be devised . . . states have responded to high current and accumulated delinquencies with laws marked by the utmost generosity . . . blanket moratoria on tax sales and foreclosures, indiscriminate penalty reductions, and miscellaneous concessions *bearing little or no relation to the condition of the individual taxpayer,* have been enacted in plenty. [Emphasis added].[2]

At the same time that extreme leniency for delinquents was favored, some commentators felt that inefficiency in collection procedures exacerbated the problem. Although the severe economic conditions of the time precipitated the high delinquency rates, it was noted:

> evidence is not lacking that a considerable share of blame for the present crisis may be laid at the door of the clumsy, inefficient, and often badly administered systems for real property tax collection which had been permitted to creak along unheeded in times of prosperity.[3]

Among these administrative shortcomings was a failure to effectively regulate the real estate market:

> The evidence points to real estate speculation and the inadequate municipal control of subdivision as generally responsible for the worst elements of tax delinquency.[4]

Solutions to the problem were not as readily forthcoming as the criticisms of the current procedures. This stemmed partly from the complexity of the problem as well as from a lack of understanding of the causes of chronic tax delinquency.

Jens P. Jensen, at that time the leading expert on real property taxation, made several suggestions to alleviate the high rate of delinquency and to make the tax collection procedure more manageable.[5] His suggestions bear a striking resemblance to those most commonly heard today. First, he suggested that the tax calendar was too long — there was too much delay between the assessment date (the date as of which the assessment takes effect) and the delinquency date (the date after which interest and penalties become effective). Less leniency on the part of tax authorities, he believed, would lead to a more effective collection process.

Another suggestion was the use of installment payments to reduce stringent effects on the owner's cash flow. Jensen felt the extra cost of more frequent collections would be more than offset by a corresponding increase in payments. For taxpayers who remained delinquent Jensen felt that there was no alternative but to levy fines through the use of penalty and interest fees. Lack of such fees would result in a lack of incentive to pay taxes promptly, if at all. Jensen also suggested experimentation with the use of discounts for the prepayment of taxes based on estimates of tax liability.

The body of thought at this time consisted primarily of the conception of the tax delinquency solution as lying somewhere along an administrative continuum with leniency at one end and rigid enforcement at the other. While some recognition was given to the existence of other — nonadministrative — dimensions yet to be analyzed, these factors remained largely unexplored. This lack of knowledge about and research into the causes of tax delinquency was best summed up by Cormick in 1936:

> The fact remains, however, that the unhealthy situation which exists with respect to tax collections in some jurisdictions has not proven readily susceptible to cure by the application of any of the remedies which have been, or which legally can be, made available in the pharmacopeia of tax administration. That some at least of the causes of this situation lie wholly beyond the reach either of the tax law itself or of the most competent administration thereunder is a fact which seems not to be given sufficient weight even in the more searching of the studies of tax delinquency which have recently been made.[6]

POST-DEPRESSION LITERATURE

As the economic recovery from the Depression continued, so did interest in the problem of tax delinquency on real property. It was increasingly realized that the economic conditions of the thirties, which earlier had led to widespread delinquency, were no longer the prime impetus behind continuing delinquency on the part of property owners. Two studies, performed in the cities of Chicago and New York at about the same time, are representative of the period and serve as interesting forerunners of contemporary research.

A 1942 study by the Chicago Housing Authority examined the incidence of tax delinquency in that city and attempted to find the housing and social characteristics of neighborhoods with high rates of delinquency.[7] The highest incidence of tax delinquent land was found on the outskirts of the city, where land was being held for speculation. The second highest incidence of tax delinquency occurred in the blighted areas characterized by "the invasion of industry and the evacuation of substantial homeowners." Neighborhoods with relatively low rates of delinquency were those with large numbers of small homes and apartment houses.[8]

The authors of the Chicago study examined correlations between neighborhood characteristics and the percentage of parcels delinquent (see Exhibit 3-2). Somewhat surprisingly, the study found a *positive* correlation between delinquency and such factors as population growth, new housing units, owner occupancy, and single-family detached units, and a *negative* correlation between delinquency and population density. Finally, there was found to be no correlation between delinquency and the incidence of mixed residential and business units, substandard units, crowding, and vacancy.

This pattern of findings, quite different from that observed in today's older central cities, is explained by the link between private speculation and tax delinquency. The link between speculation and delinquency, and the concentration of speculative activity at the outskirts of the city, explains the complementary relationship between delinquency and low density, owner occupancy, etc. Delinquency in Chicago in the 1940s appears related to the uncertainties attendant on growth, as compared to its relation today to the dynamic of decline. Nonetheless, knowledge of the underlying significance of private investment decisions is helpful in understanding the nature of the current problem.

The Citizen's Housing Council of New York investigated the tax delinquency problem in that city at approximately the same time as the Chicago study was conducted.[9] The New York study sampled 587 parcels in a twenty-five block slum area and found 107 parcels, or 18.2 percent, to be delinquent in taxes for three or more years. Over half of these long-term delinquents had been in arrears for at least six years, thus establishing that the problem in New York was more than a temporary one. The study group related tax delinquency to neighborhood "blight." In line with the reform movement's traditional concerns, the authors linked tax delinquency to the incidence of (1) poorly planned and constructed buildings; (2) lack of green space; (3) overcrowding; and (4) lack of lighting and ventilation. The authors also linked the incidence of tax delinquency to a decrease in the number of immigrants needing cheap housing.

The buildings identified as delinquent by the New York study group were primarily Old Law tenements built in the late 1800s to house the flow of immigrants from Europe. As vacancy rates in these structures rose and rental levels fell, the cash flow situation of owners worsened, eventually leading to either the inability or impracticality of paying further expenses in the form of property taxes, maintenance, or repairs. A survey of owners in the study area rendered the following reasons for the inability of owners to pay taxes: (1) insufficient income of landlords; (2) competition for tenants from low-rent public housing; (3) high cost of maintenance of older buildings; and (4) property damage from irresponsible tenants.

EXHIBIT 3-2

CHICAGO HOUSING AUTHORITY ANALYSIS OF CORRELATIONS BETWEEN NEIGHBORHOOD CHARACTERISTICS AND TWO INDICES OF TAX DELINQUENCY, 1942

	Percentage of Parcels Delinquent	Percentage of Levy Delinquent
Percentage increase in population, 1930-40	.44	.40
Percent of housing units built since 1920	.49	.34
Percent of housing units with encumbrance	.35	.29
Percent of housing units owner-occupied	.47	.37
Duration of owner occupancy of less than five years	.48	.43
Duration of tenant occupancy of less than two years	.42	*
Percent of housing units single-family detached	.54	.41
Percent of housing units converted	−.27	*
Net population density	−.51	*
Value of structure	*	−.39
Percent of business with dwelling units	*	*
Percent of housing units having no toilet and no bath	*	*
Percent of housing units physically substandard	*	*
Percent of housing units needing major repairs	*	*
Percent of units with 3 or more roomers	*	*
Percent of housing units with greater than 1.50 persons per room	*	*
Percent of population native born	*	*
Monthly rental	*	*
Percent of units vacant	*	*

Note: *These correlations were not significant.

Source: Chicago Housing Authority, "Tax Delinquency and Housing in Chicago," mimeographed (Chicago: Chicago Housing Authority, 1942).

The New York study was among the first descriptions of the inner city urban blight process, and was the first to link tax delinquency to urban structural decline. In stark contrast to the studies released during the Depression, the Council came out strongly *against* lowering the tax burden and argued forcefully for public forfeiture of derelict private ownership. The effect of tax reductions, it argued, would be that:

> Some owners might find in this reduction the difference between profitable and unprofitable operations. Yet, by that very fact they would be encouraged to maintain their slum properties longer in their present condition. The longer they could eke out a small profit on the existing tenements, the less would they be impelled to take action to bring the properties into more suitable and more rentable status. Thus, the government would be in the odd position of granting a subsidy to encourage slums.[10]

The Council's argument for a strong public role in improving the delinquency situation in New York included a call for better tax collection procedures (quicker action and stiffer penalties), the use of receivership by the city, stricter zoning regulations, and the renovation of existing structures. The Council's report pointed out, however, that these steps would provide only superficial answers to the root causes of tax delinquency and urban blight. As a further solution to the problem, the following recommendations were presented:

> Accordingly, it is recommended that the city pursue in the future the following policy with respect to properties which are tax delinquent for three or more years:
> 1. That the city sell tax liens promptly upon all properties delinquent for over three years. That it allow postponements where an honest effort to liquidate the delinquency is indicated. That it offer no special inducements to dispose of the liens to private investors and that it attempt to change the state law so it can compete with private bidders for the lien on strategic parcels.
> 2. That, except in unusual cases, the city foreclose upon those liens it owns as soon as it is legally possible. Sometimes, because of a default in current payments by the owner, liens can be foreclosed before the three year period of grace.
> 3. That the grace period for the redemption of a sold tax lien should be reduced, by an amendment of the law, from three to two, or even possibly a one year period, which is ample for redemption by conscientious taxpayers of properties worth keeping.
> 4. That the city keep title to foreclosed properties and, along with its existing holdings, use them as a nucleus for redevelopment of the area. That it acquire other parcels there by trades with private owners. Pending redevelopment or other deposition, it should maintain all of its properties in the most economical manner.
> 5. That the city continue or strengthen its present policy of tenement inspection and insistence upon renovation according to the standards of decency required by law.

6. That when the time appears ripe, the city use its acquired properties to assist either the City Housing Authority or a Redevelopment Corporation to rebuild the area. The city's holdings would be sold or leased to the agency at a fair price to serve as the strategic nucleus of land to start its operations successfully.
7. That the city immediately start the acquisition of delinquent properties and take other action indicated, on an experimental basis, either in the area covered by this study or some other blighted section, and extend this program gradually to other areas as it proves its worth.[11]

In retrospect, the Council's report realistically appraised the value of stopgap solutions as minimal and anticipated the need for more far-reaching measures to tackle the roots of the delinquency problem. The activist role proposed for municipal government was in line with the urban reform movement's traditional position favoring strong municipal responsibility for social welfare. Although the Council's report foreshadowed the current situation by more than thirty years, it has taken the full three-decade span for the Council's recommendations to be seriously considered.

CONTEMPORARY STUDIES

To the extent that references in the literature serve as a guide, interest in the tax delinquency problem was relatively dormant throughout most of the fifties and sixties. The progression of trends outlined in the previous chapter, however, led to what has been termed the "fiscal crisis" in American cities; the recognition of "crisis" has been accompanied by a resurgence of analytic interest in delinquency. We focus here on three sets of studies representative of this renewed concern:

1. Related research by the Center for Urban Policy Research
2. A study of New York City housing market trends performed by Emanuel Tobier
3. A study of delinquency in Cleveland sponsored by the Cleveland City Planning Commission

As part of continuing research into urban housing problems, George Sternlieb examined the delinquency question in the broader context of New York City's housing market processes.[12] Of all tax delinquent parcels in New York City, small Old Law structures (built before 1902) had the highest delinquency rate with 29.2 percent delinquent for two or more periods, closely followed by large Old Law tenements with 20.0 percent of them delinquent for two or more periods. The earlier study by the Citizen's Housing Council appears to have provided a brief glance into the future by examining Old Law tenements in more advanced stages of decline. It would seem as if the City were unable to prevent deterioration of such parcels during the thirty-year interval separating the two studies.

The study's findings tended to negate the hypothesis that delinquency represents a sophisticated form of borrowing money and emphasized the link between delinquency and market instability. The largest and more "sophisticated" owners generally held newer structures with low delinquency rates. Buildings with higher delinquency were typically held by smaller and less financially stable owners:

> Despite the belief among some observers that delinquencies are simply a sophisticated form of borrowing money cheaply, it is the structures which are in the largest and strongest hands which are least delinquent. The older, smaller buildings in the sample, those with typically less sophisticated owners, reveal the highest delinquency rate. This implies that a great part of the delinquency problem may be attributed to weakness in certain sectors of the real estate market, rather than the inadequacies of alternative forms of financing.[13]

The importance of market instability was stressed in a comparison of delinquent and nondelinquent parcels. According to this analysis (see Exhibit 3-3), delinquent owners were found to allocate a higher proportion of rental income to cover operating expenses. As a result, delinquent owners were found to contribute half as much as nondelinquent owners to debt retirement, depreciation, and profit. A fourth of sampled delinquents had negative yields *before* allocating funds to these budget items. Sternlieb concluded that "strictly from operations, a substantial proportion of the delinquents simply cannot carry their own weight without regard to levels of debt service."[14]

In a 1974 study of the New York City housing market, Emanuel Tobier suggested a relationship between property tax delinquency and long-run deterioration in underlying market mechanisms.[15] Tobier argued that increases in delinquency in New York City could be caused by two factors: (1) the short-run economic squeeze of rising costs with an inflexible rent structure; and (2) the long-run prospect of a weakening housing market leading to further delinquency and abandonment.

He then suggested that the New York City housing market may be faced with an increase in the latter condition:

> An increasing number of owners may now be viewing tax delinquency not as a means of short-term financing, which they eventually will repay, but as a prelude to going out of business while, in the meantime, either withdrawing as much capital from the property as possible or keeping further losses to a minimum. In other words, increased tax delinquencies are a harbinger of extensive building abandonment.

EXHIBIT 3-3

COMPARISON OF DELINQUENT AND NONDELINQUENT
RENT-CONTROLLED STRUCTURES, NEW YORK CITY, 1967

	Delinquent	Nondelinquent
Median Expenses as a Percentage of Net Rent Received	65	55
Median Cost of Repairs as a Percentage of Net Rent Received	16	12
Mean Contribution to Debt, Depreciation, and Profit as a Percentage of Net Rent Received	10	23.2
Mean Net Taxable Income as a Percentage of Net Rent Received	−11.1	0.9
Percentage of Structures with Some Commercial Occupancy	25.7	11.6
Percentage of Structures that Experienced Rising Vacancy Rate in Last Two Years	25	11

Source: George Sternlieb, *The Urban Housing Dilemma: The Dynamics of New York City's Rent Controlled Housing* (New Brunswick, N.J.: Center for Urban Policy Research, 1972).

A study prepared jointly by the Cleveland City Planning Commission and Real Estate Research Corporation examined tax delinquency in the City of Cleveland during 1974.[16] The analysis aptly tied delinquency to market collapse:

> Tax delinquent real property appears most frequently in those parts of the city that are badly deteriorated. In these areas, land has lost what is usually considered to be its intrinsic value, and owners have found it difficult — and even impossible — to maintain their properties profitably. The market for land and buildings has weakened progressively and, in some areas, has collapsed.[17]

Unfortunately, the authors examine this relationship by means of a "five-stage classification of residential areas" ranging from "healthy neighborhoods" to "nonviable and heavily abandoned neighborhoods." This typology is used on the grounds that "declining neighborhoods pass through definable stages that are consistent throughout the county."[18] Not surprisingly, the study concludes that "increases in tax delinquency correspond closely with the consecutive stages of neighborhood decline."[19]

To link delinquency with indices of market instability and collapse provides a useful exercise in the causes of the problem. To define such indices in terms of a unidirectional deterministic process, however, constitutes an extreme oversimplification that conceals true causal relationships. Deterministric stage theories have been widely criticized on numerous grounds, most notably for offering no insight into the causes of movement from one stage to the next and no explanation of wide variation in the pace and timing of such movement.

Delinquency in the Cleveland study is viewed as a function of the "inevitable" progression of neighborhoods through successive stages of decline. In contrast, a more appropriate view would consider rising delinquency as one component of the process of neighborhood change which itself is a function of housing market instability and collapse. The important research question then becomes one of identifying the causes of market collapse rather than categorizing neighborhoods according to "stage" of decline.

A final problem with neighborhood stage theories is that they tend to conceal the significance of the behavior of key actors in the housing market. Decline is viewed as an inevitable "natural" trend, while rehabilitation or renewal is viewed as an artificial intrusion into an otherwise remorseless process. A less deterministic approach sees the decisions that contribute to decline to be just as volitional as the decisions that lead to reinvestment. To view decline as a function of "natural" market processes while renewal is deemed a function of artificial intrusion by policymakers frees those who benefit from decline from responsibility for their actions and encumbers policy makers with the onus of "tampering" with the market.

SUMMARY

The historical progression of the tax delinquency literature indicates that attempts at analysis have generally derived from the heightening of the immediate urgency of the problem. Emphasis has shifted over time from a search for administrative solutions to a search for underlying causes. Suggested ameliorative strategies, however, do not appear to have developed apace. The land banking program proposed in the 1976 Cleveland study appears not to differ substantially from the Citizen's Housing Council recommendations made in New York in 1941. More importantly, no study of the problem to date has adequately examined the explicit relationship between tax delinquency and the broader processes of private disinvestment and consequent disruption of the urban system. Entrenched in an administrative and procedural perspective, most studies to date have failed to consider tax delinquency as a principal component of the breakdown in the market mechanisms that provide the underpinning for continued reproduction of the urban order. The present study serves as an initial attempt to fill this void.

NOTES

1. Paul W. Wagner, "Utilization of Reverted Tax Delinquent Land in Rural Areas," *Law and Contemporary Problems* 3 (1936): 453.

2. Wade H. Smith, "Recent Legislative Indulgences to Delinquent Taxpayers," *Law and Contemporary Problems* 3 (1936): 371-372.

3. Frederick L. Bird, "Extent and Distribution of Urban Tax Delinquency," *Law and Contemporary Problems* 3 (1936): 345.

4. David F. Cavers, "Foreword to Vol. III, No. 3," *Law and Contemporary Problems* 3 (1936): 335.

5. Jens P. Jensen, "The Tax Calendar and the Use of Installment Payments, Penalties and Discounts," *Law and Contemporary Problems* 3 (1936).

6. Philip H. Cormick, "Impediments to Tax Collection Outside the Tax Law," *Law and Contemporary Problems* 3 (1936): 445.

7. Chicago Housing Authority, "Tax Delinquency and Housing in Chicago," mimeographed (Chicago: Chicago Housing Authority, 1942).

8. Chicago Housing Authority, p. 8.

9. Citizen's Housing Council of New York, "The Relation of Tax Delinquency in Slum Areas to the Housing Problem," mimeographed (New York: Citizen's Housing Council of New York, Inc., 1941).

10. Citizen's Housing Council, p. 22.

11. Citizen's Housing Council, pp. 4-5.

12. George Sternlieb, *The Urban Housing Dilemma: The Dynamics of New York City's Rent Controlled Housing* (New Brunswick, N.J.: Center for Urban Policy Research, 1972).

13. Ibid., p. 418.

14. Ibid., p. 432.

15. Emanuel Tobier, "Aspects of the New York City Housing Market," mimeographed, 1974.

16. Susan Olson and M. Leanne Lachman, *Tax Delinquency in the Inner City* (Lexington, Mass: D.C. Heath, 1976).

17. Ibid., p. 20.

18. Ibid., p. 69.

19. Ibid., p. 79.

Chapter 4

Tax Delinquency
in National Perspective

INTRODUCTION

With this chapter, we begin an assessment of the magnitude and characteristics of tax delinquency by considering the comparative experience of a national group of forty-eight cities. As will be delineated in greater detail below, our definition of tax delinquency in this chapter is the percent of a city's property tax levy uncollected in a given year.

Preceding chapters have made reference to the fiscal problems of "older central cities." An examination of tax delinquency rates among a nationwide group of forty-eight selected cities provides abundant evidence that the delinquency problem affects cities without regard to population size and geographic location. Considering the twenty-five-year period from 1950 to 1974, the five cities with the highest delinquency rates among this national group are Houston, Chicago, Newark, Boston, and Portland, Oregon. These cities span the country and range in population size from Newark with 382,000 (as of 1970) to Chicago with over 3 million. In the single year 1970, these five cities jointly lost approximately $86 million in revenues from taxes levied but uncollected during that year.

While the problem is thus demonstrably grave, little empirical evidence is currently available as to its true scope and even less is known about the environmental and demographic factors associated with high rates of tax delinquency. We aim in this chapter to provide an overview of the delinquency problem at the national scale. Is tax delinquency a localized or a widespread problem? What can be considered a "normal" level of non-payment? Given the national experience in collections, what level of noncollection should be considered problematic? How has the scale of the problem changed over time? Finally, to what extent is it possible to identify common characteristics of high-delinquency cities?

COMPARATIVE DELINQUENCY DATA

The rate of tax delinquency is an important indicator of the fiscal posture of a municipality. The ability of a city to collect property taxes is considered by financial institutions to be an essential determinant of its fiscal stability. For this reason information on tax collections is made available to rating agencies in determining a municipality's credit rating. Because revenue sources for cities are considered of such importance in this determination, a fundamental criterion of evaluation is "(t)he community's historical tax collection record, including levies, collections and delinquencies."[1] One observer has noted that tax collection seen as a percentage of assessments is an important item in general obligation analysis and he suggests that this should not fall below 95 percent.[2]

The measure of tax delinquency used in this section of our analysis was compiled from raw data published in Moody's Municipal and Government Manual for the years 1950 to 1974.[3] These data are among the criteria employed by Moody's in assigning municipal bond ratings. For each city, Moody's provides data on total property taxes levied and the dollar amount and percent of taxes actually collected on both a current year and cumulative basis. For purposes of our analysis, the percent of each current year's taxes collected was recorded and subtracted from 100 to yield the percent of taxes uncollected for each year for each city.

Several unavoidable drawbacks associated with this measure of tax delinquency deserve mention. First, the data refer only to *current* year's collections; the possibility — and likelihood, in many cases — of collection in subsequent years are not accounted for by the data. Second, since Moody's publishes the data as reported by each city, danger of variation in accounting and reporting procedures among cities is unavoidably present. For example, the Moody's data on the total tax levy and the dollar value of taxes collected for Chicago represent an amalgamation of both real estate (real property) taxes and a municipal tax on personal property held by business firms (i.e., nonresidential establishments). While delinquency on real estate taxes is relatively low in Chicago, administrative peculiarities in the method of assessing and collecting the personal property tax result in the appearance of a relatively high level of nonpayment. Third, definitional inconsistency over time is an unavoidable concern for data covering a twenty-five-year period. Fourth, several cities have undergone significant changes in political structure, fiscal policy, accounting procedure, and geographical extent, thereby significantly altering taxing procedure over time. Finally, published figures are subject to change as adjustments are made from year to year after information is updated and corrected.

Despite these shortcomings, the Moody's data constitute the most comprehensive source available for analyzing changing patterns of delinquency rates across a large number of cities over an extended time period. In addition, an understanding of the drawbacks of the data led us to compensate in the direction of conservatism. In order not to violate the need for consistency over time numerous cities were deleted from the analysis. A change from calendar year to fiscal year accounting, or absorption of a city's tax collection function by a surrounding county government, are examples of changes that would obviate comparability of data over time and thus required elimination of the city in question from the analysis. Where discrepancies appeared, we contacted the municipal agency responsible for tax collections in each city to determine the best estimates of the collection rates for the years in question.

Given the importance of the above considerations, a prime concern in selection of the forty-eight cities examined in this analysis was the reliability of delinquency data. In addition, however, cities were selected to ensure broad representation by size, age, functional characteristics, and geographic distribution. As a result of this selection procedure, the forty-eight cities included in our analysis do not in any way constitute a randomly selected sample. The group of forty-eight cities does, however, provide a fair representation of the national system of cities.

Exhibit 4-1 provides a few selected characteristics of the cities included in the analysis. The cities range in size from Wheeling, West Virginia, the smallest with 48,000 people in 1970, to New York City with 8 million. In terms of total housing units, New York City is again the largest and the list ranges all the way down to Fargo, North Dakota with fewer than 18,000 units. The broad range of city sizes ensures that cities with all levels of population diversity, housing mix, and bureaucratic complexity are included in the analysis.

Median 1970 family income in the selected cities ranges from a high of over $11,000 in Kansas City, Missouri to a low of $7,300 in Miami, Florida. To the extent that income mirrors housing value, the spread of median incomes in the sample ensures adequate representation of a broad range of housing market conditions, consumer purchasing power, and levels of housing maintenance. Similarly, the significant variation in housing vacancy rates of the selected cities, ranging from a low of 2.8 percent in New York

EXHIBIT 4-1

SELECTED CHARACTERISTICS OF CITIES INCLUDED IN COMPARATIVE
ANALYSIS OF DELINQUENCY, 1970

City	Total Population	Median Family Income	Total Housing Units	Housing Vacancy Rate	Effective Property Tax, 1971[a]
Atlanta, Ga.	496,973	8,168	170,898	5.0	1.8
Baltimore, Md.	905,759	8,815	305,521	5.3	3.3
Birmingham, Ala.	300,910	7,737	105,370	5.1	0.8
Boston, Mass.	641,071	9,133	232,448	6.4	4.2
Bridgeport, Conn.	156,542	9,849	54,675	3.2	1.3
Cedar Rapids, Iowa	110,642	10,900	37,979	5.9	3.2
Charleston, S. Car.	66,945	7,920	23,436	5.6	1.3
Charlotte, N. Car.	241,178	9,564	80,648	4.5	1.7
Chicago, Ill.	3,366,957	10,242	1,208,771	5.8	2.5
Cincinnati, Ohio	452,524	8,894	172,551	7.3	1.6
Cleveland, Ohio	750,903	9,107	264,100	5.9	1.9
Dallas, Tex.	844,401	10,019	303,328	7.4	1.6
Denver, Colo.	514,678	9,654	193,765	4.3	1.9
Des Moines, Iowa	200,587	10,239	72,349	5.3	3.1
Detroit, Mich.	1,511,482	10,045	529,185	5.9	2.4
Fargo, N. Dak.	53,365	10,175	17,562	4.3	2.1
Fort Wayne, Ind.	117,671	10,401	61,377	6.1	2.6
Hartford, Conn.	158,017	9,108	58,495	4.2	3.9
Houston, Tex.	1,232,740	9,876	427,859	7.9	1.5
Indianapolis, Ind.	744,624	10,754	252,421	6.6	2.5
Kansas City, Mo.	507,087	11,108	192,352	8.3	n.a.
Little Rock, Ark.	132,483	8,786	48,542	6.6	1.1
Los Angeles, Calif.	2,816,061	10,535	1,077,316	4.6	2.5
Louisville, Ken.	361,472	8,564	129,689	5.4	0.9
Memphis, Tenn.	623,530	8,646	197,982	4.0	1.8
Miami, Fla.	334,859	7,304	125,278	3.6	1.5
Milwaukee, Wisc.	717,099	10,262	246,065	3.7	4.1
New Orleans, La.	593,471	7,445	208,524	7.9	0.6
New York, N.Y.	7,894,862	9,919	2,924,384	2.8	1.7
Newark, N.J.	382,417	7,735	127,424	4.9	5.8
Norfolk, Va.	307,951	7,821	91,061	4.7	1.3
Oakland, Calif.	361,561	9,626	146,615	5.3	2.6
Oklahoma City, Okla.	366,232	9,563	138,370	8.3	1.5
Philadelphia, Pa.	1,948,609	9,366	673,524	4.6	2.0
Phoenix, Ariz.	581,562	9,956	195,036	4.5	1.5
Pittsburgh, Pa.	520,117	8,800	189,840	6.2	2.3
Portland, Ore.	382,619	9,794	152,064	4.6	2.4
Richmond, Va.	249,621	8,673	87,083	4.9	1.6
St. Louis, Mo.	622,236	8,182	238,485	9.6	1.8
Salt Lake City, Utah	175,885	8,817	65,664	3.9	1.5
San Francisco, Calif.	715,674	10,503	310,402	4.9	2.2

EXHIBIT 4-1 (cont.)

Seattle, Wash.	530,831	11,037	221,973	7.1	1.3
Spokane, Wash.	170,516	9,137	64,338	5.9	1.5
Toledo, Ohio	383,818	10,474	130,340	3.8	1.5
Topeka, Kans.	125,011	9,652	43,700	3.9	2.6
Tucson, Ariz.	262,933	8,759	89,309	5.6	1.6
Wheeling, W. Va.	48,188	8,575	17,862	5.9	n.a.
Youngstown, Ohio	139,759	9,078	46,543	4.0	1.7

Notes: a. Effective property tax rate for single-family houses, 1971.
n.a. = not available.

Sources: U.S. Census of Population and Housing, 1970; U.S. Census of Governments, 1971.

City to a high of 9.6 percent in St. Louis, Missouri, guarantees that the impact of this highly important variable will be adequately considered. By the same token, the sample includes considerable variation in effective property tax rates, ranging from 0.6 in New Orleans, Louisiana to 5.8 in Newark, New Jersey.

THE MAGNITUDE OF DELINQUENCY OVER TIME

Trends in delinquency rates in the forty-eight cities over the twenty-five year period from 1950 to 1974 are tabulated in Exhibit 4-2. In order to minimize possible distortions due to a peculiarity in collection or reporting procedures that might have occurred in a particular city in a particular year, we computed the average annual percent of property taxes uncollected in each city for each successive five-year interval between 1950 and 1974. These are the data reported in Exhibit 4-2.

Comparison of delinquency rates across cities and over time reveals several interesting findings. Most noticeable is the relatively large variation among cities at any time peiod. For the full twenty-five year period, delinquency rates in the selected cities range from lows of less than one percent in the smaller Midwestern centers of Denver, Milwaukee, Des Moines, and Cedar Rapids to highs in the ten percent range in Newark, Boston, Chicago, and Houston.

The median delinquency rate for the full 1950-74 period is 3.0 percent. It can be argued that this may be the "normal level" of noncollection of a current year's tax levy. By definition, half the cities in the national group reported an average twenty-five-year delinquency rate above this figure. Both the number of cities and the length of time represented in this figure suggest that the 3.0 percent mark obtains even when cyclical swings and

EXHIBIT 4-2

AVERAGE ANNUAL UNCOLLECTED PROPERTY TAXES IN FORTY-EIGHT
CITIES, 1950 to 1974

	Average Percent Uncollected					
City	*1950-54*	*1955-59*	*1960-64*	*1965-69*	*1970-74*	*1950-74*
Atlanta, Ga.	3.4	2.5	2.3	2.2	6.4	3.2
Baltimore, Md.	3.1	2.8	2.7	2.7	3.2	2.9
Birmingham, Ala.	1.1	0.0	0.0	0.0	0.0	0.2
Boston, Mass.	8.4	9.5	7.8	8.3	12.6	9.2
Bridgeport, Conn.	0.6	1.2	1.9	2.3	4.3	2.1
Cedar Rapids, Iowa	0.0	0.3	0.9	0.2	0.8	0.4
Charleston, S. Car.	n.a.	5.3	7.5	7.1	7.7	6.7
Charlotte, N. Car.	4.9	4.2	4.6	4.1	2.6	4.1
Chicago, Ill.	8.5	10.1	10.0	10.9	14.8	10.9
Cincinnati, Ohio	1.4	1.6	2.2	2.4	2.7	2.1
Cleveland, Ohio	2.0	2.2	1.5	2.7	5.1	2.5
Dallas, Texas	1.9	1.5	1.0	1.0	1.6	1.4
Denver, Colo.	1.3	1.1	0.4	0.3	0.4	0.7
Des Moines, Iowa	0.3	n.a.	0.3	0.5	1.0	0.5
Detroit, Mich.	1.1	1.5	2.6	3.2	2.5	2.2
Fargo, N. Dak.	6.9	1.5	5.4	5.0	2.8	4.2
Fort Wayne, Ind.	1.8	6.3	3.9	n.a.	1.7	3.0
Hartford, Conn.	1.0	1.3	1.8	1.6	2.5	1.6
Houston, Texas	13.7	12.2	11.0	8.8	9.4	11.0
Indianapolis, Ind.	1.5	0.6	3.9	2.7	1.8	2.1
Kansas City, Mo.	2.7	3.1	2.6	2.1	2.9	2.7
Little Rock, Ark.	n.a.	2.7	3.6	2.9	2.7	3.0
Los Angeles, Calif.	1.5	1.4	1.9	2.7	2.5	2.0
Louisville, Ken.	7.5	6.9	5.0	3.9	4.1	5.5
Memphis, Tenn.	3.0	3.7	3.0	2.3	2.3	3.0
Miami, Fla.	1.4	0.6	1.0	1.3	3.2	1.5
Milwaukee, Wisc.	0.5	0.4	0.7	0.7	0.9	0.7
New Orleans, La.	1.6	1.4	2.4	1.8	2.1	1.9
New York, N.Y.	5.2	4.1	4.3	5.4	6.2	5.1
Newark, N.J.	5.8	7.1	8.7	11.7	12.8	9.2
Norfolk, Va.	6.7	6.8	6.4	4.4	3.1	5.4
Oakland, Calif.	1.2	1.3	1.9	2.9	3.2	2.1
Oklahoma City, Okla.	0.5	0.5	1.7	4.2	5.6	2.5
Philadelphia, Pa.	2.9	3.1	3.0	3.0	3.4	3.1
Phoenix, Ariz.	2.2	2.2	2.7	2.0	1.3	2.1
Pittsburgh, Pa.	6.3	5.3	4.5	5.0	9.2	6.1
Portland, Ore.	6.7	8.7	6.3	7.9	7.5	7.5
Richmond, Va.	5.0	4.3	3.1	3.2	3.3	3.7
St. Louis, Mo.	5.2	5.8	5.4	5.4	6.9	5.8
Salt Lake City, Utah	6.1	6.2	2.1	1.6	3.5	3.8
San Francisco, Calif.	0.8	0.9	1.2	2.1	1.5	1.3
Seattle, Wash.	2.3	1.8	2.7	2.6	5.7	3.0

EXHIBIT 4-2 (cont.)

Spokane, Wash.	2.8	2.7	3.5	4.1	5.0	3.6
Toledo, Ohio	2.7	2.5	3.3	2.8	2.7	2.8
Topeka, Kansas	0.7	2.4	1.0	1.3	1.2	1.3
Tucson, Ariz.	n.a.	1.1	2.0	4.0	5.4	3.0
Wheeling, W. Va.	n.a.	5.8	3.1	2.4	n.a.	3.8
Youngstown, Ohio	3.7	3.5	4.9	6.2	4.7	4.6

Note: n.a. = Data available for fewer than three years in the five year period.

Source: Compiled from data in *Moody's Municipal and Government Manual* (New York: Moody's Investors Services, Inc.) Annual editions, 1950 to 1975.

local peculiarities have been averaged out. A noncollection rate above 3.0 percent may thus be considered problematic.

Yet another finding that emerges from the data in Exhibit 4-2 is the relative overall stability in the scope of the problem in particular cities over time. While evident fluctuations occur, a high delinquency rate at the beginning of the period is usually maintained throughout the twenty-five year span (e.g., Boston, Chicago, New York, Newark, Pittsburgh, Portland, Oregon, etc.); likewise, relatively low delinquency in the 1950-54 period is generally maintained at a similarly low level in each successive time period (e.g., Dallas, Denver, Los Angeles, New Orleans, etc.).

Within this broad context, however, a comparison of average annual delinquency over the full twenty-five year period indicates a substantial increase in the overall extent of the problem over time. Comparing average annual delinquency rates in 1950-54 with those recorded in 1970-74, 60 percent of the 48 cities showed an increase from the first five to the last five years of the period (Exhibit 4-3).

In numerous cities, the rate of tax delinquency increased consistently over the *entire* twenty-five-year period. This list includes cities such as Bridgeport, Cincinnati, Oakland, Oklahoma City, and Tucson, which experienced relatively low delinquency levels in the 1950-54 period, as well as others, such as Chicago and Newark, which reported high delinquency rates throughout the period. Overall, the median average annual percent of taxes uncollected for the entire sample of forty-eight cities increased from 2.7 percent in 1950-54 to 3.2 percent in 1970-74.

CHARACTERISTICS OF HIGH DELINQUENCY CITIES

Initial insights into the characteristics of high delinquency cities may be gained by comparison of the highest and lowest delinquency cities. Focusing

EXHIBIT 4-3

CHANGE IN AVERAGE ANNUAL PROPERTY TAX DELINQUENCY IN A
SELECTED GROUP OF FORTY-EIGHT CITIES, 1950-54 to 1970-74

Direction of Change	Frequency	
	Number	Percent
Increase	29	60.4
Decrease	14	29.2
No Change	1	2.1
Incomplete Data	4	8.3
TOTAL	48	100.0

Source: Compiled from data in Moody's Municipal and Government Manual (see Exhibit 4-2).

on average delinquency rates for the most recent period, 1970-74, the twelve
cities falling into the highest quartile can, on inspection, be divided into two
general categories. These comprise, first, the band of large, aging industrial
cities, including Chicago, Newark, Boston, Pittsburgh, St. Louis, and New
York. The second category includes Atlanta, Charleston, South Carolina,
Houston, Oklahoma City, Portland, Oregon, and Seattle, all of which were
experiencing a climate of uncertainty due to social and economic instability
and change. In contrast, the cities in the lowest quartile during the 1970-74
period include the generally stable, medium-sized centers of the Midwest
and West: Indianapolis, Fort Wayne, Dallas, San Francisco, Phoenix,
Denver, Topeka, Des Moines, Milwaukee, Cedar Rapids, and Birmingham.
    Thus, a cursory examination of delinquency patterns suggests a
relationship between the aging of urban infrastructure, the uncertainty con-
tingent on social and economic instability, and nonpayment of property
taxes. These data provide an initial indication of the context of tax delinquency.
    Further insight can be gained by examining the changing rank of cities in
the selected group in 1950-54 compared to 1970-74. By ranking cities according to delinquency rate at both periods, cities with a persistent high
delinquency rate can be differentiated from those in which high delinquency
has been a relatively short-term phenomenon and, in turn, from those cities
which consistently report a low delinquency rate over time. Toward this
end, cities have been categorized into groups indicating (1) those cities in the
highest quartile (highest delinquency rate) in 1950-54 but not in 1970-74; (2)
cities in the top quartile in 1970-74 but not in 1950-54; (3) cities that ranked
in the highest quartile during both periods; (4) cities in the bottom quartile

EXHIBIT 4-4

CITIES RANKING IN THE HIGHEST AND LOWEST QUARTILES IN PROPERTY TAX DELINQUENCY AMONG FORTY-EIGHT SELECTED CITIES, 1950-54 AND 1970-74

(1) *Highest Quartile* *1950-54 Only*	(2) *Highest Quartile* *1970-74 Only*	(3) *Highest Quartile* *1950-54 & 1970-74*	(4) *Lowest Quartile* *1950-54 Only*	(5) *Lowest Quartile* *1970-74 Only*	(6) *Lowest Quartile* *1950-54 & 1970-74*
Fargo, N. Dak. Louisville, Ky. Norfolk, Va. Salt Lake City, U.	Atlanta, Ga. Charleston, S.C. Oklahoma City, O. Seattle Wash.	Boston, Mass. Chicago, Ill. Houston, Tex. New York, N.Y. Newark, N.J. Pittsburgh, Pa. Portland, Ore. St. Louis, Mo.	Bridgeport, Conn. Detroit, Mich. Hartford, Conn. Oakland, Ca. Oklahoma City, O.	Dallas, Tex. Fort Wayne, Ind. Indianapolis, Ind. Phoenix, Ariz. New Orleans, La.	Birmingham, Ala. Cedar Rapids, Iowa Denver, Colo. Des Moines, Iowa Milwaukee, Wisc. San Francisco, Ca. Topeka, Kan.

Source: Compiled from data in *Moody's Municipal and Government Manual* (see Exhibit 4-2).

in 1950-54 but not in 1970-74; (5) cities ranked in the lowest quartile in 1970-74 but not in 1950-54; and (6) cities that consistently ranked among the lowest quartile at both dates. The results of this categorization, tabulated in Exhibit 4-4, reveal a striking typology of urban economic health.

The analysis indicates that—as was the case nationally during the Depression years of the 1930s—property tax delinquency is closely associated with the incidence of social and economic uncertainty, upheaval, and realignment leading to instability in the housing market. The cities listed in column (1) of Exhibit 4-4, for instance, experienced substantial upheavals during the early fifties, reflected in relatively high delinquency rates, with subsequent stabilization resulting in removal of these cities from the highest quartile category. In this category, for example, is Norfolk, Virginia, which experienced serious dislocations in the early 1950s associated both with the post-World War II closing of extensive military facilities and with a major building boom that occurred in outlying areas of the city. Similarly, both Louisville and Salt Lake City, in the same category, experienced rapid suburbanization during the 1950s, requiring major readjustments in the central city housing markets in these two cities. Between 1950 and 1960, the population of the Salt Lake City SMSA increased by 46.5 percent while the population of the central city increased by only 4.0 percent; corresponding figures for the Louisville SMSA and central city are 25.7 percent and 5.8 percent, respectively.[4] Such rapid suburban growth, in contrast to the slow growth in the central city, suggests a substantial realignment of the nature of supply and demand for housing in the central city. The uncertainty and instability associated with such realignment appear in turn to be related closely to the incidence of a high rate of property tax delinquency. With the return of relative stability in subsequent periods, delinquency rates in these cities no longer ranked in the highest quartile among the forty-eight selected cities.

A similar pattern is reflected in the cities listed in column (2) of Exhibit 4-4, cities that rank in the highest quartile in the 1970-74 period but not in the 1950-54 period. In these cities, a recent increase in the tax delinquency rate may serve as a leading indicator of incipient housing market instability. For example, average annual tax delinquency in the five successive five-year intervals between 1950 and 1974 in Atlanta was as follows: 3.4 percent, 2.5 percent, 2.3 percent, 2.2 percent, and 6.4 percent. In Oklahoma City, respective delinquency rates were: 0.5 percent, 0.5 percent, 1.7 percent, 4.2 percent, and 5.6 percent. The remaining cities in column (2) reflect a similar substantial increase in the most recent period.

The cities listed in column (3) of Exhibit 4-4 ranked in the highest delinquency quartile in both 1950-54 and 1970-74. This list represents the older, declining industrial cities of the Northeast and Midwest. The longstanding nature of the delinquency problem in these cities suggests that the present "fiscal crisis" affecting these cities is not a recent phenomenon. The inclusion of Portland, Oregon in this list may also reflect the longstanding instability in that city associated with fluctuations in the aircraft and aerospace industries.

The remaining three columns in Exhibit 4-4 indicate those cities ranked in the lowest quartile in property tax delinquency among the forty-eight cities. The cities in column (4) ranked in the lowest quartile in 1950-54 but not in the 1970-74 period. This category appears to include older second-order industrial cities that have only recently begun to confront the problems of an aging infrastructure and a decline in function. It is interesting to note that Oklahoma City ranked in the lowest quartile in 1950-54 [column (4)] and in the highest quartile in 1970-74 [column (2)].

The cities in column (5), ranking in the lowest quartile in 1970-75 but not in the 1950-54 period, appear to include those that experienced an earlier period of often explosive expansionary growth and have now stabilized. Finally, the cities in column (6), in general smaller cities of the Midwest and West, consistently rank in the lowest delinquency quartile.

This very general overview of the relationship between city characteristics and the tax delinquency rate suggests that the nonpayment of property taxes is likely to occur most frequently in those cities in which the housing market and, more directly, property owners are operating in a climate of instability and uncertainty. In the most recent period, the sources of such instability appear to be the loss of economic viablilty of older, central city housing and an aura of investment uncertainty in cities that are losing their traditional economic functions. In order to develop a more explicit identification of the factors associated with delinquency at the citywide scale, we tested this hypothesis by means of statistical analysis relating delinquency data to city characteristics provided by the Census Bureau.

THE ENVIRONMENT OF DELINQUENCY — THE CITY SCALE

Our purpose in this section is to identify the environmental conditions at the citywide scale associated with a high incidence of owner's decisions not to pay real estate taxes. A high rate of tax delinquency results directly from the aggregate decisions of individual property owners not to pay real estate taxes. For any individual, this decision is likely to be due to some combination of personal idiosyncracies and the impact on the individual of demographic, environmental, and fiscal conditions extant in a given city.

This section of the analysis is addressed to assessing the latter set of factors responsible for real estate tax delinquency. The idiosyncratic characteristics of an individual's situation are difficult to assess and, by definition, vary by individual. On the other hand, the social, economic, and administrative environment of a city is common to, and affects in varying degrees, *all* residents. Further, the aggregated population and housing characteristics of a city to a large extent result from the combined characteristics of property owners and the properties they own, so in a sense the latter set of environmental correlates of tax delinquency subsumes the former set of idiosyncratic factors. As a result, not only may we identify contextual or environmental factors associated with high rates of tax delinquency but we may also be confident that these factors contribute to an explanation of differences in delinquency rates among cities.

The specific means employed in the analysis involve the statistical testing of the nature and strength of the relationship between the rate of tax delinquency and selected characteristics of the city's demographic and housing environment. Analysis based on the national group of cities described earlier permits us to identify those factors or conditions which, when present in a city, result in the greater propensity of owners to become delinquent in tax payments. The broad range of delinquency levels in the selected cities allows us to proceed in the identification of city characteristics that vary in proportion to the variation in the delinquency rate.

The nature of our discussion thus far leads to a number of working hypotheses regarding the factors associated with high citywide rates of tax delinquency. Specifically, we have identified five general sets of city characteristics that we expect will be closely related to variation in the rate of tax delinquency across the national group of cities. These five sets of characteristics are (1) total population, (2) demographic characteristics, (3) "quality of life", (4) housing market viability, and (5) housing value. The hypotheses related to these city characteristics are as follows:

Population. We expect larger cities to have higher delinquency rates than smaller cities. To the extent that total size of the population serves as a proxy for age and period of development, the larger cities are those which reached their prominence during the period of industrial development in the nineteenth century. These larger and older cities are thus likely to have benefitted the least from more recent patterns of economic growth and, in turn, are more likely to be experiencing the process of instability and decline discussed in Chapter 2. In addition, it can be expected that the largest cities bear the greatest likelihood of extreme complexity in the administrative and collection procedures associated with the property tax and that this complexity will be reflected in higher rates of noncollection of current year's taxes.

Demographic Characteristics. In addition to total size of the population, we hypothesize that specific aspects of population growth and composition will be related to variations in the level of tax delinquency across cities. In terms of population growth, we expect that cities with high birth rates and/or high net in-migration will have low delinquency. In terms of demographic composition, we expect that cities with high proportions of persons over sixty-five years of age will have high delinquency rates, while a high proportion of families with young children will be associated with low delinquency. We expect these relationships to hold not because of a presumed propensity toward delinquency on the part of the elderly but rather because the age structure of the population is indicative of the extent of housing turnover and the relative asset position of a city's population.

Quality of Life. The elusive concept of the "quality of life" in a city is expected to be associated with levels of tax delinquency to the extent that it reflects the social and economic climate in the city and the nature of residents' commitment and attachment. As one indicator of this "qualitative" dimension of city life, we expect that a high crime rate will be associated with high delinquency. Again, this is not to suggest that tax delinquents necessarily commit crimes. Rather, a high crime rate is likely to reduce residents' attachment and commitment to an area and is likely to be associated with increased difficulty in and cost of property maintenance. In addition, we tentatively expect that low income, high concentrations of families below the poverty level, and high proportions of the population receiving welfare benefits are associated with high delinquency rates. We offer this only as a tentative hypothesis, however, because of the bimodal income distribution observed in many cities and because of the common observation that concentrations of low-income population in a city contribute to maintaining a high level of demand for low-cost housing.

Housing Market Viability. The same expectations regarding the influence on tax delinquency of population dynamics and quality of life indicators apply to our hypotheses pertaining to housing market viability. High vacancy rates, high proportions of older housing units, and low housing turnover are expected to be associated with high delinquency. Conversely, a high proportion of new housing is expected to be associated with low delinquency. In a somewhat related area, we anticipate that a high tax rate will be related to high delinquency.

Housing Value. The outright value of housing in a city can be expected to have the same effect on tax delinquency as is expected of the general viability of the housing market. Higher median value and higher gross rent are likely to be indicative of more affluent areas in which delinquency should be correspondingly low. Similarly, the change in housing value over time should be a powerful predictor of delinquency, with housing that maintains its value over time conducive to lower delinquency levels.

DATA

Data on a broad range of these characteristics of cities were extracted from various Census Bureau publications. Given the constraints of data availability between census years, most data are for 1970; the few exceptions are noted below. In those cases where we computed rates of change in various city characteristics, we used Census Bureau information for 1960 and 1970. The specific measures used in each of the five general sets of city characteristics are summarized in Exhibit 4-5. These data require little further elaboration.

Since our information on city characteristics was derived from 1970 data, we computed a measure of tax delinquency to coincide with this time frame. In this segment of the analysis, our measure of tax delinquency for each city is the average annual percent of real property taxes uncollected for the period 1968 to 1973. These six years include the 1970 benchmark set by the Census data. Computation of the average annual rate of delinquency over the six-year period again allows us to counter the possible negative effects of a peculiarity in tax collection or reporting for any given year. Three cities were deleted from the national group because of incomplete delinquency data during the 1968-1973 period, leaving a total of forty-five cities in the analysis. Average delinquency in the group during the six-year period was 3.97 percent, with a minimum of 0.25 percent and a maximum value of 12.35 percent.

CORRELATES OF DELINQUENCY

Analysis of simple correlations between delinquency and the city characteristics tabulated above provides a first test of hypothesized relationships.[5]

City Size The correlation between total population size and tax delinquency is positive and moderately strong, as expected (See Exhibit 4-6): larger cities have higher delinquency rates. In addition, the measure of the proportion of assessed value of property categorized as commercial or industrial is also positively related to delinquency. These relationships provide initial support for the contention that delinquency is a problem that is greatest in the larger industrial cities.

Demographic Characteristics Exhibit 4-7 summarizes the simple correlations between demographic characteristics and tax delinquency. A number of surprising findings emerge from this analysis. Both median age and the percent of population over 65 are moderately and positively associated with delinquency, supporting the contention that cities with an older age structure have a greater delinquency problem; both of these relationships, however, achieve only marginal statistical significance, suggesting the need for caution in interpreting these results. Both the birth rate and the death rate perform as expected: the higher the birth rate, the lower the delinquency level, while a higher death rate is associated with higher delinquency. The

EXHIBIT 4-5

CITY CHARACTERISTICS USED IN CROSS-CITY ANALYSIS
OF TAX DELINQUENCY

Characteristic	Mean	Standard Deviation	Minimum	Maximum
I. POPULATION SIZE				
Total population	733,009	—	48,000	7,895,000
% of assessed value of property classified as commercial/industrial	37.7	9.1	16.6	55.5
II. DEMOGRAPHIC CHARACTERISTICS				
Median age	29.5	2.8	23.9	37.2
% over 65	11.1	2.1	6.5	15.0
Birth rate	18.9	2.3	14.3	23.9
Death rate	11.6	2.1	7.3	15.8
% foreign born	17.5	12.4	3.1	54.4
% black	23.1	15.3	0.1	57.2
% families with children under 6	24.9	2.8	18.6	31.5
% female-headed households	16.0	4.0	8.0	26.8
Population growth rate, 1960-1970	4.3	15.1	−17.0	56.7
Black population growth rate, 1960-1970	31.7	21.0	− 9.8	79.2
III. QUALITY OF LIFE				
Crime rate (Index crimes per 1,000)	48.8	20.0	5.1	84.4
% households receiving welfare benefits	7.2	3.3	2.1	18.5
Median family income	9,348	985	7,304	11,108
% households below poverty level	11.3	3.9	5.3	21.9
Male civilian unemployment rate	4.4	1.7	1.9	8.8
Persons per unit (density)	3.0	0.2	2.4	3.6
IV. HOUSING MARKET VIABILITY				
% housing units vacant for sale	4.3	2.2	1.4	9.1
Change in vacancy rate, 1960-1970	0.1	1.8	− 5.3	5.6
% housing units built pre-1939	49.0	17.8	11.2	77.2
New housing units (built 1960-70) as % of total units	17.2	8.4	4.1	35.4
% renter occupied units	50.0	12.8	30.8	79.4
% households in same unit, 1965 and 1970	50.0	6.1	38.1	63.3
% units lacking plumbing	3.8	1.7	1.1	7.9
Effective tax rate, single-family units, 1971	2.0	0.9	0.6	5.1
Effective tax rate, single-family units, 1966	1.8	0.7	0.5	3.6
Change in effective tax rate, 1966 to 1971	0.1	0.5	− 0.9	1.5
V. HOUSING VALUE				
Median value, owner-occupied units ($)	15,814	4,127	9,614	27,814
Median gross rent, renter-occupied units ($)	98	12	72	130
Change in median value, 1960-70, of units built by 1960 ($)	3,248	2,186	760	10,565
Change in median rent, 1960-70, of rental units built by 1960 ($)	25	8	12	56

Sources: U.S. Census of Population and Housing, 1970; U.S. Census of Housing, Metropolitan Housing Characteristics, 1960 and 1970; U.S. Bureau of the Census, County and City Data Book, 1972; U.S. Census of Governments, 1967 and 1972.

EXHIBIT 4-6

SIMPLE CORRELATION COEFFICIENTS BETWEEN CITY SIZE
CHARACTERISTICS AND TAX DELINQUENCY

City Characteristic	Simple Correlation	Level of Significance (p ⩽)	Number of Cases
Total Population	.379	.01	45
% assessed value of property classified as commercial or industrial	.299	.05	41

former measure suggests the importance of population growth in limiting delinquency, while the latter measure might provide the strongest indication of the impact of an older age structure on the delinquency rate. The presence of families with children under six is also negatively related to delinquency (i.e., the more such families, the lower the delinquency rate). While the statistical significance of this last measure is again only marginal, that the sign of the relationship is as expected suggests that each of these demographic characteristics indicates the importance of families in the childbearing years in limiting delinquency. At the same time, however, the presence of female-headed households is positively and significantly associated with high delinquency, perhaps because of the relatively low income of such families. Finally, the general measure of total population growth is inversely, though marginally, related to delinquency. This may suggest that it is not simply population growth *per se* that limits delinquency but rather growth based on a particular pattern of family composition.

The larger the proportion of foreign born population in a city, the higher the delinquency rate, although this relationship must be approached cautiously because of the marginal significance level and the likelihood that the proportion of foreign-born is closely tied to total population size. The percentage black population in a city is *not* correlated with delinquency, nor is the growth of the black population betweeen 1960 and 1970.

Quality of Life Correlations between quality of life measures and tax delinquency are tabulated in Exhibit 4-8. Most notably in this section, a high crime rate is directly related to a high delinquency rate. As suggested earlier, this finding lends support to the hypothesis that a high crime rate prompts decreased commitment and attachment to the community — a situation conducive to high delinquency. In addition, a high crime rate may contribute to delinquency to the extent that it results in increased property maintenance costs. The proportion of households receiving welfare benefits is also positively associated with delinquency. This measure (as well as the crime rate measure) may be related to delinquency only to the extent that it correlates with city size. It is possible, however, to suggest that the presence of a large dependent population is indicative of the absence of private sector commitment which, it was hypothesized in Chapter 2, is directly related to high delinquency.

EXHIBIT 4-7

SIMPLE CORRELATION COEFFICIENTS BETWEEN DEMOGRAPHIC
CHARACTERISTICS AND TAX DELINQUENCY

City Characteristic	Simple Correlation	Level of Significance $(p \leqslant)$	Number of Cases
Median age	.207	.10	45
% over 65	.227	.10	45
Birth rate	.291	.05	45
Death rate	.241	.05	45
% foreign born	.229	.10	45
% black	.106	ns	45
% families with children under 6	.225	.10	45
% female-headed households	.312	.05	45
Population growth rate, 1960-1970	.171	.10	45
Black population growth rate, 1960-1970	.091	ns	45

Note: ns = not significant.

EXHIBIT 4-8

SIMPLE CORRELATION COEFFICIENTS BETWEEN QUALITY OF LIFE
CHARACTERISTICS AND TAX DELINQUENCY

City Characteristic	Simple Correlation	Level of Significance $(p \leqslant)$	Number of Cases
Crime rate	.344	.01	45
% households receiving welfare benefits	.264	.05	43
Median family income	.002	ns	45
% households below the poverty level	.069	ns	45
Male civilian unemployment rate	.212	.10	45
Persons per unit (density)	.169	.10	45

Note: ns = not significant.

Neither median family income nor the percent of households below the poverty level are significantly correlated with tax delinquency. This finding also holds when median family income is disaggregated between median income in owner-occupied units and median income in renter-occupied units. As suggested before, the presence of low-income households may indeed limit delinquency by maintaining the level of demand for low-cost and marginal housing units that otherwise would be withdrawn from the market.

Housing Market Viability The relationship between housing market viability and tax delinquency is indicated by the correlation coefficients tabulated in Exhibit 4-9. Once again, the findings that emerge are not as clear-cut as might be expected.

The percent of housing units vacant and for sale is positively related to delinquency: the higher the vacancy rate, the higher the level of delinquency. The measure of vacant units available for sale is particularly important as an indicator of the ability of owners to realize their equity through resale. A high rate of unsold vacant units is indicative of a slow market in which owners may find it difficult to obtain a return on their investment. A decision to minimize expenditures (including tax payments) on the property is a likely response to such a situation. However, a change in the vacancy rate between 1960 and 1970 is not significantly related to variations in delinquency. While it might be expected that an increasing vacancy rate might accelerate the level of nonpayment of taxes, this supposition is not supported by the analysis.

A concentration of older housing units (built pre-1939) is positively correlated with delinquency, while a concentration of new units (built 1960-70) is inversely related to delinquency. These finding support the hypotheses that the presence of new private investment limits the incidence of delinquency and that a housing market marked by a low level of new construction is conducive to delinquency. In a related fashion, housing markets characterized by low turnover (as measured by the proportion of households in the same unit in 1965 and 1970) are also marked by high delinquency.

Contrary to expectations, the effective tax rate is not significantly related to the delinquency level. This is the case regardless of whether the 1966 or the 1971 tax rate is considered, or even an average of the two, and whether the tax rate for single-family or all residential units is considered. Similarly, while it might be hypothesized that an increasing tax rate might spur delinquency, the change in the effective tax rate between 1966 and 1971 is not significantly related to delinquency. Again, this finding holds whether the absolute difference or the ratio between the two rates is used as the change measure.

EXHIBIT 4-9

SIMPLE CORRELATION COEFFICIENTS BETWEEN HOUSING MARKET
CHARACTERISTICS AND TAX DELINQUENCY

City Characteristic	Simple Correlation	Level of Significance (p ⩽)	Number of Cases
% housing units vacant for sale	.267	.05	42
Change in vacancy rate, 1960-1970	.133	ns	45
% housing units built pre-1939	.276	.05	45
New housing units (built 1960-70) as % of total units	−.211	.10	42
% renter occupied units	.333	.01	45
% households in same unit, 1965 and 1970	.227	.10	45
% units lacking plumbing	.139	ns	45
Effective tax rate, single-family units, 1971	.115	ns	43
Effective tax rate, single-family units, 1966	.105	ns	42
Change in effective tax rate, 1966 to 1971	.084	ns	41

Note: ns = not significant.

EXHIBIT 4-10

SIMPLE CORRELATION COEFFICIENTS BETWEEN HOUSING VALUE
CHARACTERISTICS AND TAX DELINQUENCY

City Characteristic	Simple Correlation	Level of Significance (p ⩽)	Number of Cases
Median value, owner-occupied units	.263	.05	42
Median gross rent, renter-occupied units	.260	.05	42
Change in median value, 1960-70, of units built by 1960 ($)	.365	.01	42
Change in median rent, 1960-1970, of units built by 1960 ($)	.366	.01	42

Housing Value.   The final set of correlations — those between housing value and tax delinquency — are tabulated in Exhibit 4-10. The basic hypothesis here is that housing value is inversely related to delinquency: the higher the value of housing in a city, the lower the delinquency rate.

Examination of the data, however, indicates that this is not the case. Disregarding for the moment the possible intervening influence of other factors, higher median value is positively and significantly related to delinquency: the higher the median value of housing, the higher the delinquency rate. Moreover, this relationship holds regardless of which value measure is used: 1970 median value of owner-occupied units, 1970 median rent of renter-occupied units, or change in median value or rent of occupied units from 1960-1970.[6]

These results, at first apparently counterintuitive, at second glance suggest the link between delinquency and market instability. The median value and median rent data refer only to occupied units, High values on these measures might be indicative, then, either of a housing market composed of generally high-quality and high-value units, or of a setting in which low-quality and low-value units have dropped out of the occupied market through vacancy and abandonment. It is the presence of the latter "excess" units that is likely to account for a high level of tax delinquency.

This phenomenon explains the apparently contradictory finding of high tax delinquency in cities that appear to be experiencing a significant upgrading in the quality of the housing stock. As will be discussed in greater detail in Chapter 5, data for Pittsburgh indicate that while the tax delinquency rate was rising between 1960 and 1970, the city experienced a 50 percent decrease in the number of housing units lacking plumbing facilities and a 42 percent drop in units with more than 1.01 persons per room. At first glance, the decrease in the number of substandard and crowded housing units suggests a strengthening of the housing market, in contrast to the weak market suggested by increasing delinquency. The seeming improvement in the housing stock, however, is less likely to be the result of upgrading of existing units, but is more likely to be the result of the outright abandonment of marginal units and their elimination from the stock of occupied or vacant-and-available units that constitute the city's housing market. While it gives the appearance that the quality of the remaining stock has been upgraded, the illegal abandonment of these marginal structures tends to swell the nonpayment of taxes that have been assessed and levied.

A similar argument holds for the finding that an *increase* in median value and rent is associated with higher tax delinquency. An increase in value (or rent) may come about as a result of a wholesale rise in values or, alternatively, the median will rise if a large proportion of structures at the *low end* of the value scale are deleted from the occupied housing stock from which the median is calculated. Further, the withdrawal of such lower value units from the market will increase the pressure on the remaining units, thus forcing rent and value up further.

The large number of factors considered thus far in part illuminate and in part conceal the nature of the factors most directly associated with variation in the level of tax delinquency across cities. Several factors, such as percent black, median income, and the effective tax rate, can be eliminated from the analysis based on the finding of no statistically significant correlation between these factors and delinquency. For a second set of factors, such as total population, birth rate, housing vacancy, and housing value, the analysis has provided initial support for hypothesized relationships. The analytic and methodological concern at this point is to identify the smallest possible set of city characteristics that independently explain the greatest possible amount of variation in the level of tax delinquency across our national group of cities. Since the items grouped *within* each of the five basic sets of city characteristics are likely to be closely related to each other, we identified the one characteristic in each set which contributes the most to an explanation of the variation in delinquency. We would thus expect to identify five characteristics of our group of cities which each contribute independely to an explanation of the variation in delinquency rates.

The results of this analysis, presented in the form of a regression equation, are summarized in Exhibit 4-11. (See Appendix A for a brief description of regression analysis.) The final equation contains four variables which together explain 43.3 percent of the variation in delinquency across the national group of cities.

Each of these four variables represents one factor from the population size, demographic, housing market, and housing value data sets. None of the "quality of life" measures contributes independently to explain the variation in delinquency levels when the other four variables are considered simultaneously. For example, crime rate was shown to be moderately strongly and significantly correlated with delinquency ($r = .344$, $p \leq .01$), as was indicated in Exhibit 4-8. When considered simultaneously with the four key characteristics tabulated in Exhibit 4-11, however, crime rate fails to contribute any additional explanation of variation in delinquency beyond that contributed by the first four variables. The same finding holds true for each of the remaining city characteristics considered. (Intercorrelations among the four variables in the regression range from .02 to .10).

SUMMARY

The four characteristics that contribute most to an explanation of variations in delinquency levels lend considerable support to the model of tax delin-

EXHIBIT 4-11

FINAL REGRESSION EQUATION EXPLAINING VARIATION IN DELINQUENCY ACROSS FORTY-TWO CITIES

City Characteristic	Coefficient	Standard Error	Level of Significance ($p \leq$)
Total population	.0766	.0305	.001
Change in median rent, 1960-1970	.1379	.0475	.001
% units vacant-for-sale	5.0021	1.7494	.001
Birth rate	−.3818	.1653	.01
Constant	4.9451		
F	7.0067		
R^2	0.4331		

quency discussed in Chapter 2. The analysis at the citywide scale suggests that, all other things being equal, the larger the total population, the greater the increase in rent, the higher the vacancy rate, and the lower the birth rate, the higher will be the delinquency rate. Delinquency, in other words, tends to be highest in large cities with high vacancy rates, where there is a withdrawal of low value units from the occupied housing market, and with a lack of young families in the childbearing years who might sustain a viable level of demand for housing.

This analysis of delinquency rates at the city-wide scale provides initial support for the descriptive model of tax delinquency introduced in Chapter 2. In further testing of the relationships suggested by this model, we turn next to an intensive case study of one key city — Pittsburgh — in which delinquency has been a long-standing, chronic, and serious problem.

NOTES

1. Brenton W. Harries, Statement in U.S. Congress, Subcommittee on Economic Progress, Joint Economic Committee, *Financing Municipal Facilities,* Vol. II 90th Congress, 1968; cited in Twentieth Century Fund Task Force on Municipal Bond Credit Ratings, *The Rating Game* (New York: The Twentieth Century Fund, 1974), p. 78.

2. John E. Peterson, "Background Paper," in Twentieth Century Fund, *The Rating Game,* p. 79.

3. Moody's Investors Services, Inc., *Moody's Municipal and Government Manual* (New York: Moody's Investors Services, Inc.). Annual editions, 1950 to 1975.

4. U.S. Bureau of the Census, *County and City Data Book, 1967.* A Statistical Abstract Supplement (Washington, D.C.: U.S. Government Printing Office, 1967).

5. The simple correlation coefficient varies between −1.000 and 1.000 and provides a measure of the degree of association between two variables (sets of characteristics) of the population analyzed (in this case, cities). A correlation of 1.000 indicates a perfect positive relationship; −1.000 indicates a perfect negative relationship; and a correlation of zero indicates complete independence between the two variables. The associated measure of statistical significance indicates the probability that the observed correlation could have occurred by chance; a probability of 5 percent or less (.05) is usually required to reject the hypothesis of randomness and impute statistical significance to the observed relationship.

6. In computing the measures of change in housing value used here, we first obtained the median value (or median rent) of all units for each city in 1960; then, from the 1970 Census, we obtained the median value (or median rent) of all units built pre-1960. Change values (absolute difference or ratio) were then calculated using these two data points for each city. These measures thus indicate the extent to which units built by 1960 had gained or lost value ten years later.

Part 2

Narrowing The Focus:
The Pittsburgh
Case Study

Chapter 5

Population Trends and Neighborhood Structure in Pittsburgh

INTRODUCTION

In Chapter 4, we examined differences in delinquency levels at the citywide scale, attempting to identify the characteristics of high-delinquency cities. Chapters 5 and 6 are devoted to replicating this analysis at the neighborhood scale in the context of a single city.

We have argued that tax delinquency is part of a citywide structural process involving individual owners' decisions concerning private capital expenditure and investment. That negative decisions cluster in particular neighborhoods is not a function of the particular "stage of decline" characterizing a given neighborhood. Rather, our analysis at the city scale suggests that neighborhood concentration of delinquency is a function of citywide softness in private investment, with the least economically viable real estate — wherever it may be located — feeling the brunt of capital withdrawal first. The significance of this distinction is that it ties concentrations of delinquency not to neighborhoods *per se* but rather to the pattern of investment and ownership decisions that are played out in, and have an impact on, neighborhoods. Policy responses, then, can be keyed not to changing the characteristics of neighborhoods, but rather to influencing the pattern of ownership and investment decisions that have an impact on neighborhoods.

Our objective in this section is thus to identify patterns and clusters of delinquency at the neighborhood level. If, as we suggested in Chapter 1, an equal probability exists for any given parcel in a city to be either renovated or abandoned, what neighborhood characteristics are associated with a high propensity to disinvestment rather than reinvestment? What neighborhood environmental factors, in other words, are associated with owners' decisions to move in one direction or the other?

Our discussion in this chapter serves as an introduction to an intensive case study of tax delinquency at the neighborhood scale in Pittsburgh. The focus on Pittsburgh as a case study is significant for several reasons. The evidence indicates that Pittsburgh has experienced a rate of tax delinquency significantly in excess of the national average over an extended number of years. With a 6.1 percent average annual noncollection rate between 1950 and 1974, Pittsburgh ranks sixth in a measure of tax delinquency rates among the forty-eight cities discussed in Chapter 4. Viewed year by year, Pittsburgh's average annual rate of uncollected property taxes exceeded the national average by more than two full percentage points each year, a rate which represents a revenue loss of several million dollars a year. Not only is delinquency a currently manifested problem but it is also of longstanding signifiance. Pittsburgh's delinquency rate ranked the city in the top quartile of the group of forty-eight cities in all but three of the twenty-five years between 1950 and 1974 (the exceptions were 1948, 1964, and 1965). Further, the delinquency problem in Pittsburgh has taken on even greater significance in recent years. For the 1970-74 period, Pittsburgh tallied a 9.2 percent average annual delinquency rate, reflecting a noticeable increase over the preceding five year period and measuring substantially above the median level of 3.2 percent for the forty-eight cities as a whole. By the 1970-74 period, Pittsburgh recorded the fifth highest delinquency rate among the forty-eight cities.

The evidence thus clearly suggests that tax delinquency is both a longstanding and a growing problem in Pittsburgh. Given this city's role in America's urban history, it is an excellent example of an older industrial city confronting the brunt of urban change. As such, it provides perhaps one of the best possible examples of the trends described in Chapter 2.

Our discussion in this chapter sets the stage for the analysis of delinquency presented in the next chapter. We begin here with a brief overview of recent population and housing trends in the City of Pittsburgh. Second, we report the results of a statistical analysis designed to uncover the pattern and characteristics of neighborhood structure in Pittsburgh. In Chapter 6, we present a summary of the magnitude and characteristics of tax delinquency in Pittsburgh, address the question of the neighborhood environment of de-

linquency, and report the outcome of analysis linking neighborhood structure and delinquency levels.

POPULATION AND HOUSING TRENDS IN PITTSBURGH

Tax delinquency in Pittsburgh is occuring in the context of significant
changes in the city's population and housing market characteristics.
Between 1960 and 1970, the city lost 84,000 people, its total housing stock
declined by 6,000 units, and housing vacancy increased by 50 percent. From
1970 to 1975, the city's total population fell by another 61,500 people, so
that, by 1975, Pittsburgh had lost nearly a fourth (24.1 percent) of its 1960
population. At the same time, some characteristics such as the growth of the
black population showed signs of stabilization over the decade, and
improvement was evident in the rate of crowding and the incidence of sub-
standard housing units.

A detailed examination of these recent changes in population and housing
characteristics helps to place the analysis of delinquency in the broader
perspective of overall trends affecting the city. The changing characteristics
of the city's population define the parameters of housing demand while a
view of changes in the city's housing stock indicates the nature of housing
supply. Data from the U.S. Census of Population and Housing, comparing
Pittsburgh with the surrounding suburban region, provide an introduction
to the context of tax delinquency in the city.

TOTAL POPULATION

The city's total population has declined dramatically over the last twenty-
five years, falling 11 percent in the 1950-60 decade, 14 percent from 1960 to
1970, and another 12 percent between 1970 and 1975. The city's loss of
84,000 people during the sixties was not quite matched by an increase of
80,000 in the suburban sections of the metropolitan area (see Exhibit 5-1), as
the SMSA as a whole failed to maintain its size with an overall loss of 4,000
people. Between 1970 and 1975, even the suburbs experienced a net population loss with a decrease of 18,000. This changing distribution of population
within the metropolitan area resulted in a decrease in the city's representation in the SMSA — from 25.1 percent of the area's population in 1960 to
21.7 percent in 1970 — and a corresponding increase in the proportion of
the population living in the suburbs.

RACE AND ETHNICITY

Within this general context of diminishing size, the racial and ethnic
composition of the city's population changed only slightly between 1960 and
1970. This is in sharp contrast to the experience of some other cities in which
the black population is achieving majority status and a rapidly growing
Spanish-speaking population is continuing the tradition of ethnic in-migra-

EXHIBIT 5-1

COMPOSITION OF THE POPULATION, PITTSBURGH, 1960 AND 1970

	1960		1970		Change 1960-1970	
	Number	Percent of Total Population	Number	Percent of Total Population	Number	Percent
Total Population						
City	604,332	100.0	520,117	100.0	− 84,215	−13.9
Suburbs	1,801,103	100.0	1,881,128	100.0	+ 80,025	+ 4.4
White Population						
City	502,593	83.2	412,280	79.3	− 90,313	−17.9
Suburbs	1,739,316	96.6	1,812,741	96.4	+ 73,425	+ 4.2
Black Population						
City	100,692	16.7	104,904	20.2	+ 4,212	+ 4.2
Suburbs	60,808	3.7	64,980	3.5	+ 4,172	+ 6.9
Native of Native Parentage						
City	421,220	69.7	385,468	74.1	− 35,753	− 8.5
Suburbs	1,292,207	71.7	1,443,044	76.7	+150,837	+11.7
Native of Foreign or Mixed Parentage						
City	137,859	22.8	103,403	19.9	− 34,456	−24.9
Suburbs	398,488	22.1	361,471	19.2	− 37,017	− 9.3
Foreign Born						
City	45,253	7.5	31,275	6.0	− 13,978	−30.9
Suburbs	110,408	6.1	76,556	4.1	− 33,852	−30.7

Source: U.S. Census of Population and Housing, 1960 and 1970.

tion established by European immigrants of an earlier period. For the city of Pittsburgh, the growth of the black population slowed significantly in the 1960-70 decade while in absolute numbers the foreign-born population decreased steadily over time.

More specifically, the black population in the city increased each decade from 1940 to 1970 but at a rapidly diminishing rate. Starting with 62,000 in 1940, the black population increased 32 percent between 1940 and 1950, 22 percent from 1950 to 1960, and only 4 percent from 1960 to 1970. This 4 percent increase between 1960 and 1970 — an increase of only 4,000 people (see Exhibit 5-1) — represents a significant stabilization in the size and growth of the city's black population.

Despite the decreasing black population growth rate, and primarily as a result of the 18 percent decline in the city's white population, black representation in the city increased from slightly under 17 percent of total population in 1960 to slightly over 20 percent in 1970. Also, largely as a result of the movement to the suburbs by white population, black representation in the suburbs *decreased* from 3.7 percent of the suburban population in 1960 to 3.5 percent in 1970 (see Exhibit 5-1). At the same time, a very slight trend toward suburbanization of the black population became evident between 1960 and 1970 as the proportion of the metropolitan area's black population living in the city declined from 62.3 percent to 61.8 percent while the proportion living in the suburbs increased correspondingly from 37.7 percent to 38.2 percent. The change was so slight, however, as to be hardly noticeable.

The stabilization in the size of the black population was accompanied by an absolute decrease in the foreign-born ethnic population throughout the metropolitan area over the same period. Between 1960 and 1970, the foreign-born population decreased at a uniform 31 percent in both the city and the surrounding suburban area (see Exhibit 5-1). Accordingly, as the foreign-born proportion of the city's total population fell from 7.5 percent in 1960 to 6.0 percent in 1970, the proportion of the population in the "native born of native parentage" category increased from 69.7 percent of the city's total in 1960 to 74.1 percent in 1970. The change in the representation of the foreign-born population in the suburban portion of the metropolitan area was similar in direction and magnitude, decreasing from 6.1 percent in 1960 to 4.1 percent in 1970. The areal distribution of foreign-born in the metropolitan area remained exactly the same over the decade, with 29 percent of the area's first-generation immigrants living in the city and 71 percent resident in the suburban portions of the SMSA in both 1960 and 1970. Only one-fourth of the metropolitan area's Spanish-speaking population — fewer than 3,000 people — lived within the city in 1970, constituting only one-half of one percent of the city's total population.

Although the census data on racial and ethnic characteristics of the population provide only circumstantial evicence, some conclusions can be inferred regarding the components of Pittsburgh's population growth. The significant overall loss of population in Pittsburgh is explained as the end-product of a large-scale white out-migration which has been only slightly offset by natural increase (births over deaths) of the black population. The rapid decline in the black growth rate suggests that in-migration of blacks to Pittsburgh has slowed substantially in recent years, leaving only natural increase to augment population size. The decline, both in absolute and relative terms, of the foreign-born population suggests similarly that in-migration of foreign-born ethnics has played an insignificant role in Pittsburgh's population dynamics in recent years, further accounting for the city's overall population decline.

RESIDENTIAL MOBILITY

Further insight into the nature of changes in Pittsburgh's population is gained by examining the volume and pattern of residential moves over the 1960-70 decade. Although the census again offers only circumstantial evidence, analysis of available data suggests both a relative stabilization of residential patterns within the city and a continuing trend toward suburbanization. A more detailed examination of these trends provides further indication of changing patterns of demand for housing in Pittsburgh.

The proportion of residents in the city who, at each census period, reported living in the same house five years prior to the census increased from 57 percent in 1960 to 62 percent in 1970 (see Exhibit 5-2). A similar tendency is apparent in the suburban portions of the metropolitan area (60 percent in 1960 and 67 percent in 1970), suggesting an *areawide trend involving fewer per capita moves and therefore a relatively less-active housing market and increasing residential stabilization.*

The pattern of changes in the number of residents who did report residential moves indicates a continuing trend to suburbanization. Considering those residents who moved out of a house in the central city five years before the census and still lived in the SMSA, the proportion who had moved into another house in the central city fell from 73 percent to 60 percent between 1960 and 1970 while, correspondingly, the proportion who had moved to the suburbs increased from 27 percent to 40 percent over the same decade. A more direct measure of continuing suburbanization is revealed by the 14 percent increase over the decade (from 63,000 in 1960 to 72,000 in 1970) in the number of suburban residents who at each Census period reported living in the central city five years prior to the census (see Exhibit 5-2).

Finally, the data provide little indication of an accelerating return-to-the-city movement in Pittsburgh. While 22,000 city residents in 1960 had lived in the suburbs five years before, the number had increased only slightly to a level of 24,000 in 1970 and, at both census dates, this number was still less than a third of those who made the trip in the opposite direction (see Exhibit 5-2.)

IN-MIGRATION

In addition to data on overall population growth rates discussed earlier, data on residents who reported living in a different house outside the SMSA or abroad five years prior to the census provide a further measure of in-migration to the Pittsburgh area.

Expressed as a proportion of the total population, the number of people who reported living outside the SMSA five years before the census increased slightly from 1960 to 1970 for both the city and the surrounding suburbs. This proportion rose between 1960 and 1970 from 4.7 percent to 6.5 percent

EXHIBIT 5-2

PREVIOUS RESIDENCE AND RESIDENTIAL MOBILITY, PITTSBURGH, 1960
AND 1970

	1960		1970		Change 1960-1970	
	Number	*Percent of Persons ⩾ 5 Years Old*	*Number*	*Percent of Persons ⩾ 5 Years Old*	*Number*	*Percent*
Same House						
City	312,475	57.2	302,473	62.3	− 10,002	− 3.2
Suburbs	954,440	59.5	1,156,932	66.6	+202,492	+21.2
Different House in Central City						
City	174,182	31.9	107,140	22.1	− 67,042	−38.5
Suburbs	63,471	3.9	72,389	4.2	+ 8,918	+14.1
Different House in Suburbs						
City	22,308	4.1	23,546	4.9	+ 1,238	+ 5.5
Suburbs	473,533	29.5	334,331	19.2	−139,202	−29.4
Different House Outside SMSA and Abroad						
City	25,692	4.7	31,758	6.5	+ 6,066	+23.6
Suburbs	97,319	6.1	119,908	6.9	+ 22,589	+23.2
Different House — North and West						
City	16,053	2.9	21,565	4.4	+ 5,512	+34.3
Suburbs	69,395	4.3	86,635	4.9	+ 17,240	+24.8
Different House — South						
City	6,145	1.1	5.523	1.1	− 622	−10.2
Suburbs	21,059	1.3	24,537	1.4	+ 3,478	+16.5
Different House — Abroad						
City	3,494	0.6	4,670	0.9	+ 1,176	+33.7
Suburbs	6,865	0.4	8,736	0.5	+ 1,871	+27.3

Source: U.S. Census of Population and Housing, 1960 and 1970.

for the city and from 6.1 percent to 6.9 percent for the suburban portion of
the SMSA (see Exhibit 5-2). Concurrently with this slight increase, however,
the relative city-suburb distribution of this in-migrant population remained
the same over the decade, with 21 percent located in the city and 79 percent
in the suburbs in both 1960 and 1970, with the result that the suburbs
received the bulk of new arrivals.

A breakdown of the data for total in-migration to the city reveals that the largest increase over the decade represented in-migration from the North and West, while the number of Pittsburgh residents who lived in the South five years before each census fell by 10 percent (see Exhibit 5-2). In-migration from abroad increased slightly, but still represented less than 1 percent of the city's population over five years old at both the beginning and end of the decade. As suggested earlier, the data on previous residence indicate that in-migration has contributed only minimally to population growth in Pittsburgh over the last decade.

OCCUPATION

Between 1960 and 1970, Pittsburgh lost 29,000 resident employed workers, a 13 percent decrease in the total number employed. This is commensurate with the city's loss of total population over the decade (see Exhibit 5-3). The 11 percent increase in employed workers in the surrounding suburbs more than accounted for the city's loss. As a result, the city's share of the metropolitan area's employed workers dropped from 27 percent to 22 percent while the suburb's share increased from 73 percent to 78 percent, over the decade.

Comparison of unemployment rates between censuses bears the danger of confusing secular trends with cyclical fluctuations. However, it is worthy of note that both the city and the surrounding suburbs showed substantial decreases in unemployment over the decade, with the unemployment rate dropping by 2.8 percentage points in both areas. Nonetheless, the unemployment rate in the city was considerably higher than the rate for the suburbs in both 1960 and 1970. The comparable figures are 8.1 percent for the city and 6.7 percent for the suburbs in 1960 and 5.3 percent for the city compared to 3.9 percent for the suburbs in 1970 (see Exhibit 5-3). Viewed in absolute terms, the city seems to have done better than the suburbs in improving its unemployment picture, with the decrease of 11,000 unemployed workers over the decade amounting to a 47 percent improvement for the city while the decrease of 16,000 unemployed in the suburbs amounted to only a 36 percent improvement.

A breakdown of total employment by occupation reveals that, while the suburbs gained substantially in all categories commensurate with their overall population growth, the city gained only slightly in higher status occupations and lost workers in all other categories (see Exhibit 5-3). Between 1960 and 1970, Pittsburgh experienced a net gain of 2,000 residents employed as professionals, managers, and administrators, an increase of 6 percent over the decade, while it lost 12,000 craftsmen and operatives, 4,000 laborers and service workers, and 2,000 sales and clerical workers. While these data represent residence by occupation rather than the number of jobs in the city, the increase from 18 percent to 22 percent in the proportion of the city's residents employed in higher status jobs may well mirror the national trends toward central city specialization in managerial and administrative functions and the decentralization of industry. An equally like-

EXHIBIT 5-3

CHARACTERISTICS OF THE LABOR FORCE, PITTSBURGH, 1960 AND 1970

	1960		1970		Change 1960-1970	
Residence	*Number*	*Percent of Employed Workers*	*Number*	*Percent of Employed Workers*	*Number*	*Percent*
Total Employed						
City	221,906	100.0	192,565	100.0	−29,341	−13.2
Suburbs	610,232	100.0	678,337	100.0	+68,105	+11.2
Professionals, Managers, and Administrators						
City	39,208	17.7	41,400	21.5	+ 2,192	+ 5.6
Suburbs	123,210	20.2	159,235	23.5	+36,025	+29.2
Sales and Clerical						
City	57,490	25.9	55,160	28.6	− 2,330	− 4.1
Suburbs	139,298	22.8	171,923	25.3	+32,625	+23.4
Craftsmen and Operatives						
City	61,972	27.9	50,049	25.9	−11,923	−19.2
Suburbs	221,084	36.2	230,292	33.9	+ 9,208	+ 4.2
Laborers and Service Workers						
City	49,863	22.5	45,956	23.9	− 3,907	− 7.8
Suburbs	105,278	17.3	116,887	17.2	+11,609	+11.0
Occupation Not Reported						
City	13,373	6.0	(a)	(a)	(−13,373)	(a)
Suburbs	21,362	3.5	(a)	(a)	(−21,362)	(a)
Unemployed						
City	19,564	8.1[b]	10,838	5.3[b]	− 8,726	−44.6
Suburbs	43,969	6.7[b]	28,149	3.9[b]	−15,820	−35.9

Notes: a: Changes in census enumeration procedures resulted in the elimination of the category "occupation not reported" from 1970 data. In this table, the 1960-70 change in this category is given in parenthesis to indicate the change in census methods while providing a full accounting of aggregate changes in employment over the period.

b: Percent of civilian labor force.

Source: U.S. Census of Population and Housing, 1960 and 1970.

ly and not contradictory interpretation of the data reflects the increasing ability of blue-collar workers to move from city to suburb: the decrease in the city of 12,000 craftsmen and operatives represented almost twice the decrease in all other occupations combined, with a 19 percent decrease in craftsmen and operatives, an 8 percent decrease in laborers and service workers, and a 4 percent decrease in residents reporting sales and clerical occupations. As a result of these changes, the city has experienced a slight upgrading in the occupational level of its work force despite the decrease in the overall size of the work force. At the same time, the suburban areas of the SMSA registered sizable increases in all occupations and also seem to have experienced a slight improvement in occupational level: professionals, managers, and administrators increased their representation in the suburban work force from 20.2 percent in 1960 to 23.5 percent in 1970 while craftsmen and operatives decreased from 36.2 percent of employed workers in 1960 to 33.9 percent in 1970.

To the extent that occupational categories reflect income and resultant purchasing power, changes in labor force characteristics in Pittsburgh between 1960 and 1970 suggest that while aggregate demand is most likely decreasing as a result of the overall loss of employed workers, average per capita consumption may be increasing commensurate with the gradual improvement in occupational level.

RESIDENCE AND WORKPLACE

The data on residential patterns and job distributions coalesce in journey-to-work patterns determined by the aggregate relationship between residence and workplace. The residence-workplace relationship between city and suburbs provides a useful indicator of the economic viability of the central city.

As measured by place of work reported by residents of the SMSA, Pittsburgh experienced a net gain of almost 13,000 jobs during the 1960-70 decade, countering a loss of 40,000 resident city workers with a 53,000 gain in the number commuting to the city to work (see Exhibit 5-4). Thus, while Pittsburgh had 29,000 fewer resident *workers* in 1970 than it had in 1960, the city gained in number of *jobs* as it continued to be able to attract commuters from the suburbs. In other words, the 23 percent drop in the number of residents who both work and live in Pittsburgh was more than offset by the 56 percent increase in the number of suburban residents who work in the central city. While the proportion of workers in the SMSA working in the city of Pittsburgh remained the same over the decade (33.6 percent in 1960 and 33.5 percent in 1970), the proportion of Pittsburgh's workers who lived in the city dropped from 83 percent in 1960 to 74 percent in 1970 and the proportion living in the suburbs rose accordingly from 16 percent to 22 percent.

Summarized, these data portray a significant trend toward suburbanization of Pittsburgh's work force and an increasing flow of commuters into the city. While in 1960, 65 percent of the people who worked in Pittsburgh lived in the city, by 1970 more people who worked in Pittsburgh lived in the suburbs (147,433 — 51.5 percent) than lived in the city (138,742 — 48.5 percent) (see Exhibit 5-4). Several studies have documented the extent to which suburban commuters drain the city's resources by imposing a daytime demand for public transportation, sanitation, safety, and similar services from the city while spending their incomes and paying property taxes in their home suburban communities. On the other hand, it has also been argued that large-scale commuting provides the city with revenue generated by consumer expenditures, payment for services, and taxes paid by employers, while freeing the city from substantial expenditures for schools and other services the costs of which are borne by the suburban municipalities. Regardless of this

EXHIBIT 5-4

JOURNEY-TO-WORK PATTERNS, PITTSBURGH, 1960 AND 1970

	1960		1970		Change 1960-1970	
Residence	*Number*	*Percent of All Workers*	*Number*	*Percent of All Workers*	*Number*	*Percent*
All Workers						
City	216,598	100.0	187,994	100.0	−28,604	−13.2
Suburbs	597,299	100.0	665,157	100.0	+67,858	+11.4
Work in Pittsburgh						
City	179,075	82.7	138,742	73.8	−40,333	−22.5
Suburbs	94,545	15.8	147,433	22.2	+52,888	+55.9
Work in Suburbs						
City	22,618	10.4	35,297	18.8	+12,679	+56.1
Suburbs	465,579	77.9	464,752	69.9	− 827	− 0.2
Work Outside SMSA						
City	1,682	0.8	1,857	0.9	+ 175	+10.4
Suburbs	15,756	2.6	19,349	2.9	+ 3,593	+22.8
Place of Work Not Reported						
City	13,223	6.1	12,098	6.4	− 1,125	− 8.5
Suburbs	21,419	3.6	33,623	5.1	+12,204	+56.9

Source: U.S. Census of Population and Housing, 1960 and 1970.

debate, Pittsburgh is likely to benefit from its evident ability to generate economic activity and attract commuters to city jobs. As commuting time and distance lengthens, it is also likely that the city's continued economic viability may begin to attract residents back from the suburbs.

At the same time that the city gained a net 13,000 jobs (the excess of new commuters over the loss of resident workers), it also gained an equal number of reverse commuters, with 13,000 more Pittsburgh residents working in the suburbs in 1970 than in 1960 (see Exhibit 5-4). This 56 percent increase in reverse commuting probably reflects the decentralization of employment and provides further evidence of the functional interdependence of city and suburb. *The city's ability to provide viable housing for the 19 percent of its residents who work in the suburbs and at the same time to continue to attract large numbers of suburban commuters will in large measure determine how the city will fare in economic competition with the surrounding suburbs.*

THE SUPPLY OF HOUSING

Changes in the supply of housing in the city of Pittsburgh between 1960 and 1970 provide a vivid portrait of housing market conditions in the city. Between 1960 and 1970, the city lost 3 percent — over 6,000 units — of its 1960 housing stock (see Exhibit 5-5). This decrease affected all housing categories: both total owner-occupied and total renter-occupied units decreased in number over the decade (−2.4 percent and −8.4 percent, respectively) as did the total number of units occupied by whites (−9.8 percent). These losses for the city were offset by only moderate increases in black owner-occupied (+23 percent) and black renter-occupied (+11 percent) units.

At the same time that the city's total housing stock decreased, the surrounding suburbs gained 55,000 new units, an increase of 10.2 percent for the ten-year period (see Exhibit 5-5). Within this suburban growth pattern, owner-occupied units increased by 14 percent and renter-occupied units increased by 5 percent.

Several noticeable changes occurred in the make-up of the city's housing stock over the decade. While in 1960 slightly more units in the city were renter-occupied, by 1970 the balance had tipped so that there were slightly more owner-occupied than renter-occupied units. The breakdown by tenure for occupied units in 1960 was 48.8 percent owner-occupied and 51.3 percent renter-occupied; in 1970, 50.3 percent were owner-occupied and 49.7 percent were renter-occupied.

The racial composition of occupied units in the city indicated that while the gap narrowed slightly over the decade, the vast majority of units were

EXHIBIT 5-5

HOUSING SUPPLY, PITTSBURGH, 1960 AND 1970

Housing Units	1960 Number	1960 Percent of All Housing Units	1970 Number	1970 Percent of All Housing Units	Change 1960-1970 Number	Change 1960-1970 Percent
Total Housing Units						
City	196,168	100.0	189,840	100.0	− 6,328	− 3.2
Suburbs	544,472	100.0	599,931	100.0	+55,459	+10.2
Owner-occupied						
City	91,825	46.8	89,626	47.2	− 2,199	− 2.4
Suburbs	372,200	68.4	424,877	70.8	+52,677	+14.2
White Owner-occupied						
City	82,854	42.2	78,397	41.3	− 4,457	− 5.4
Suburbs	365,218	67.1	415,349	69.2	+50,131	+13.7
Black Owner-occupied						
City	8,971	4.6	10,991	5.8	+ 2,020	+22.5
Suburbs	6,982	1.3	9,011	1.5	+ 2,029	+29.1
Renter-occupied						
City	96,511	49.2	88,390	46.6	− 8,121	− 8.4
Suburbs	149,207	27.4	156,281	26.0	+ 7,074	+ 4.7
White Renter-occupied						
City	76,076	38.9	64,912	34.2	−11,164	−14.7
Suburbs	140,397	25.9	146,451	24.4	+ 6,054	+ 4.3
Black Renter-occupied						
City	20,435	10.4	22,721	11.9	+ 2,286	+11.2
Suburbs	8,810	1.6	9,410	1.6	+ 600	+ 6.8
Vacant						
City	7,832	3.9	11,793	6.2	+ 3,961	+50.6
Suburbs	23,065	4.2	17,466	2.9	− 5,599	−24.3
Vacant-For-Sale						
City	655	0.3	957	0.5	+ 302	+46.1
Suburbs	4,060	0.8	2,784	0.5	− 1,276	−31.4
Vacant-For-Rent						
City	4,570	2.3	7,362	3.9	+ 2,792	+61.1
Suburbs	7,908	1.5	7,665	1.3	− 243	− 3.1
Other Vacant						
City	2,607	1.3	3,474	1.8	+ 867	+33.3
Suburbs	11,097	2.0	7,017	1.2	− 4,080	−36.8

Source: U.S. Census of Population and Housing, 1960 and 1970.

occupied by whites in both 1960 and 1970: blacks occupied 15.6 percent of the city's occupied units in 1960 and 18.9 percent by 1970.

Considering differences in tenure by race, white owners in the city slightly outnumbered white renters while black renters predominated over black owners at both the beginning and end of the decade. Fifty-two percent of white-occupied units compared to only 31 percent of black-occupied units were owner-occupied in 1960, with the proportions substantially unchanged (55 percent of white units and 33 percent of black units owner-occupied) in 1970.

Summarizing the results of these changes for the city between 1960 and 1970, white occupancy decreased substantially while black occupancy increased (see Exhibit 5-5). Within these categories, white renter-occupancy decreased at the fastest rate (−14.7 percent) while black owner-occupancy increased the fastest (+22.5 percent). Since white-occupied units far outnumbered black-occupied units in absolute terms, the black growth rate was insufficient to offset entirely decreases in white-occupied housing, with the net effect being an overall decrease in both owner- and renter-occupancy in the city.

The single most critical change in occupancy characteristics in the city is the vacancy rate. *Between 1960 and 1970, total vacancies in the city increased 51 percent, from a 1960 rate of 3.9 percent to a 1970 vacancy rate of 6.2 percent* (see Exhibit 5-5). Comparatively, the vacancy rate in the suburban portions of the metropolitan area decreased by a fourth, from a 1960 level of 4.2 percent to 2.9 percent in 1970. Thus, vacancy in the city was increasing even as the total number of available housing units was decreasing, while the suburbs experienced a significant decline in vacancies at a time of substantial expansion of the supply of housing. *The data provide conclusive evidence of a slackening of housing demand in the city combined with a growing demand for housing in the suburbs,* as would be expected from the analysis of population provided above.

Examination of city vacancy data by housing tenure indicates that vacant-for-rent units far outnumbered vacant-for-sale units in both 1960 and 1970, and that the disparity increased over the decade: in 1960, 58 percent of vacant units were vacant-for-rent compared to only 8 percent vacant-for-sale, while in 1970 the proportions were 62 percent and 8 percent, respectively. Approximately a third of all vacant structures in the city were not available for sale or rent in both 1960 and 1970: this latter category of vacant units accounted for 1.3 percent of the city's total housing units in 1960 and 1.8 percent in 1970 (see Exhibit 5-5).

CHARACTERISTICS OF THE HOUSING STOCK

Within the context of an overall decrease in the housing stock, significant

EXHIBIT 5-6

CHARACTERISTICS OF THE HOUSING STOCK, PITTSBURGH, 1960 AND 1970

Housing Units	1960 Number	1960 Percent of All Housing Units	1970 Number	1970 Percent of All Housing Units	Change 1960-1970 Number	Change 1960-1970 Percent
Total Housing Units						
City	196,168	100.0	189,840	100.0	− 6,328	− 3.2
Suburbs	544,472	100.0	599,931	100.0	+55,459	+10.2
Units Lacking Plumbing Facilities						
City	26,535	13.5	13,422	7.1	−13,113	−49.4
Suburbs	45,828	8.4	23,886	3.9	−21,942	−47.9
Three Rooms or Less						
City	54,492	27.8	49,755	26.2	− 4,737	−17.9
Suburbs	68,155	12.5	59,858	9.9	− 8,297	−12.2
Eight Rooms or More						
City	14,696	7.5	14,383	7.6	− 313	− 2.1
Suburbs	36,231	6.7	51,346	8.6	+15,115	+41.7
Median Number of Rooms						
City	4.6	—	4.7	—	—	—
Suburbs	5.3	—	5.9	—	—	—
Persons per Room ≥1.01						
City	19,622	10.0	11,481	6.0	− 8,141	−41.5
Suburbs	47,024	8.6	34,318	5.9	−12,706	−27.0
One Unit per Structure						
City	110,044	56.1	100,367	52.9	− 9,677	− 8.8
Suburbs	456,243	83.8	467,756	78.1	+11,513	+ 2.5
Two Units per Structure						
City	33,206	16.9	28,747	15.1	− 4,459	−13.4
Suburbs	39,574	7.3	54,908	9.2	+15,334	+38.7
Three to Four Units per Structure						
City	22,128	11.3	20,064	10.6	− 2,064	− 9.3
Suburbs	23,131	4.2	29,231	4.9	+ 6,100	+26.4
Five or More Units per Structure						
City	30,721	15.7	40,642	21.4	+ 9,921	+32.3
Suburbs	25,375	4.7	46,885	7.8	+21,510	+84.8

Source: U.S. Census of Population and Housing, 1960 and 1970.

changes in the type and quality of housing in Pittsburgh were indicated by several measures.

A 50 percent decrease was evident in the incidence of substandard housing as measured by the presence of units lacking some or all plumbing facilities (see Exhibit 5-6). Crowding of housing units also decreased substantially over the decade, with a 42 percent decrease in the number of housing units with a persons per room ratio of 1.01 or more. Both the large-scale out-migration from the city and its high vacancy rate, which were reported earlier, suggest that with housing supply exceeding demand, the worst housing is most likely being removed from the existing housing stock.

A further indication of the withdrawal of marginal units from the housing market derives from the significant decrease in the city's supply of very small units: between 1960 and 1970, small units (three rooms or fewer) decreased by 18 percent while very large units (eight rooms or more) decreased by only 2 percent. Simultaneously, the median number of rooms per unit in the city remained essentially unchanged over the decade, amounting to 4.6 in 1960 and 4.7 in 1970.

The nature of housing abandonment as well as of new construction is suggested in part by relative housing losses and gains by structure size. The city's net loss of 6,000 units between 1960 and 1970 was accounted for entirely by single-family, duplex, and small multifamily structures: the number of single-family structures fell by 9 percent, the number of units in duplexes by 13 percent, and the number of units in small multifamily structures (three to four units per structure) by 9 percent. At the same time, the number of units in larger multifamily structures (five or more units per structure) increased significantly, by 32 percent (see Exhibit 5-6). In absolute terms, the increase of 9,921 units in large multifamily structures offset more than half (61.2 percent) of the city's loss of units in all other types of structures. As a result of this increase in the number of units in large structures, one-unit (single-family) structures declined slightly from 56.1 percent of all units in 1960 to 52.9 percent of all units in 1970. Similarly, units in large multifamily structures increased proportionally from 15.7 percent of all units in 1960 to 21.4 percent in 1970.

The rise in multifamily construction in the city mirrored a similar trend in the suburbs, where units in large multifamily structures increased by 85 percent over the decade. The rapid increase in the size of the suburban housing stock resulted in a decrease in the city's share of units in the SMSA for all size categories. Between 1960 and 1970, the city's share of the SMSA's single-unit structures fell from 19.4 percent to 17.7 percent; its share of units in duplexes fell from 45.6 percent to 34.4 percent; the city's share of units in three- to four-unit structures fell from 48.9 percent to 40.7 percent; and the

city's proportion of the SMSA's units in structures with five or more units
fell from 54.8 percent to 46.4 percent.

SUMMARY

*The data on Pittsburgh's population and housing characteristics for 1960 and
1970 indicate a clear trend toward an excess of housing supply over demand.*
While total population fell 14 percent the city's housing stock decreased by 3
percent. The slackening of demand has had the positive effect of allowing
the retirement of the worst structures from the housing market, but also it
has had the negative effect of greatly increasing the vacancy rate. In sum, the
data suggest that Pittsburgh represents a first-rate example of the structural
shifts outlined for the general case in the descriptive model of tax delinquency in Chapter 2. Relationships between these structural shifts and the
level of tax delinquency in Pittsburgh will be examined in Chapter 6.

NEIGHBORHOOD STRUCTURE IN PITTSBURGH

The ebbs and flows of population and housing trends over time coalesce at
any given time in a particular pattern of neighborhoods. The number, size,
and location of affluent, deteriorated, or transitional neighborhoods in
Pittsburgh in 1970 are the direct manifestations of the population and housing trends just described. Our discussion above of population and housing
trends described the dynamic processes at work; we focus now on the underlying structure of the resulting neighborhood pattern. Our aim here is to
delineate the City's neighborhood structure, not necessarily in terms of
traditionally recognized neighborhood units, but rather, through the
statistical technique of factor analysis, by identifying neighborhood areas in
terms of shared communalities of population and housing characteristics.
These functionally defined neighborhoods will then be used in Chapter 6 to
identify the neighborhood characteristics associated with a high rate of tax
delinquency.

Neighborhoods, or any other subareas within the city, can be identified
on the basis of any of a wide range of characteristics. Thus, neighborhoods
may be identified on the basis of shared population characteristics or
homogeneity of housing characteristics or some combination of the two.
Following well-worn techniques of urban analysis, our approach is to consider a wide range of population and housing characteristics and to attempt
to identify the key factors underlying the citywide diversity in the incidence
of these characteristics.

Focusing on the census tract as our unit of analysis, we collected data on
fifty population and housing characteristics for each of 182 census tracts in
Pittsburgh. (Five of the city's total of 187 tracts were deleted from the

analysis because of their entirely institutional nature or because of major boundary changes that were made between 1960 and 1970.) Then, we subjected this matrix of fifty variables (characteristics) by 182 tracts to the statistical procedure of factor analysis. This procedure is designed to identify statistically the smallest possible number of factors that summarize clusters of related characteristics underlying the apparent diversity observed among census tracts in the city. (For a more detailed discussion of factor analysis, see Appendix A.)

In the Pittsburgh case, we identified nine principal factors that summarize the distribution of the fifty census characteristics across the 182 tracts. Examination of the particular clusters of characteristics included in each factor indicates the nature of the factors underlying the structure of population and housing characteristics of Pittsburgh's neighborhoods.

The nine factors that define the basic structure of population and housing characteristics in Pittsburgh are: (1) homeownership, (2) race and resources, (3) low rent, (4) affluence, (5) old age, (6) boarding house areas, (7) declining housing value, (8) vacancy, and (9) redevelopment areas. These nine factors and the clusters of population and housing characteristics associated with each one are summarized in Exhibit 5-7. Together, these nine factors capture 73 percent of the variation across census tracts of the fifty population and housing characteristics. A map of Pittsburgh's census tracts is provided in Exhibit 5-8, and the distributions of tracts according to their scores on each of the nine factors are mapped in Exhibits 5-9 through 5-17.

The data reported in Exhibit 5-7 warrant significant attention. The entries in the body of the Exhibit indicate the correlation between each census tract characteristic and its factor. (These are termed factor "loadings.") Only strong correlations are reported (i.e., those greater than .40 or less than $-.40$), so that our factors are defined only in terms of their most important constituent variables. The extent to which our factors succeed in accounting for the variation over census tracts in each of the fifty characteristics is indicated by the column to the far right of the Exhibit, headed "Communality." The closer this value is to 1.000, the larger the proportion of variation in the characteristic that has been accounted for by all the factors. The values reported at the bottom of the Exhibit indicate the relative importance of *each factor* in contributing to the underlying structure of neighborhood characteristics in Pittsburgh. The higher the proportion of total variation explained by each factor, the more important the factor. Armed with these definitions, we can proceed to an examination of the principal factors underlying the structure of neighborhoods in Pittsburgh.

FACTOR I: HOMEOWNERSHIP.

The first and most important factor identifies areas characterized by a high

EXHIBIT 5-7

POPULATION AND HOUSING STRUCTURE OF PITTSBURGH CENSUS TRACTS, 1970

Variables	I Homeowner	II Race & Resources	III Low Rent	IV Affluence	V Old Age	VI "Boarding House"	VII Declining Value	VIII Vacancy	IX Redevelopment Areas	Communality h^2
1. % of units in 5 or more-unit structures	-.878	—	—	—	—	—	—	—	—	.943
2. Median number of rooms	.854	—	—	—	—	—	—	—	—	.902
3. % of housing units owner-occupied	.853	—	—	—	—	—	—	—	—	.892
4. % of persons 5 years and over in same house, 1965 & 1970	.739	—	—	—	—	—	—	—	—	.812
5. Median persons per unit, renter-occupied	.725	—	—	—	—	—	—	—	—	.649
6. Median persons per unit, owner-occupied	.707	—	—	—	—	—	—	—	—	.669
7. Median persons per unit, all units	.652	—	—	—	-.493	—	—	—	—	.903
8. % of population over 14 years married	.642	—	—	—	—	-.512	—	—	—	.867
9. % of owner-occupied units with value less than $7,500	-.594	—	—	—	—	—	.439	—	—	.690

EXHIBIT 5-7 (cont'd)

POPULATION AND HOUSING STRUCTURE OF PITTSBURGH CENSUS TRACTS, 1970

	I Homeowner	II Race & Resources	III Low Rent	IV Affluence	V Old Age	VI "Boarding House"	VII Declining Value	VIII Vacancy	IX Redevelopment Areas	Communality h^2
10. % of units with more than one bathroom	.535	—	—	.502	—	—	—	—	—	.825
11. Median income of families and un-related individuals	.530	−.477	—	—	—	—	—	—	—	.840
12. % of units with same occupant in 1949	.518	—	—	—	—	—	—	—	—	.704
13. % change in rent of renter-occupied units, 1960 to 1970	−.450	—	−.448	—	—	—	—	—	.494	.770
14. % black	—	.940	—	—	—	—	—	—	—	.943
15. % of families with female head	—	.749	—	—	—	—	—	—	—	.791
16. % of families with income below poverty level	—	.747	—	—	—	—	—	—	—	.867
17. % service workers	—	.733	—	—	—	—	—	—	—	.791
18. % foreign stock	—	−.714	—	—	—	—	—	—	—	.640
19. % of workers using mass transit to get to work	—	.665	—	—	—	—	—	—	—	.598
20. % of families with public assistance or public welfare income	—	.589	.425	—	—	—	—	—	—	.770
21. % government workers	—	.553	—	—	—	—	—	—	—	.376

EXHIBIT 5-7 (cont'd)

POPULATION AND HOUSING STRUCTURE OF PITTSBURGH CENSUS TRACTS, 1970

22. % of population 16 to 21 years not high school graduates and not enrolled	.483	—	—	—	—	—	—	.431
23. % clerical and kindred workers	-.470	—	—	—	—	—	—	.426
24. % of male civilian labor force unemployed	.462	—	—	—	—	—	—	.513
25. % of females in labor force	-.698	—	—	—	—	—	—	.602
26. Median rent, renter-occupied units	-.680	.570	—	—	—	—	—	.928
27. % of renter-occupied units with gross rent less than $60	.629	—	—	—	—	—	—	.558
28. % professional, technical, and kindred workers	-.613	.481	—	—	—	—	—	.860
29. % of units with income $5,000 to $9,999 paying more than 25% for gross rent	-.567	.453	—	—	—	—	—	.667
30. Median school years completed	-.544	—	—	—	—	-.450	—	.882
31. % craftsmen, foremen, and kindred workers	.450	—	—	—	—	—	—	.552

EXHIBIT 5-7 (cont'd)

POPULATION AND HOUSING STRUCTURE OF PITTSBURGH CENSUS TRACTS, 1970

Variables	I Homeowner	II Race & Resources	III Low Rent	IV Affluence	V Old Age	VI "Boarding House"	VII Declining Value	VIII Vacancy	IX Redevelopment Areas	Communality h^2
32. % of families with income $25,000 or more	—	—	—	.786	—	—	—	—	—	.818
33. % self-employed workers	—	—	—	.769	—	—	—	—	—	.662
34. % managers and administrators, except farm	—	—	—	.652	—	—	—	—	—	.795
35. Median age	—	—	—	—	.920	—	—	—	—	.918
36. % of population over 65 years old	—	-.405	—	—	.784	—	—	—	—	.836
37. Change in median age, 1960 to 1970	—	—	—	—	.776	—	—	—	—	.740
38. % of families with children under 18 years old	—	—	—	—	-.538	—	—	—	—	.803
39. % of families with social security income	—	—	—	—	.452	—	—	—	—	.525
40. % of units built in 1939 or earlier	—	—	—	—	—	.573	—	—	—	.664
41. % of units with roomers, boarders, or lodgers	—	.425	—	—	—	.528	—	—	—	.556
42. % of units with 1.51 or more persons per room	—	—	—	—	—	.515	—	—	—	.448
43. % of units lacking all or some plumbing facilities	-.484	—	—	—	—	.502	—	—	—	.695

EXHIBIT 5-7 (cont'd)
POPULATION AND HOUSING STRUCTURE OF PITTSBURGH CENSUS TRACTS, 1970

44. % of units with no heat or with non-conventional heating	—	—	—	—	—	.486	—	—	—	.754
45. % population less than 5 yrs. old	.416	.447	—	—	—	—	—	—	—	.751
46. Median value, owner-occupied units	—	—	—	—	—	−.447	—	—	—	.889
47. % increase in median value, owner-occupied units, 1960 to 1970	—	—	.610	—	—	—	−.613	—	—	.501
48. Change in vacancy rate, 1960 to 1970	—	—	—	—	—	—	−.605	—	—	.822
49. % of units vacant for-sale or vacant-for-rent	—	—	—	—	—	—	—	.824	—	.810
50. % increase in median income 1960-1970	−.414	—	—	—	—	—	—	.726	.838	.817
% of total variation explained by each factor	16.00	13.97	9.70	8.29	7.30	5.59	4.27	4.01	3.77	72.90
Eigenvalues	8.001	6.984	4.851	4.147	3.652	2.796	2.133	2.007	1.885	

Technical Notes: Factors rotated to normal varimax position. Squared multiple correlations were inserted in the main diagonal of the correlation matrix as communality estimates, and only common factors with eigenvalues ≥ 1.00 were extracted. Only factor loadings greater than + .40 or less than − .40 have been reported. The percent of *total* variation explained by each factor is equal to the sum of the squared factor loadings (i.e., the eigenvalues) divided by the total number of variables (50) times 100. See Appendix A for a further description of the factor analysis procedure.

EXHIBIT 5-8

PITTSBURGH WARDS AND CENSUS TRACTS, 1970

28 – Ward Number

━━━ Ward Boundary

──── Tract Boundary

* *Not Applicable / No Data*

degree of homeownership. Housing units in these areas tend to be large
(variable 2, loading .854); owner-occupied (variable 3, loading .853);
relatively stable (variable 4, loading .739 and variable 12, loading .518); and
have more than one bathroom (variable 10, loading .535). Households in
these areas are generally characterized by larger families (variable 5, loading
.725; variable 6, loading .707; variable 7, loading .652); married persons
(variable 8, loading .642); and high median income (variable 11, loading
.530). Conversely, areas with low scores on the homeownership factor are
characterized by multifamily units (variable 1, loading −.878); of low value
(variable 9, loading −.594); with little increase in rent (variable 13, loading
−.450); a high proportion of units lacking plumbing facilities (variable 43,
loading −.484); and high vacancy (variable 49, loading −.414).

The distribution of census tracts in Pittsburgh according to their scores on the Homeownership factor is mapped in Exhibit 5-9, where a darker shading indicates a higher score. A relatively strong concentric pattern is evident, with low-scoring tracts clustered in the city center through parts of the fourth, fifth, seventh, and eighth wards, and north of the Ohio River in the twenty-second and twenty-third wards. Conversely, tracts scoring high

EXHIBIT 5-9
FACTOR I: HOMEOWNERSHIP

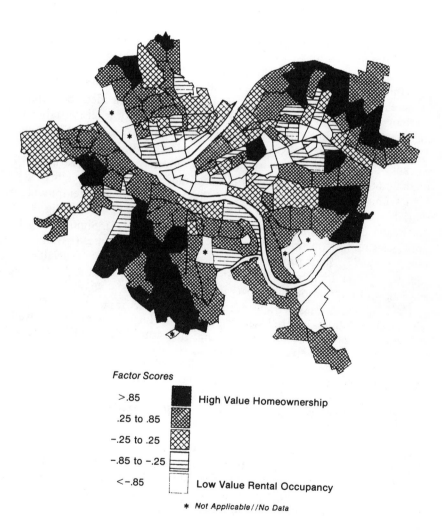

Factor Scores

>.85	■	High Value Homeownership
.25 to .85		
−.25 to .25		
−.85 to −.25		
<−.85		Low Value Rental Occupancy

* *Not Applicable//No Data*

on the Homeownership factor are spread around the outskirts of the City, with major concentrations in parts of the nineteenth, twentieth, and thirty-second wards to the south and the tenth, eleventh, and twelfth wards to the north. Census tracts scoring in the middle ranges on the Homeownership factor occupy the remainder of the city, with higher scores grading outward in increasing intensity from the center to the periphery. This pattern is as may be expected given the outward growth and decreasing density with distance from the center of the city.

FACTOR II: RACE AND RESOURCES

The second factor in importance in defining the structure of neighborhoods in Pittsburgh is one composed of indicators of racial composition and poor economic resources. This factor is defined by a cluster of characteristics entirely different than those of the first factor. Census tracts with high scores on the Race and Resources factor have a high percent black population (variable 14, loading .940) and high loadings for characteristics indicating a poor economic base: high percentages of female-headed households (variable 15, loading .749); families below the poverty level (variable 16, loading .747); persons employed in service occupations (variable 17, loading .733) and government jobs (variable 21, loading .553); high proportions of workers using public transportation in the journey to work (variable 19, loading .665); families receiving public assistance (variable 20, loading .589); high school "drop outs" (variable 22, loading .483); high unemployment (variable 24, loading .462); transient residents (variable 41, loading .425); and many children under five (variable 45, loading .416). Simultaneously, areas scoring low on this factor report high median incomes (variable 11, loading −.477); high proportions of foreign-born residents (variable 18, loading −.714); high proportions of clerical workers (variable 23, loading −.470); and population over 65 (variable 36, loading −.405).

The mapping of census tracts according to their scores on Factor II is indicated in Exhibit 5-10. High-scoring tracts are clustered in extremely well-defined areas of the city: in the third and fifth wards close to the center of the city, in wards twelve and thirteen to the east, in the twenty-first and twenty-fifth wards, and in several additional isolated tracts scattered throughout the city. Most of the remaining tracts in the city scored in the lowest category on the Race and Resources factor, underlining the rigid nature of low-income racial segregation: very few mixed or integrated tracts appear on the map.

FACTOR III: LOW RENT

The third factor, again identified by a completely different cluster of variables, appears to identify low-rent blue-collar communities. Census tracts with high scores on this factor tend to contain housing units which rent (in 1970) for less than $60 a month (variable 27, loading .629); and have high proportions of craftsmen, foremen, and kindred workers (variable 31, loading .450). Units in these tracts often have no heat or have non-conventional heating (variable 44, loading .447); and a high proportion of families receive public assistance (variable 20, loading .425). At the opposite end of the scale, census tracts with low scores on the Low Rent factor are characterized by a high percent of females in the labor force (variable 25, loading −.698); professional and technical workers (variable 28, loading −.613); and high education (variable 30, loading −.544). Rents in low-

EXHIBIT 5-10

FACTOR II: RACE AND RESOURCES

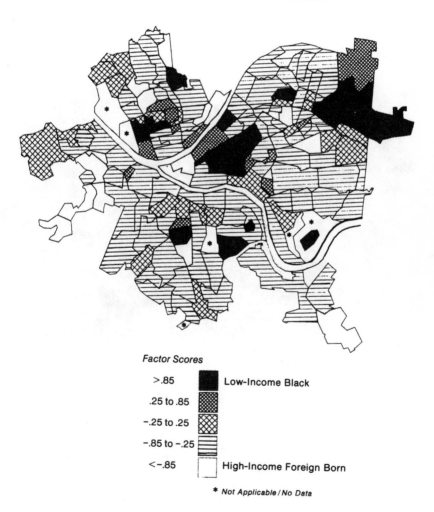

Factor Scores

>.85	Low-Income Black
.25 to .85	
−.25 to .25	
−.85 to −.25	
<−.85	High-Income Foreign Born

* *Not Applicable / No Data*

scoring tracts increased between 1960 and 1970 (variable 13, loading −.448), and median rent is high (variable 26, loading −.680). Perhaps as a result of these two characteristics, middle-income households in low-scoring tracts tend to pay more than 25 percent of their income for rent (variable 29, loading −.567). In summary, tracts scoring high on the Low Rent factor appear to represent blue-collar workers (craftsmen) living in low-rent units; tracts scoring low on the Low Rent factor appear to represent white-collar (professional), well-educated workers (with many women in the labor force)

EXHIBIT 5-11

FACTOR III: LOW RENT

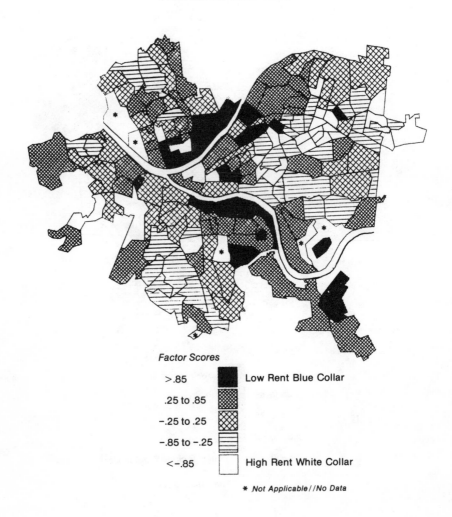

Factor Scores

>.85	■	Low Rent Blue Collar
.25 to .85		
−.25 to .25		
−.85 to −.25		
<−.85	□	High Rent White Collar

* Not Applicable//No Data

living in relatively high-rent units to which they allocate a high proportion of their income.

The distribution of census tracts by scores on Factor III is indicated in Exhibit 5-11. High-scoring tracts tend to be adjacent to and beyond (i.e., further from the city center) the tracts that scored high on Race and Resources. Low rent, blue-collar, communities in Pittsburgh, in other words, tend to be located adjacent to the low-income black communities but with little or no overlap. Thus, Low Rent census tracts are generally concentrated in wards twenty-two, twenty-three, and twenty-four, and in the industrial areas along the river in wards sixteen, seventeen, and thirty-one. Census tracts with low scores on the Low Rent factor appear to be scattered among the higher-rent areas in the center of the city, areas in which the accessibility of the center would be seen as advantageous by the white-collar renter population. These tracts thus appear in wards two and three adjacent to the center, in the fourth and seventh wards which are close to the center, and in ward thirteen. Tracts scoring in the middle ranges on the Low Rent factor tend to be dispersed throughout the remaining industrial and older residential sections of the city, along the Allegheny River to the north, in wards six and nine, in ward thirty-one to the south, and in parts of wards twenty and twenty-eight.

FACTOR IV: AFFLUENCE

The fourth factor underlying the structure of neighborhoods in Pittsburgh is a measure of socioeconomic status and affluence. To some extent, it appears to be the opposite or the complement of the Low Rent factor. The characteristic with the highest loading on the Affluence factor is very high income (variable 32, loading .786). Census tracts with high scores on Factor IV are also characterized by high proportions of self-employed workers (variable 33, loading .769); managers and administrators (variable 34, loading .652); and professional and technical workers (variable 28, loading .481). Median value of housing in these tracts is high (variable 46, loading .610), as is median rent (variable 26, loading .570). A high proportion of units have more than one bathroom (variable 10, loading .502). Perhaps because of the high median rent, middle-income residents in these tracts tend to pay more than a fourth of their income on rent (variable 29, loading .453).

The map of census tract scores on the Affluence factor (see Exhibit 5-12) indicates that high-scoring tracts on this factor form a strongly marked cluster that is almost coterminous with the low-density residential area of ward fourteen. Adjacent segments of wards seven and twelve are also included in this cluster. Several other scattered tracts also score high on the Affluence factor: those segments of the second and third wards that are close to the city center and have undergone urban renewal, and segments of wards eleven and twenty at outlying, and opposite, corners of the city.

FACTOR V: OLD AGE

Factor V identifies the "age ghettos" of the city: areas with concentrations of elderly residents. The highest loading characteristic on the Old Age factor is, clearly, median age (variable 35, loading .920). In addition, tracts with high scores on this factor have concentrations of population over sixty-five (variable 36, loading .784); reflect *increasing* concentrations of the elderly

EXHIBIT 5-12

FACTOR IV: AFFLUENCE

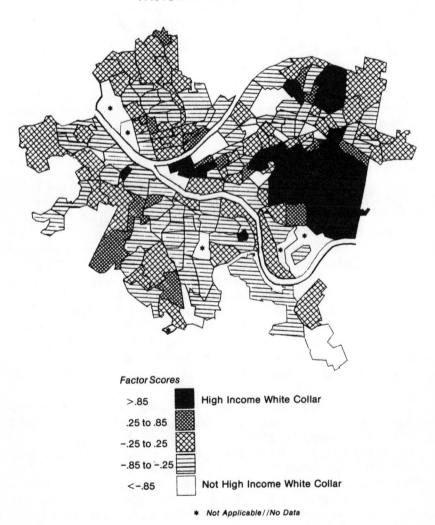

Factor Scores

>.85	High Income White Collar
.25 to .85	
−.25 to .25	
−.85 to −.25	
<−.85	Not High Income White Collar

* *Not Applicable//No Data*

between 1960 and 1970 (variable 37, loading .776); and have a high proportion of families receiving social security income (variable 39, loading .452). As would be expected, census tracts scoring low on the Old Age factor have high proportions of families with children under eighteen (variable 38, loading −.538) and a high median number of persons per unit, i.e., large families (variable 7, loading −.493).

EXHIBIT 5-13

FACTOR V: OLD AGE

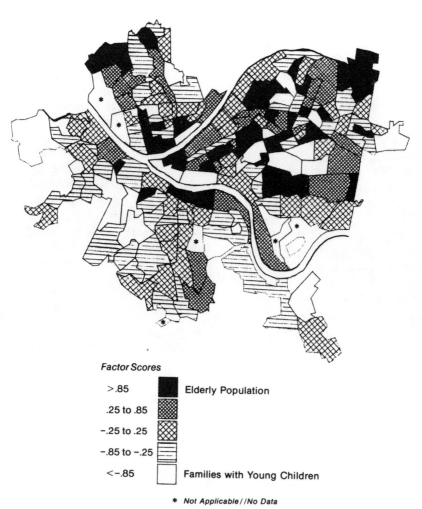

Factor Scores

> .85	Elderly Population
.25 to .85	
−.25 to .25	
−.85 to −.25	
< −.85	Families with Young Children

* *Not Applicable//No Data*

The map of census tract scores on Factor V demonstrates the widespread distribution of the elderly population in Pittsburgh (see Exhibit 5-13). High-scoring tracts are dispersed throughout much of the city: concentrations of the elderly are found in wards two, three, five, seven, eight, nine, ten, eleven, twelve, and thirteen, on one axis, and in wards twenty-two, twenty-three, twenty-five, twenty-six, and twenty-seven, on a second axis. Additional concentrations are to be found in the seventeenth and nineteenth wards south of the Monongahela River. The scattered but widespread nature of this distribution seems to indicate that the elderly constitute an important segment of Pittsburgh's population, but that their residences are scattered in the interstitial areas vacated by other groups.

FACTOR VI: "BOARDING HOUSE" AREAS

The "Boarding House" factor identifies areas most strongly characterized by sub-standard housing. Census tracts with high scores on Factor VI have high proportions of housing units that were built pre-1939 (variable 40, loading .573); are occupied by roomers, boarders, or lodgers (variable 41, loading .528); are crowded (variable 42, loading .515); lack adequate plumbing facilities (variable 43, loading .502); and lack adequate heating facilities (variable 44, loading .486). Residents of census tracts scoring low on the "Boarding House" factor tend to be married (variable 8, loading −.512) and have children under five (variable 45, loading −.447). "Boarding house" areas thus appear to be those characterized by a transient single (unmarried) population having few or no children and living in substandard housing.

The map of census tract scores on Factor VI (Exhibit 5-14) shows high-scoring tracts to be the "skid row" areas just outside and surrounding the central business district. The outlying high-scoring tracts (e.g., tract 1201 in ward 12) contain institutional populations (e.g., prisons, state hospitals, etc.) whose characteristics most resemble those of the skid row areas (e.g., crowding, no children, etc.).

FACTOR VII: DECLINING (LOW) VALUE

The seventh factor defining Pittsburgh's neighborhood structure is based on variables that indicate very low — and declining — housing value and the absence of high-value units. Census tracts that score high on Factor VII contain high proportions of owner-occupied units with a 1970 value of less than $7,500 (variable 9, loading .439). Conversely, low-scoring tracts have high-median-value units (variable 46, loading −.613); and evidenced an increase in median value between 1960 and 1970 (variable 47, loading −.605). Residents of low-scoring tracts tend to be well-educated (variable 30, loading −.450).

Census tracts with high scores on the Declining (Low) Value factor tend to be concentrated in the industrial belt along the Monongahela River in wards sixteen, seventeen, and thirty-one, in the twentieth ward, and scattered throughout the north-west corner of the city (see Exhibit 5-15). Correspondingly, low-scoring tracts (i.e., those with high and increasing median housing values) are generally concentrated in a sectoral pattern extending along the main northeast axis. This latter area appears to comprise the city's healthiest housing submarket.

EXHIBIT 5-14

FACTOR VI: "BOARDING HOUSE" AREAS

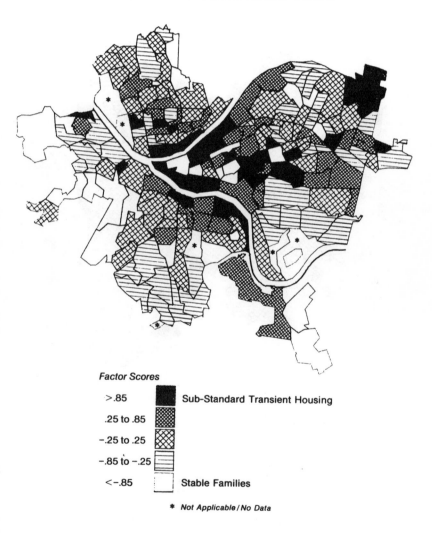

Factor Scores

> .85	■	Sub-Standard Transient Housing
.25 to .85	▨	
−.25 to .25	▧	
−.85 to −.25	☰	
< −.85	▢	Stable Families

* *Not Applicable/No Data*

FACTOR VIII: VACANCY
Two variables, vacancy rate and change in the vacancy rate, create their own independent and significant dimension underlying Pittsburgh's neighborhood structure. Census tracts scoring high on Factor VIII have high vacancy in both for-sale and rental units (variable 49, loading .726); and experienced an increase in the vacancy rate between 1960 and 1970 (varaible 48, loading .824).

EXHIBIT 5-15

FACTOR VII: DECLINING LOW VALUE

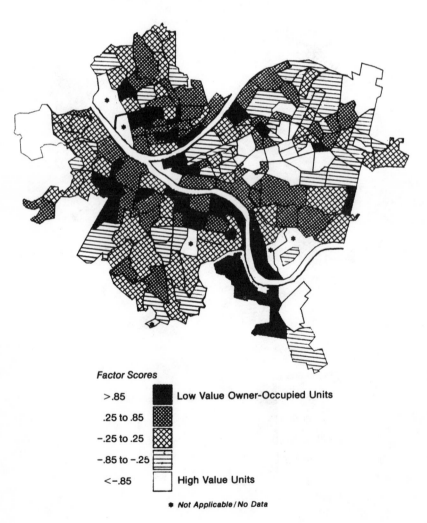

Factor Scores

>.85	■	Low Value Owner-Occupied Units
.25 to .85	▦	
−.25 to .25	▨	
−.85 to −.25	▤	
<−.85	□	High Value Units

✶ Not Applicable / No Data

As indicated in the map in Exhibit 5-16, the vacancy problem appears to be largely concentrated in a rather extensive area of the center of the city. Wards one, two, three, and parts of five are the most heavily affected.

FACTOR IX: REDEVELOPMENT AREAS

The final unique dimension of neighborhood structure is created through high loadings of two variables, one indicating an increase in median income between 1960 and 1970 (variable 50, loading .838), and the second indicating an increase in median rent between 1960 and 1970 (variable 13, loading .494). To score high on Factor IX, a tract must exhibit an increase in median income and median rent levels substantially greater than the overall citywide increases due to inflation.

EXHIBIT 5-16

FACTOR VIII: VACANCY

Factor Scores

>.85	High Vacancy
.25 to .85	
−.25 to .25	
−.85 to −.25	
<−.85	Low Vacancy

* Not Applicable / No Data

   Examination of the distribution of high-scoring tracts (see Exhibit 5-17) indicates that these tracts are essentially synonymous with the city's redevelopment projects of the 1960s. Complete clearance and redevelopment of large tracts of land provide one of the few plausible explanations for local increases in income and rent substantially above the citywide rate.

   The nine factors described above represent the principal components of population and housing characteristics of Pittsburgh's neighborhoods. In the following chapter, we first present a brief description of the magnitude of tax delinquency within the City of Pittsburgh, and then examine the relationships between the distribution of tax delinquency and the distribution of census tract scores on the nine neighborhood factors.

EXHIBIT 5-17

FACTOR IX: REDEVELOPMENT AREAS

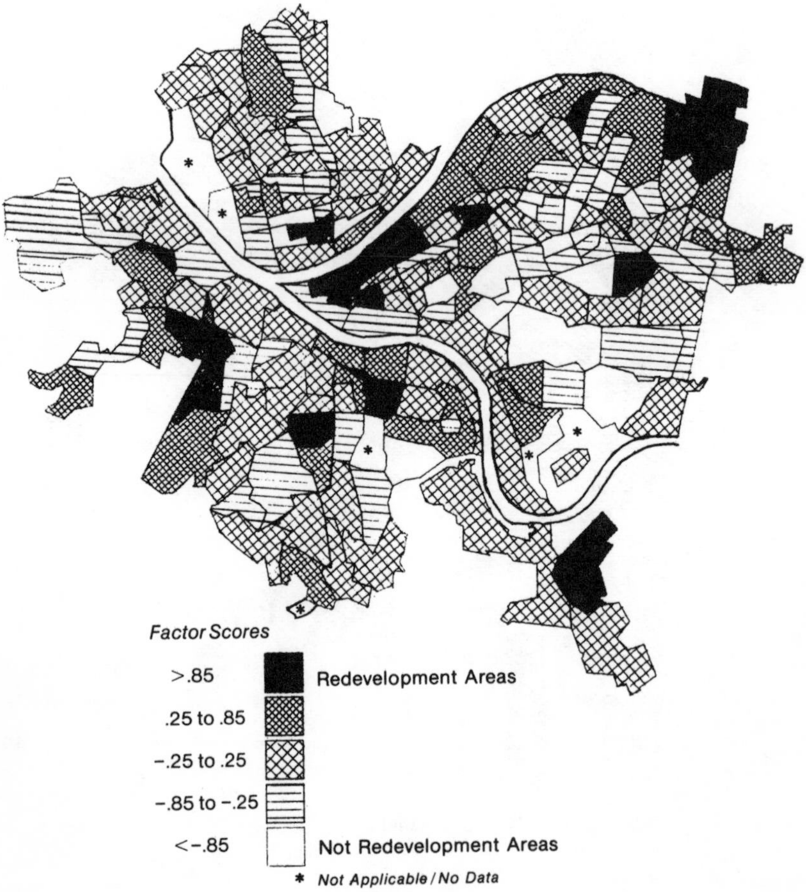

Factor Scores

>.85   ⬛ Redevelopment Areas

.25 to .85

−.25 to .25

−.85 to −.25

<−.85   ☐ Not Redevelopment Areas

* Not Applicable / No Data

Chapter 6

The Neighborhood Environment of Delinquency

INTRODUCTION

The population and housing trends described in Chapter 5 summarize the parameters of housing market activity in Pittsburgh and suggest the city-wide context of tax delinquency. In this chapter, we proceed to a specific focus on the magnitude, geographic distribution, and neighborhood environment of tax delinquency within the city.

Our discussion is organized as follows. First, we examine the overall magnitude and the size distribution of taxes owed, by property type, as indicated by city tax records. We then narrow our focus to concentrate on delinquency on *residential* parcels. As of year-end 1973, city records indicated real estate taxes in arrears on some 6200 residential properties in the city.

Maintaining our focus on residential parcels, we next examine the geographic distribution of four different but inter-related measures of delinquency. Each of these measures provides information on a different aspect of the overall problem, reflecting the multi-faceted complexity of the delinquency question. The four measures serve as indicators of (a) *frequency* — the proportion of delinquent parcels in a census tract; (b) *magnitude* — the average amount of back taxes owed per parcel in a tract; (c) *extreme delinquency* — the proportion of delinquent parcels with back tax bills above the

113

city-wide average; and (d) *chronic delinquency* — the proportion of delinquent parcels in a tract with ratios of delinquency to assessed value above
the city-wide average. Mapping the geographic distributions of these four
delinquency measures provides a graphic illustration of the incidence of
delinquency in Pittsburgh.

With information in hand on the magnitude and distribution of the
problem, we then turn to the question of defining the neighborhood environment of tax delinquency. We first uncover the complexity of the
problem by identifying the specific population and housing characteristics
associated with each of the four delinquency measures, thus clarifying the
particular dimension of delinquency reflected in each measure. Then, the
distribution of each measure of residential tax delinquency in Pittsburgh is
analyzed in light of the underlying dimensions of Pittsburgh's neighborhood
structure identified in Chapter 5.

THE MAGNITUDE OF TAX DELINQUENCY IN PITTSBURGH

Data on the magnitude of tax delinquency in Pittsburgh are maintained in
computerized files in the City Treasurer's office. (See Appendix A for details
on the methodology employed in extracting these data and linking them to
related data on land use characteristics, structure type, assessed value, etc.)
The discussion in this section covers city records on taxes owed as of
December 31, 1973. Our definition of tax delinquency in this section is
therefore the amount of taxes owed as of that date as indicated in the tax
delinquency file of the Pittsburgh City Treasurer's office.

TOTAL TAXES OWED

As of December 31, 1973, some combination of real estate taxes, water
charges and sewer charges were in arrears on 31,926 real properties in the
city of Pittsburgh, or on approximately one-quarter of the real properties in
the city.[1] Total tax arrears on active accounts amounted to $21.4 million, or
approximately 10 percent of the locally raised annual revenues of the city,
school district, and county government[2] (see Exhibit 6-1). Considering all
properties listed in city records as delinquent, improved properties account
for 84 percent of taxes owed and 87 percent of the total number of delinquent properties; unimproved parcels (i.e. vacant land) account for 16 percent of taxes owed and 13 percent of the number of delinquent properties.
Within the category of improved parcels, residential properties account for
the lion's share of the *number of delinquent parcels* (71 percent of *all* delinquent parcels; 82 percent of *improved* delinquent parcels). Improved properties in non-residential use, however, account for a disproportionate share of
taxes owed: 36.7 percent of all delinquent parcels, versus 31.6 percent accru-

EXHIBIT 6-1

TOTAL REAL ESTATE, WATER, AND SEWER TAXES OWED THE CITY, SCHOOL DISTRICT, AND COUNTY ON DECEMBER 31, 1973, BY PROPERTY LAND USE AND OWNERSHIP, PITTSBURGH

	Privately Owned Properties					Publicly Owned Properties					All Properties				
	Taxes Owed (000s)		Delinquent Properties		Dollars per Delinquent Property	Taxes Owed (000s)		Delinquent Properties		Dollars per Delinquent Property	Taxes Owed (000s)		Delinquent Properties		Dollars per Delinquent Property
	$	%	Number	%	$	$	%	Number	%	$	$	%	Number	%	$
Improved Properties[a]															
Residential[b]	6,455	37.2	21,912	74.3	295	301	7.5	721	29.8	417	6,756	31.6	22,633	70.9	299
Non-residential[b]	6,562	37.8	1,779	6.0	3,689	1,288	31.9	177	7.3	7,280	7,850	36.7	1,956	6.1	4,013
Type Unknown[c]	1,997	11.5	2,994	10.1	667	1,284	31.8	83	3.4	15,475	3,281	15.3	3,077	9.6	1,066
Total Improved	15,014	86.5	26,685	90.4	563	2,873	71.2	981	40.5	2,929	17,887	83.6	27,666	86.7	647
Vacant Land[d]	2,350	13.5	2,820	9.6	833	1,164	28.8	1,440	59.5	808	3,514	16.4	4,260	13.3	825
TOTAL[e]	17,364	100.0	29,505	100.0	589	4,037	100.0	2,421	100.0	1,667	21,401	100.0	31,926	100.0	670

Notes:
a. Improved properties are defined as parcels with an assessed value of improvements greater than zero.
b. Land uses were determined using the 1967 Land Use Survey; see Appendix A for full description.
c. These delinquent properties could not be matched with reports in the Land Use Survey.
d. Vacant land is defined as a property with an assessed value of improvements equal to zero.
e. Totals may not be exactly comparable from Exhibit to Exhibit due to missing data for some properties. Properties lacking relevant data are excluded from affected tabulations.

Sources: Pittsburgh Tax Delinquency File, Real Property File, Land Use Survey; see Appendix A for full description.

ing to residential properties. As a result of these disparities, average delinquency on residential parcels amounted to only $299 while average delinquency on non-residential parcels was $4013. (These data must be interpreted with caution, however, because of the relatively large proportion of parcels for which property type could not be determined - these parcels account for 15 percent of taxes owed and 10 percent of the total number of delinquent properties.) Average delinquency on unimproved (vacant) parcels amounted to $825, substantially above the average for delinquent residential parcels but far below the average for non-residential properties. For all delinquent parcels in the city, the average amount of taxes owed was $670.

Of the 32,000 nominally delinquent parcels in Pittsburgh at year end 1973, 8 percent - owing over 4 million dollars in back taxes - are parcels owned by public agencies. The bulk of these publicly owned properties are held by the Urban Redevelopment Authority. Parcels of vacant land substantially outnumber improved properties, accounting for 60 percent of total delinquent publicly owned properties. In contrast, unimproved parcels comprise only 10 percent of privately-owned delinquent properties. Residential properties comprise a far smaller proportion of publicly owned delinquent parcels (30 percent) than is the case for total (71 percent) and privately-owned (74 percent) delinquent properties.

City records indicate that on average publicly owned properties owe $1667 of back taxes per property, almost three times the average amount owed on privately owned properties. Except for parcels of vacant land, publicly owned properties of every type owe substantially more than do privately owned delinquent properties. However, the bulk of the difference in average taxes owed on public and private properties results from the enormous value of taxes owed on publicly owned improved properties of unknown type. Almost one-third of the back taxes owed by public authorities is due on the 83 properties in this group. On average, these 83 properties owe $15,000 in back taxes. Privately owned properties in this class owe only $667 on average.

It is difficult to determine the validity of the tax delinquency records of publicly owned properties. In many cases, the tax bills of these nominally delinquent properties were undoubtedly accrued by private owners before the property was acquired by public agencies. In other cases, tax delinquency records may simply result from delays in acknowledging the property tax exemption of many of these properties. Independent research conducted by the Center for Urban Policy Research in New York City, Newark, and Trenton, New Jersey (in addition to Pittsburgh) indicates that the delinquency records in each of these cities often include substantial amounts of taxes owed on properties in public ownership. To the extent that maintaining delinquency records on exempt properties artificially swells the magnitude of the problem, it is likely that most municipalities would benefit greatly from a record-cleaning operation designed to delete these nominally delinquent accounts from the delinquent file.

Even if all tax bills in arrears on publicly owned properties in Pittsburgh proved to be invalid, however, delinquent real estate, water, and sewer taxes owed the city, county, and school district on privately-owned parcels amounted to $17.4 million and involved nearly 30,000 parcels. Almost three-fourths of these privately-owned delinquent properties were residential, although an average of only $295 was owed on these properties. Nine out of ten privately owned properties were improved and the remaining 10 percent were vacant land.

SIZE DISTRIBUTION OF TAXES OWED

Exhibits 6-2 to 6-4 provide further insight into the nature of property tax delinquency in Pittsburgh. As was indicated above, on December 31, 1973 back taxes were owed on 31,926 real properties in Pittsburgh. Of this total 82 percent of the bills amounted to less than $500. Bills of over $1000 were owed on only 2,099 (6.6 percent) of the 31,926 delinquent properties. Thus, most back tax bills were quite small. Nonresidential improved properties stand out as being most likely to have built up substantial tax bills, and even here, bills of less than $500 are owed on two out of every three properties of this type.

As is shown in Exhibits 6-3 and 6-4, large individual amounts more commonly tend to be owed on publicly owned properties. Only 6 percent of the bills for back taxes on *privately* owned parcels are greater than $1000; over 14 percent of the bills owed on *publicly* owned properties fall into this size class. Nevertheless, almost three-quarters of the tax bills owed on publicly owned properties are less than $500.

The high proportion of delinquent parcels owing relatively small tax bills is undoubtedly influenced by the inclusion in these data of properties on which only water and/or sewer charges (as opposed to real extate taxes) are owed. The data in Exhibit 6-5 show this to be the case. Here, focusing only on privately-owned residential structures, the size distribution of taxes owed is shown separately for those structures on which real estate taxes are in arrears and those owing only water and/or sewer charges. Fully 94 percent of the latter category but only 58 percent of the former owed less than $500 in payments due the City. Conversely, 15 percent of parcels owing real estate taxes but only 1 percent of parcels in arrears on water or sewer charges owed $1,000 or more. Privately owned residential parcels delinquent in real estate taxes owed $658 on average; equivalent parcels delinquent on only water or sewer charges owed an average of only $151.

EXHIBIT 6-2

SIZE DISTRIBUTION OF REAL ESTATE, WATER, AND SEWER TAXES OWED ON ALL DELINQUENT PROPERTIES IN PITTSBURGH, DECEMBER 31, 1973

| Dollars Owed Per Property | Improved Properties[a] | | | | | | | | Vacant Land[d] | | Total Delinquent Properties | |
| | Residential[b] | | Non-Residential[b] | | Unknown Land-Use[c] | | Total Improved Properties | | | | | |
	Number	Percent	Number	Percent	Number	Percent	Number	Percent	Number	Percent	Number	Percent
Less than $500	18,871	83.4	1,297	66.3	2,574	83.7	22,742	82.2	3,440	80.8	26,182	82.0
$500-999	2,629	11.6	240	12.3	348	11.3	3,217	11.6	428	10.0	3,645	11.4
$1000 or more	1,133	5.0	419	21.4	155	5.0	1,707	6.2	392	9.2	2,099	6.6
TOTAL[e]	22,633	100.0	1,956	100.0	3,077	100.0	27,666	100.0	4,260	100.0	31,926	100.0

Notes:
a. Improved properties are defined as parcels with an assessed value of improvements greater than zero.
b. Land uses were determined using the 1967 Land Use Survey; see Appendix A for full description.
c. These delinquent properties could not be matched with records in the Land Use Survey.
d. Vacant land is defined as a property with an assessed value of improvements equal to zero.
e. Totals may not be exactly comparable from Exhibit to Exhibit due to missing data for some properties. Properties lacking relevant data are excluded from affected tabulations.

Sources: Pittsburgh Tax Delinquency File, Real Property File, Land Use Survey; see Appendix A for full description.

EXHIBIT 6-3

SIZE DISTRIBUTION OF REAL ESTATE, WATER, AND SEWER TAXES OWED ON PRIVATELY OWNED PROPERTIES IN PITTSBURGH, DECEMBER 31, 1973

| Dollars Owed Per Property | Improved Properties[a] | | | | | | | | Vacant Land[d] | | Total Delinquent Properties | |
| | Residential[b] | | Non-Residential[b] | | Unknown Land-Use[c] | | Total Improved Properties | | | | | |
	Number	Percent	Number	Percent	Number	Percent	Number	Percent	Number	Percent	Number	Percent
Less than $500	18,297	83.5	1,213	68.2	2,520	84.2	22,030	82.6	2,408	85.4	4,438	82.8
$500-999	2,535	11.6	204	11.5	343	11.5	3,082	11.5	234	8.3	3,316	11.2
$1000 or more	1,080	4.9	362	20.3	131	4.4	1,573	5.9	178	6.3	1,751	5.9
TOTAL[e]	21,912	100.0	1,779	100.0	2,994	100.0	26,685	100.0	2,820	100.0	29,505	100.0

Notes: a. Improved properties are defined as parcels with an assessed value of improvements greater than zero.
b. Land uses were determined using the 1967 Land Use Survey; see Appendix A for full description.
c. These delinquent properties could not be matched with records in the Land Use Survey.
d. Vacant land is defined as a property with an assessed value of improvements equal to zero.
e. Totals may not be exactly comparable from Exhibit to Exhibit due to missing data for some properties. Properties lacking relevant data are excluded from affected tabulations.

Source: Pittsburgh Tax Delinquency File, Real Property File, Land Use Survey; see Appendix A for full description.

EXHIBIT 6-4

SIZE DISTRIBUTION OF REAL ESTATE, WATER, AND SEWER TAXES OWED ON PUBLICLY OWNED PROPERTIES IN PITTSBURGH, DECEMBER 31, 1973

| Dollars Owed Per Property | Improved Properties[a] | | | | | | Total Improved Properties | | Vacant Land[d] | | Total Delinquent Properties | |
| | Residential[b] | | Non-Residential[b] | | Unknown Land-Use[c] | | | | | | | |
	Number	Percent	Number	Percent	Number	Percent	Number	Percent	Number	Percent	Number	Percent
Less than $500	574	79.6	84	47.5	54	65.1	712	72.6	1,032	71.7	1,744	72.0
$500-999	94	13.0	36	20.3	5	6.0	135	13.8	194	13.5	329	13.6
$1000 or More	53	7.4	57	32.2	24	28.9	134	13.7	214	14.9	348	14.4
TOTAL[e]	721	100.0	177	100.0	83	10.0	981	100.0	1,440	100.0	2,421	100.0

Notes: a. Improved properties are defined as parcels with an assessed value of improvements greater than zero.
b. Land uses were determined using the 1967 Land Use Survey; see Appendix A for full description.
c. These delinquent properties could not be matched with records in the Land Use Survey.
d. Vacant land is defined as a property with an assessed value of improvements equal to zero.
e. Totals may not be exactly comparable from Exhibit to Exhibit due to missing data for some properties. Properties lacking relevant data are excluded from affected tabulations.

Sources: Pittsburgh Tax Delinquency File, Real Property File, Land Use Survey; see Appendix A for full description.

EXHIBIT 6-5

SIZE DISTRIBUTION OF TAX DELINQUENCY ON PRIVATELY OWNED
RESIDENTIAL STRUCTURES IN PITTSBURGH, BY TYPES OF TAXES OWED,
DECEMBER 31, 1973

Dollars Owed Per Structure	Structures Owing Real Estate Taxes		Structures Owing Only Water or Sewer Charges		Total Delinquent Privately Owned Residential Structures	
	Number	Percent	Number	Percent	Number	Percent
Less than $500	3,598	58.1	14,699	93.5	18,297	83.5
$500-999	1,672	27.0	863	5.5	2,535	11.6
$1000 or more	928	15.0	152	1.0	1,080	4.9
Total Structures	6,198	100.0	15,714	100.0	21,912	100.0
Average Taxes Owed Per Structure	$ 658		$ 151		$ 295	'

Source: Pittsburgh Tax Delinquency File, Real Property File, Land Use Survey.

From the viewpoint of municipal officials, overdue payment on any of these charges would classify a property as delinquent in its tax payments. Public utility charges represent an important component of total city revenues. Nonetheless, the remainder of our discussion will focus on those parcels delinquent in real estate tax payments, and will omit parcels owing only water or sewer charges. (Parcels delinquent in real estate tax payments may owe water and sewer charges as well.)

Further, we narrow our focus to consider only delinquent privately-owned residential parcels. The omission of publicly-owned delinquent parcels from further consideration derives from the ambiguous status of these parcels. The focus on residential parcels is motivated by the finding that the largest proportion of delinquent properties in Pittsburgh are housing structures. It follows, then, that the problems producing delinquency are typically housing problems with their locus in the operation of the housing market. The data indicate that while delinquency in non-residential property and vacant land tends to represent large dollar-value accounts, it is concentrated in a relatively small number of accounts. This suggests in turn that delinquency in non-residential parcels may typically stem from particular problems unique to particular properties or particular owners. The focus on residential delinquency tends to minimize the impact of idiosyncratic factors on the overall delinquency rate. Thus, for the remainder of our discussion, the definition of a tax delinquent parcel will be limited to improved privately owned residential properties on which real estate taxes were owed as of December 31, 1973.

RESIDENTIAL TAX DELINQUENCY

The analysis of residential tax delinquency will focus on three housing structure types: (1) single-family homes in both attached and detached structures; (2) duplexes; and (3) apartments with some commercial use. No information was available to make it possible to accurately identify apartments lacking commercial occupancy. Information on the stock of housing structures in Pittsburgh was drawn from the 1970 Census of Housing. Numbers of single family, duplex and apartment buildings in the city were estimated using census data. Information on delinquency was current in 1973; information on the land use of delinquent structures was current in 1967; and information on neighborhood housing and population characteristics was collected in 1970. Thus, all figures must be considered approximations of current reality.

Of the 6198 privately owned residential parcels with delinquent property taxes, 5887 (95 percent) could be classified as one-family homes, duplexes or apartment structures with some commercial occupancy. The remaining 311 properties were classified in a miscellaneous category, encompassing apartments, rooming houses, dormitories, etc. Exhibit 6-6 presents estimates of the numbers of properties of the various types, and their tax delinquency.

The exhibit presents delinquency rates and the size distribution of taxes owed for the three residential structure types. Overall, 5 percent of residential structures in Pittsburgh had outstanding real estate tax bills on December 31, 1978. Duplexes show the highest rate of delinquency of the three structure types - 7.6 percent. Apartments evidence the lowest delinquency rate. This low rate is in part attributable to the fact that only mixed use delinquent apartment structures could be identified. However, even if a major portion of the miscellaneous unclassified residential structures are apartment structures, the delinquency rate of apartments would not rise much above 5 percent.

Delinquent apartment structures tend to owe larger back tax bills than do either one-family or duplex structures. Taxes owed exceed $1,000 for over a third of apartment structures but only 15 percent of total delinquent residential structures. This might be expected given higher assessed values of multi-family structures.

GEOGRAPHIC DISTRIBUTION OF RESIDENTIAL
TAX DELINQUENCY

Four different measures of the incidence or severity of residential tax delin-

EXHIBIT 6-6
RESIDENTIAL TAX DELINQUENCY IN PITTSBURGH ON DECEMBER 31, 1973, BY STRUCTURE TYPE

A. Percent of Residential Structures Tax Delinquent, by Structure Type

Number of Properties	Single-Family Homes	Duplexes	Mixed-Use Apartments[b]	Other Residential Properties[c]	Total Privately-Owned Real Estate Tax Delinquent Properties
Delinquent Structures	4,598	1,096	193	311	6,198
Total Structures[a]	100,106	14,379	8,810	na	123,295
Percent Delinquent	4.55	7.62	2.19	na	5.03

B. Size Distribution of Back Taxes Owed on Residential Properties, By Structure Type

Dollars Owed Per Property	Single-Family Homes		Duplexes		Mixed-Use Apartments[b]		Other Residential Properties[c]		Total Privately-Owned Real Estate Tax Delinquent Properties	
	Number	Percent	Number	Percent	Number	Percent	Number	Percent	Number	Percent
Less than $500	2,820	61.3	581	53.0	74	38.3	123	39.5	3,598	58.1
$500-999	1,210	26.3	323	29.5	53	27.5	86	27.7	1,672	27.0
$1000 or more	568	12.4	192	17.5	66	34.2	102	32.8	928	15.0
Total Delinquent	4,598	100.0	1,096	100.0	193	100.0	311	100.0	6,198	100.0

Notes: a. Estimates based on the 1970 Census of Housing.
b. Data were unavailable for apartments lacking commercial uses.
c. Includes apartments, dormitories, rooming houses, etc.; na = data not available.

Sources: 1970 Census of Housing. Pittsburgh Tax Delinquency File. Land Use Survey.

quency have been devised. Each measure sheds light on a different component of the overall problem. Mapping the geographic patterns of these four
delinquency measures graphically illustrates the neighborhood distribution
of delinquency in Pittsburgh. Definitions of the four measures are summarized below and in Exhibit 6-7.

(1) *Frequency.* The first measure indicates the frequency or incidence of
residential delinquency in a census tract. It is calculated as the number of
delinquent residential structures in a tract, divided by the total number of
structures in the tract, times 100. This measure takes no account of the dollar value of delinquency involved, weighting equally the large multi-family
structure and the single-family dwelling. The frequency measure thus iden-

EXHIBIT 6-7

MEASURES OF RESIDENTIAL TAX DELINQUENCY,
PITTSBURGH CENSUS TRACTS, 1973

Measure	Definition	Mean	Standard Deviation	Minimum	Maximum
Frequency of Delinquency	Number of delinquent residential structures as a percent of total structures in a census tract.	6.14	5.38	0.0	36.60
Magnitude of Delinquency	Dollar value of real estate taxes owed on residential structures divided by the number of structures in the census tract.	74.09	647.48	0.0	8754.96
Extreme Delinquency	Number of delinquent residential structures owing more than $658, as a percent of total structures in a census tract.	0.95	1.11	0.0	9.39
Chronic Delinquency	Number of delinquent residential structures owing more than 15 percent of assessed value in taxes, as a percent of total structures in a census tract.	1.72	2.29	0.0	13.37

Note: N = 182 census tracts.

tifies census tracts in which delinquency is a common or widespread occurrence, independent of the dollar amount of back tax bills involved. Among the 182 Pittsburgh census tracts included in our analysis, the frequency measure ranges from a low of 0.0 percent to a high of 36.6 percent, with an average value of 6.14 percent.

EXHIBIT 6-8

FREQUENCY OF DELINQUENCY

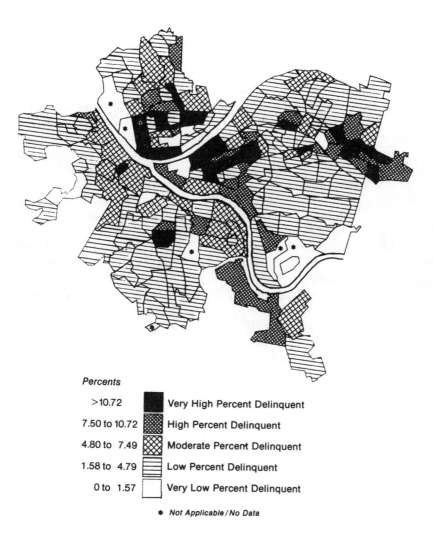

Percents

>10.72	■	Very High Percent Delinquent
7.50 to 10.72	▨	High Percent Delinquent
4.80 to 7.49	▨	Moderate Percent Delinquent
1.58 to 4.79	▤	Low Percent Delinquent
0 to 1.57	□	Very Low Percent Delinquent

✳ *Not Applicable / No Data*

The frequency of tax delinquency in Pittsburgh census tracts is mapped in Exhibit 6-8. A major concentration of high frequency tracts is clustered in the Strip and Lower Hill areas adjacent to the CBD (but not in the heart of the CBD itself) and continuing eastward throught the low-income areas of Middle and Upper Hill (ward 5). Smaller scattered pockets of high frequency are found in the Shadyside area of ward 8 and the Garfield neighborhood (ward 10). This eastward axis continues through the Larimer area of East Liberty (ward 12) and Homewood (ward 13), one of the most ·deteriorated sections of the city. Additional pockets with a high frequency of delinquency are located in Beltzhoover (ward 18) and the West End Valley area of ward 20. The remaining large concentration of high frequency is found to the north in the Manchester and California Avenue sectors of ward 21, the North Shore neighborhood in the Central North Side (ward 22), the Spring Hill section of ward 24, and Perry South in wards 25 and 26.

(2) *Magnitude.* The second measure reflects the average dollar value of delinquency in a census tract. This measure is computed as the total dollar value of real estate taxes owed on private residential structures in a tract, divided by the total number of structures (delinquent and non-delinquent) in the tract. The higher this figure, the greater the magnitude of delinquency per structure in the tract. Those census tracts with a very high measure of magnitude are the most responsible for the gap between total property taxes levied and total revenue collected. The average per structure magnitude of residential delinquency in Pittsburgh's census tracts ranges from a low of zero to a high of $8755, with a mean of $74.

Exhibit 6-9 indicates the distribution of delinquency by average magnitude in Pittsburgh. The major areas of high magnitude delinquency parallel the distribution of high frequency but appear to be somewhat more concentrated. High average delinquency is found within the CBD itself, in the adjacent Strip, in the close-in low-income neighborhoods of Lower Hill (ward 3), Middle and Upper Hill (ward 5), and spilling over into North Oakland (ward 4). Parts of Bloomfield in ward 8 and major sections of Shadyside (ward 7), East Liberty (ward 12), and Homewood (ward 13) are impacted by high delinquency. An outlying high magnitude pocket is found in the Stanton Heights neighborhood of ward 10 in the northeastern corner of the city, and we again find scatterings in Beltzhoover (ward 20) to the South and West. As was true for the frequency of delinquency, Manchester (ward 21) and the North Shore neighborhood, together with Allegheny West in the Central North Side (ward 22) evidence large concentrations of high magnitude delinquency.

The frequency and magnitude measures are useful in identifying census tracts with large amounts of either parcels delinquent or dollars delinquent, respectively. They are not entirely adequate, however, for pinpointing census tracts with either extremely high or chronic delinquency. The two remaining measures attempt to fill this gap.

(3) *Extreme delinquency.* This measure focuses on the frequency of delinquent residential parcels in a tract which owe back taxes above the city-wide average for such parcels. As indicated earlier, delinquent privately-owned residential parcels in Pittsburgh owe an average of $658 in back real

EXHIBIT 6-9

MAGNITUDE OF DELINQUENCY

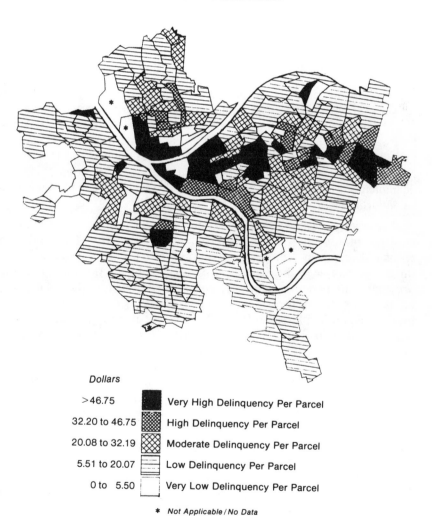

Dollars

>46.75	■	Very High Delinquency Per Parcel
32.20 to 46.75	▦	High Delinquency Per Parcel
20.08 to 32.19	▨	Moderate Delinquency Per Parcel
5.51 to 20.07	≡	Low Delinquency Per Parcel
0 to 5.50		Very Low Delinquency Per Parcel

* *Not Applicable / No Data*

estate taxes. Thus, the measure of extreme delinquency is defined as the number of delinquent residential parcels in a census tract owing more than $658 in real estate taxes, divided by the total number of structures in the tract, times 100. The incidence of extreme delinquency in Pittsburgh's census tracts ranges from 0 to 9.39 percent of structures in a tract, with an average among all tracts of 0.95 percent. High values on this measure identify census tracts which impact most negatively on city revenue collections in terms of dollar amounts. We would not expect to find the worst cases of extreme dollar delinquency in the city's poorest areas: the generally low housing values in these areas would tend to preclude the assessment of high tax bills on these parcels, and only extremely prolonged non-payment would accumulate such above-average delinquency.

As indicated in Exhibit 6-10, the pattern of extreme delinquency mirrors the distribution of high magnitude delinquency but it is concentrated in fewer areas. Once again, portions of the CBD and the Strip evidence a high incidence of extreme delinquency, extending into smaller sections of the Lower and Middle Hill areas, and including a cluster in the Upper Hill neighborhood and the adjacent section of North Oakland (ward 4). A portion of Shadyside (ward 7) and neighboring Larimer (in ward 12) are impacted by extreme delinquency, as are the central segments of Homewood North and Homewood South. The second major concentration of extreme delinquency is located in the North Shore, Allegheny West, and Manchester neighborhoods in wards 21 and 22.

(4) *Chronic delinquency.* The extreme delinquency measure rests on the existence of a severe problem expressed in absolute terms. The measure of chronic delinquency represents the amount of back taxes owed relative to the assessed value of the delinquent parcel. The higher this ratio, the more prolonged the period of non-payment of taxes. Further, this relationship holds regardless of the value of the property. The average delinquent residential parcel in Pittsburgh owes back taxes equal to 15 percent of its assessed value. Our measure of chronic delinquency is thus defined as the number of delinquent residential parcels in a census tract with unpaid taxes amounting to more than 15 percent of assessed value, divided by the total number of structures in the tract, times 100. Census tracts with a high index of chronic delinquency will therefore contain relatively large numbers of delinquent parcels that are either of very low value, of very high delinquency, or both. These tracts will also contain relatively large concentrations of structures on which delinquency represents such a high proportion of value that redemption is increasingly unlikely. A high incidence of chronic delinquency thus identifies those areas of the city most impacted by tax delinquency. Chronic delinquency in Pittsburgh census tracts ranges from a low of 0 to a high of 13.37 percent, with a mean of 1.72 percent.

The geographic distribution of chronic delinquency is the most concentrated of all four measures (Exhibit 6-11). The largest area of high chronic delinquency includes the Strip, the portion of the CBD adjacent to Lower
Hill, the Lower, Middle, and Upper Hill neighborhoods, and Bedford
Dwellings. All of these areas are clustered near the center of the city. The

EXHIBIT 6-10

EXTREME DELINQUENCY

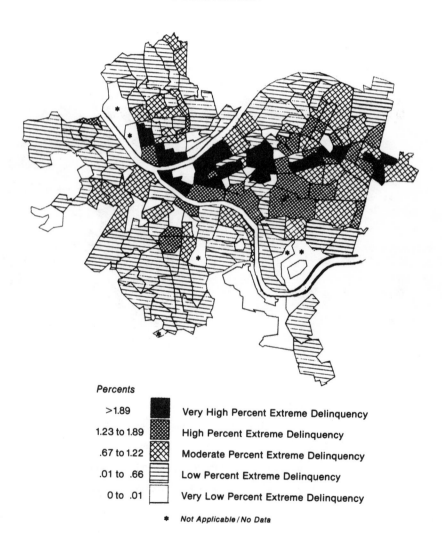

Percents

> 1.89   Very High Percent Extreme Delinquency

1.23 to 1.89   High Percent Extreme Delinquency

.67 to 1.22   Moderate Percent Extreme Delinquency

.01 to .66   Low Percent Extreme Delinquency

0 to .01   Very Low Percent Extreme Delinquency

*   *Not Applicable / No Data*

Garfield neighborhood in ward 10 presents another pocket of chronic delinquency. East Liberty and Homewood (wards 12 and 13) evidence serious
chronic delinquency, but the pattern is concentrated in fewer census tracts
as compared to the other delinquency measures. Once again, the North
Shore and Manchester neighborhoods, and portions of the Central North
Side, stand out as severly impacted. Smaller pockets of chronic delinquency

EXHIBIT 6-11
CHRONIC DELINQUENCY

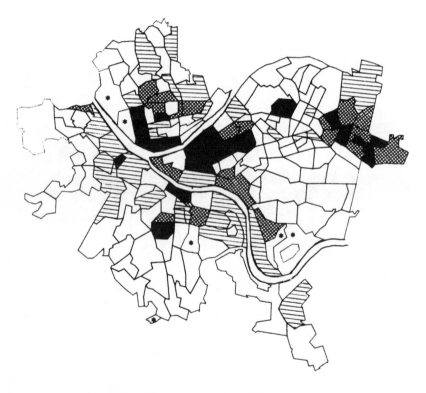

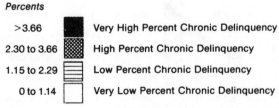

Percents

>3.66	■	Very High Percent Chronic Delinquency
2.30 to 3.66	▨	High Percent Chronic Delinquency
1.15 to 2.29	▤	Low Percent Chronic Delinquency
0 to 1.14	□	Very Low Percent Chronic Delinquency

* *Not Applicable//No Data*

are located to the south in Beltzhoover (ward 18), West End Valley (ward 20), and Southside Flats (ward 17).

THE NEIGHBORHOOD ENVIRONMENT OF TAX DELINQUENCY

Having mapped the geographic distribution of tax delinquency in Pittsburgh, we turn next to the question of the population, housing, and neighborhood characteristics associated with a high delinquency rate. If the descriptive model of delinquency outlined in Chapter 2 bears any validity, then we would expect that those neighborhoods most impacted by the forces described in the model will evidence the highest delinquency rate. In this segment of the analysis, we are explicitly testing the relationships specified in the first two segments of the model, i.e., the effect of structural change and housing market processes on delinquency. Thus, we are here concerned with factors such as population age and income, and housing condition and vacancy. Analysis of the behavioral components of delinquency is addressed in Chapters 7 and 8.

Examination of the neighborhood environment of tax delinquency entails two separate components. Four measures of delinquency have been created, each highlighting a different dimension of the whole. We therefore sought to identify the particular neighborhood characteristics associated with each of the four measures. By identifying particular characteristics associated with one measure but not others, we further classify the meaning of the delinquency measures and the differences between them. For instance, we might expect a high proportion of families below poverty to be associated with high frequency delinquency (indicating a high proportion of parcels in a tract delinquent) but not with extreme delinquency (indicating an above-average dollar value of taxes owed per parcel). Similarly, we might expect a given characteristic to be positively related to one delinquency measure but negatively related to another. The first step in our analysis examines these different patterns of association for each delinquency measure in order to further clarify their meaning. We then examine the relationship between the four delinquency measures and the patterns of neighborhood structure identified through factor analysis in the preceding chapter.

CHARACTERISTICS OF HIGH DELINQUENCY AREAS— THE FOUR MEASURES

The selection of population, housing, and neighborhood characteristics related to tax delinquency is motivated by the same hypotheses that prevailed in the city-level analysis reported in Chapter 4. The principal difference is that total population size has less meaning at the neighborhood level than was true at the city scale, and "quality of life" indicators may be expected to play a stronger role. Based on the findings at the national scale and hypotheses suggested by the descriptive model of tax delinquency, we selected thirteen variables related to neighborhood variations in delinquency levels. These thirteen variables, and their simple correlations with the four delinquency measures, are summarized in Exhibit 6-12. The pattern of correlations with the different measures of delinquency supports our expectation that the four measures reflect different dimensions of the overall problem.

Median age. The median age of all persons in a census tract bears a complex relationship to tax delinquency. To the extent that a high median age reflects fixed low incomes or the absence of families in the child-bearing years, it will be associated with a high frequency but a low dollar magnitude of delinquency. To the extent that housing value increases with age, however, a high median age might also be associated with a high index of extreme delinquency (i.e., a high proportion of delinquent accounts above the city-wide average).

Percent population under five years. A high percent of children under five indicates a concentration of young families. These in turn reflect a high rate of new family formation and continued demand for housing. We therefore expect that a high percent of population under five shoud be indicative of a low frequency of delinquency. Where such families are concentrated in high delinquency areas, however, they should contribute to a low average magnitude of delinquency and a low proportion of extreme delinquency.

Percent foreign stock. Foreign stock refers to persons born abroad or whose parents were born abroad. To the extent that this variable reflects a high rate of in-migration, it suggests continued strong demand for housing and consequent low delinquency. Both the frequency of delinquency and the extent of chronic delinquency should be low in areas with high concentrations of foreign born; to the degree that recent in-migration is indicative of low income, such areas should also be marked by a low dollar magnitude and low incidence of extreme dollar delinquency.

Median family income. This variable is defined as the median family income of families and unrelated individuals in a census tract. A high median income should be related to a low delinquency rate on all measures.

Percent of families below poverty. The indication of concentrations of poverty is expected to exert an influence on the delinquency rate independent of the median income variable. Families below the poverty line who own their homes will no doubt be hard pressed to meet tax payments; poverty families in rental units suggest a minimal financial return to owners. Either case would lead to a high frequency of delinquency and serious chronic delinquency. Since delinquent structures are likely to be of low value, however, this should be accompanied by a low average magnitude and low incidence of extreme dollar delinquency.

Housing units with more than 1.50 persons per room. Crowding and high density occupancy are typically associated with impoverished areas of the city. At the same time, however, this measure is indicative of unsatisfied demand for housing. Thus, crowding is likely to be associated with high frequency and chronic delinquency but this may in part be offset by the continued economic viability of otherwise inadequate housing. The ultimate impact of crowding on delinquency rates is therefore ambiguous.

Families receiving public assistance. It is no secret that families on welfare are consigned to the least desirable sectors of the city. The frequency and incidence of chronic delinquency is expected to be high in such areas. To the extent that welfare families are typically housed in large multi-family structures with a nominally high assessed value, chronic delinquency in such structures will contribute to a high dollar magnitude and high incidence of extreme dollar delinquency.

Units in multi-family structures. This variable is defined as the percent of housing units in structures containing five or more units. It is thus a measure of large multi-family rental structures. Such structures are uncommon in Pittsburgh's most deteriorated neighborhoods, that more typically contain duplexes and small rental units. Tracts containing high proportions of units in large rental structures might therefore be associated with a low frequency of delinquency. Since the assessed value of such structures is likely to be quite high, these tracts are likely to contribute to low chronic delinquency as measured by the delinquency-to-assessment ratio. When such structures do become delinquent, however, they contribute to a high dollar magnitude of delinquency in the tract and high incidence of extreme (above average) dollar delinquency.

Percent of units lacking plumbing facilities. As an indicator of sub-standard housing, the absence of plumbing facilities is likely to be associated with a high delinquency rate. Units lacking plumbing are likely to be among the most marginal in the city and the first to be abandoned given any slackening in the housing market.

Percent of units built 1939 or earlier. Older housing units require higher maintenance costs and are most subject to declining value. For these reasons, we would expect high proportions of older units to be positively related to tax delinquency. This relationship might also be strongest for delinquency frequency and the incidence of chronic delinquency.

Change in the vacancy rate: 1960-1970. An increasing vacancy rate signals a diminishing cash flow and the unlikely prospect of adequate economic return or equity recapture. A rising vacancy rate should therefore be associated with a high delinquency rate across all measures.

EXHIBIT 6-12

MEANS AND SIMPLE CORRELATIONS OF DEMOGRAPHIC AND HOUSING CHARACTERISTICS ASSOCIATED WITH FOUR TAX DELINQUENCY MEASURES, PITTSBURGH CENSUS TRACTS

Variable	Mean	Standard Deviation	Minimum	Maximum	Simple correlations with:			
					Frequency of Delinquency	Magnitude of Delinquency	Extreme Delinquency	Chronic Delinquency
DEMOGRAPHIC								
Median Age of Population	34.90	7.46	14.04	56.95	.007	−.126*	.263***	.003
Percent Population Under 5 Years	6.47	2.47	0.0	18.97	.051	−.170**	−.263***	.097
Percent Foreign Stock	24.98	12.21	0.0	57.59	−.482***	−.042	−.189**	−.467***
QUALITY OF LIFE								
Median Family Income	6,544	2,442	920	13,640	−.373***	−.170**	−.257***	−.328***
Percent Families Below Poverty Line	12.00	10.97	0.0	67.19	.338***	−.074	.093	.361***
Percent Housing Units ≥ 1.51 Persons Per Room	1.29	1.51	0.0	11.94	.189**	.144*	.202**	.164**
Percent Families Receiving Public Assistance	10.88	11.74	0.0	62.50	.503***	.341***	.317***	.510***

HOUSING QUALITY							
Percent of Units in Multi-family Structures (5+ units)	21.65	26.43	0.0	99.36	−.130*	.202**	.276***	−.128*
Percent of Units Lacking Plumbing Facilities	7.80	11.01	0.0	97.38	.265***	.617***	.454***	.248***
Percent of Units Built Pre-1940	74.11	22.97	1.22	100.00	.311***	.074	.177**	.231***
HOUSING MARKET							
Change in Vacancy Rate, 1960-1970	2.00	3.78	−7.93	15.70	.354***	.181**	.327***	.347***
Percent Residing in Same Unit in 1949	21.56	9.76	0.0	51.10	.055	−.080	−.185***	.038
Percent of Units with Roomers or Lodgers	2.86	2.52	0.0	16.37	.438***	.016	.273***	.356***

Notes: Number of cases = 182. All census data for 1970; delinquency data for 1973.

 * = significant at p ≤ .05
 ** = significant at p ≤ .01
 *** = significant at p ≤ .001

Percent residing in same unit in 1949.   This variable measures the percent
of 1970 housing units occupied by the same household in 1949 — a twenty-
one year span. A high proportion of such units in a census tract is indicative
of an admirable stability, and may be taken to indicate further the existence
of strong community loyalty and social ties. On the other had, this same
variable might indicate extreme market stagnation, low turnover, and
stability bred not of choice but of lack of options. The latter dynamic would
suggest a high frequency of low dollar magnitude delinquency.

Percent of units with roomers or lodgers.   A high proportion of dwelling
units occupied by roomers, boarders, or lodgers is indicative of low demand
for such units, weak family structure, low income, and a high incidence of
social disorganization. This "skid row" syndrome, typically concentrated
close-in adjacent to the CBD, is likely to be associated with high values on
all delinquency measures.

The results of the analysis linking these variables to the four measures of
tax delinquency are summarized in Exhibit 6-13. Two general observations
precede interpretation of the results. First, three variables - median family
income, units built 1939 or earlier, and units with more than 1.50 persons
per room - failed to exert an independent effect on any of the tax delinquency measures in addition to that exerted by the ten remaining variables.
Secondly, as expected, the variables interact differently with each of the
delinquency measures, thus clarifying the differences between the measures.
However, the pattern of relationships summarized in Exhibit 6-13 indicates
a clear affinity between the frequency of delinquency and the incidence of
chronic delinquency. Widespread and persistent delinquency appear to go
hand in hand. A somewhat more diffused but still clearly evident
relationship also exists between the dollar magnitude of delinquency and the
incidence of very extreme dollar delinquency.

The equations summarized in Exhibit 6-13 account for between 31 and 53
percent of the census tract variation in the four delinquency measures. Up to
a half of the variation in tax delinquency across census tracts is thus attributable to the direct effects of these structural and housing market indicators. The specific variables associated with each of the four delinquency
measures can be summarized briefly.

Frequency of delinquency.   The proportion of delinquent parcels in a
census tract appears to be a function of deteriorating housing market conditions. Large multi-family structures, a high proportion of foreign born in-
migrants, and concentrations of families with young children - all indicators
of viable housing demand - are all related to a *low* frequency of delinquency.
Conversely, an increasing vacancy rate, a high proportion of welfare
families, and units occupied by roomers or boarders contribute to a *high* frequency of delinquency. Not surprisingly, the most widespread delinquency

is to be found where vacancy is high and the remaining residents are among the most economically marginal segments of the population. These are the areas that have been most consistently by-passed in the geographic reorientation of private capital investment.

Magnitude of delinquency. A high average dollar value of delinquency in a census tract is related to the presence of large sub-standard multi-family

EXHIBIT 6-13

NEIGHBORHOOD LEVEL CHARACTERISTICS ASSOCIATED WITH
FOUR TAX DELINQUENCY MEASURES,
PITTSBURGH CENSUS TRACTS, 1970

Independent Variables	Dependent Variables [a]			
	Frequency of Delinquency	Magnitude of Delinquency	Extreme Delinquency	Chronic Delinquency
Percent of units in Multi-Family Structures (5+)	−.0720 (.0124)	3.0295 (1.3326)		−.0311 (.0054)
Change in Vacancy Rate, 1960-1970	.1713 (.0881)		.0448 (.0198)	.0997 (.0385)
Percent Households on Public Assistance	.2099 (.0331)			.0946 (.0145)
Percent Foreign Stock	−.1148 (.0312)			−.0502 (.0131)
Percent Population under 5 Years	−.5171 (.1573)			−.2055 (.0658)
Percent Units with Roomers or Lodgers	.3350 (.1353)			
Percent Units Lacking Plumbing Facilities		41.8186 (3.2412)	.0363 (.0067)	
Median Age of Population		−29.2089 (4.7763)	.0326 (.0097)	
Percent Families Below Poverty Line		−20.1398 (3.3299)		
Percent Residing in Same Unit in 1949			−.0212 (.0074)	
Constant	10.3304	943.3698	−.1064	3.7440
F	29.2675	50.1193	19.4362	29.3270
R^2	.5009	.5311	.3052	.4545
N	182	182	182	182

Note: (a) Standard errors of regression coefficients indicated in parentheses. All coefficients statistically significant at $p \leq .05$.

rental structures. The higher the median age of the population and the higher the proportion of families below poverty, the *lower* the average dollar magnitude of delinquency per parcel. That median age negatively effects the magnitude of delinquency independently of the effect of families below poverty, suggests a bifurcation in the elderly population. Since the effect of poverty-level elderly households is presumably expressed in the poverty variable, elderly but non-poverty households evidently suppress the average magnitude of delinquency further. This may be due either to a lower delinquency rate in this segment of the population, or to a generally low value of housing occupied by the elderly which would be unlikely to amass large delinquent accounts.

Extreme delinquency. A large proportion of delinquent parcels with above-average back tax bills appears to be associated with areas marked by increasing vacancy in substandard units and a remaining population of transient elderly residents. In contrast to the average dollar magnitude measure, median age of the population is positively related to extreme delinquency: the higher the median age, the higher the proportion of parcels in the tract with above-average back tax bills. Taken in combination with the negative effect exerted by extreme stability, substandard units occupied by a transient elderly population appear to contribute to the incidence of extreme delinquency.

Chronic delinquency. The variables defining chronic and widespread delinquency are identical with the exception of the roomers and lodgers variable which failed to attain significance in this equation. As was the case with the frequency measure, chronic delinquency - a high proportion of units with above-average delinquency to assessment ratios - is symptomatic of market collapse: increasing vacancy and families on welfare are directly related to chronic delinquency. Foreign in-migration and family formation contribute to low levels of chronic delinquency.

In sum, it appears that the frequency and chronic delinquency measures are correlates of market collapse in the most deteriorated areas of the city. Widespread and chronic delinquency are most evident where deterioration has progressed the furthest: the market here has ceased to function, owners have ceased tax payments, and the existing units serve only as partial shelter for the poorest and most welfare-dependent segments of the population. High dollar magnitude and extreme dollar delinquency are correlates of increasing market obsolesence and declining demand in individual increasingly substandard larger structures. The market in these areas has seriously weakened, with the remaining elderly population unable to maintain adequate demand. Deterioration has not progressed as far in these areas as in the former case, and values are still high enough to generate large back tax bills.

NEIGHBORHOOD CORRELATES OF DELINQUENCY

It is only a small jump from the preceding descriptions to specification of the neighborhood correlates of tax delinquency. The basic structure of Pittsburgh's neighborhoods was described in Chapter 5 in terms of nine basic dimensions. Exhibit 6-14 summarizes the relationships between these nine dimensions of neighborhood structure and the four measures of tax delinquency. These nine factors — indicative of the basic structure of housing sub-markets in the city — account for between 29 and 45 percent of the variation in delinquency rates across census tracts. Explanation is most successful for the frequency of delinquency and chronic delinquency. This is to

EXHIBIT 6-14

DIMENSIONS OF NEIGHBORHOOD STRUCTURE INFLUENCING
FOUR TAX DELINQUENCY MEASURES,
PITTSBURGH CENSUS TRACTS, 1970

Independent Variables	Frequency of Delinquency	Dependent Variables [a] Magnitude of Delinquency	Extreme Delinquency	Chronic Delinquency
Factor I Homeowner		−201.4862 (41.1077)	−.3262 (.0713)	
Factor II Race & Resources	2.6171 (.2988)	−125.0692 (40.4819)	.1483 (.0702)	1.1063 (.1288)
Factor III Low Rent				.3672 (.1330)
Factor IV Affluence	−.6355 (.3138)	−117.7419 (42.5584)		
Factor V Old Age		−135.8025 (41.4380)	.2717 (.0719)	
Factor VI "Boarding House"	1.9127 (.3164)	158.4292 (42.8657)	.2409 (.0743)	.5873 (.1364)
Factor VII Declining Value		−110.8333 (42.8696)	−.1949 (.0742)	
Factor VIII Vacancy	1.4678 (.3219)	124.2210 (43.6112)	.2791 (.0756)	.7126 (.1388)
Factor IX Redevelopment Areas				.3188 (.1362)
Constant	6.1458	74.1415	.9456	1.7161
F	36.1112	11.3717	12.1925	27.3270
R^2	.4494	.3140	.2948	.4370
N	182	182	182	182

Note: (a) Standard errors of regression coefficients indicated in parentheses. All coefficients statistically significant at $p \leq .05$.

be expected since, as indicated by the analysis above, the remaining two measures appear to reflect the vagaries of individual parcels in an uncertain market and thus are more subject to the behavioral factors discussed in the following chapters.

The neighborhood patterns summarized in Exhibit 6-14 require little amplification. A high rate of homeownership has the effect of reducing dollar magnitude of delinquency and the incidence of extreme dollar delinquency. This substantiates the finding that high scores on these measures are associated with multi-family rental structures in which high assessed values lead to large back tax bills. Neighborhoods predominantly characterized by low-income minority residents are impacted by both widespread and chronic delinquency, again in accord with previous findings. The average magnitude of taxes levied in these neighborhoods is low, but prolonged non-payment appears to contribute to a high incidence of extreme (i.e., above-average dollar value) delinquency, most likely in large rental structures. Low rent neighborhoods, characterized by often sub-standard low-value rental units occupied by blue-collar workers dependent on public assistance, are associated with chronic delinquency. The most affluent neighborhoods, in contrast, are marked by a low frequency of delinquency and a low average magnitude of taxes owed in those cases where it does occur. As indicated in the analysis above, neighborhood concentrations of the elderly tend to decrease the average magnitude of delinquency per parcel but contribute to a high incidence of extreme delinquency. "Boarding house" neighborhoods, among the most deteriorated in the city, reflect high scores on all four delinquency measures. The presence of low-value owner-occupied units in a neighborhood tends to depress the average magnitude of taxes owed and the incidence of extreme delinquency. Neighborhoods marked by a high and increasing vacancy rate are strongly impacted by delinquency as indexed by all four measures. Finally, redevelopment areas are associated with a high rate of chronic delinquency, due no doubt to the existence of conditions prompting redevelopment as well as the uncertainty generated by the redevelopment process.

In sum, the findings at the neighborhood level augment and reflect the city-level findings reported above, and lend further support for the descriptive model of delinquency proposed in Chapter 2. At the neighborhood scale as at the city-wide scale, tax delinquency is both a function and a symptom of market weakness and collapse generated by the withdrawal of private investment commensurate with structural change in the nature of the city. The explicit linkages leading to the individual owner's decision to discontinue property tax payments are examined in the following two chapters.

NOTES

1. Total properties were estimated on the basis of sampling the 1974 Real Property File (see Appendix A). In 1966, there were 131,920 real properties in the city. See U.S. Bureau of the Census, *1967 Census of Governments,* 2, *Taxable Property Values,* Table 19.

2. During fiscal year 1972, locally raised revenues of the City amounted to $83.7 millions; local taxes of the school district amounted to $49 millions; and taxes of Allegheny County collected $69 millions. Total locally raised revenues amounted to $201.7 millions. See U.S. Bureau of the Census, *1972 Census of Government,* 4, Government Finances. Numbers 1, 3 and 4.

Chapter 7

Characteristics of Delinquent Property Owners and Their Properties

INTRODUCTION

Our discussion thus far has focused on the structural and market process influences on tax delinquency. We turn now to the question of individual owner behavior set within these broader contextual bounds.

The broad-scale analysis suggests two delinquency scenarios which inform the direction of our discussion in these next two chapters. On the one hand, delinquency may arise as part and parcel of the disinvestment decision: inadequate return on income producing property leads directly to the delinquency decision. On the other hand, homeowners caught within a deteriorating housing market may be forced into delinquency through increasing maintenance costs, vanishing equity, and illiquidity. The significance of each of these scenarios is examined through a comparison of delinquency in a sample of homeowners and landlords in Pittsburgh.

The data base for this discussion is derived from an intensive survey of 158 delinquent owners of residential properties conducted in Pittsburgh during the Summer of 1974. Furnished with this unique data source, we can begin in this chapter to study some of the vexing and thus far unanswered questions concerning the dynamics of the delinquency process.

We focus in this chapter on four principal issues:

1. *Identification of the characteristics of delinquent owners and their properties.* This aspect of the analysis offers answers to the questions: "Who are the delinquent property owners?" and "What types of properties do they own?"

2. *Clarification of the decision-making process whereby owners discontinue paying property taxes.* What factors are cited by owners as the reasons for their initial delinquency or for ceasing payments altogether? What are the detailed components of the delinquency decision?

3. *Examination of the relationship between tax delinquency and abandonment.* For what proportion of owners is nonpayment a temporary or transitory phenomenon and for what proportion is delinquency a forerunner of property neglect and ultimate abandonment? What are the characteristics of owners and properties associated with each of these dynamics?

4. *Identification of the characteristics of properties most likely to be acquired by the city.* Which owners report an intention to let title be acquired by the city? What are the characteristics of their properties? Identification of owners who intend ultimately to abandon their properties offers a preview of the type of properties to which the city is likely to become heir through enforcement of its acquisition program.

THE MAGNITUDE OF TAX DELINQUENCY AMONG SAMPLED PROPERTIES

Exhibits 7-1 and 7-2 summarize the magnitude and distribution of tax delinquency for the 158 properties in the sample. Considering property taxes, sewer, and water charges, the 158 properties together account for some $94,000 of back taxes owed the City on December 31, 1973.

EXHIBIT 7-1

TOTAL TAXES OWED ON SAMPLED PROPERTIES ON DECEMBER 31, 1973, BY STRUCTURE TYPE

Structure Type	Dollars	Delinquent Properties	Dollars Per Delinquent Property
Single-Family	68,283	117	584
Duplex	14,310	24	596
Apartment	8,158	11	742
Rooming House	1,252	3	417
Other	2,389	3	796
TOTAL	94,392	158	597

Sources: Tax Delinquency File; CUPR Pittsburgh Delinquency Survey, Summer 1974.

As was reported for the City as a whole, the average level of delinquency for single-family homes in the sample ($584) is substantially below the average level for apartment structures ($742). Structures in the "other" category — essentially mixed-use commercial structures — have the highest level of average delinquency in the sample at close to $800 per structure.

Reflecting this higher average level of delinquency, both apartment and "other" structures are overrepresented in the highest category of taxes owed (see Exhibit 7-2). While 17 percent of single-family structures have accumulated back taxes of $1,000 or more, 27 percent of apartments and 33 percent of "other" structures are in this category. Correspondingly, single-family structures have the highest proportionate representation in the less than $500 category of taxes owed. Again mirroring the distribution of taxes owed by all delinquent properties in the City, well over half of all properties in the sample have accumulated less than $500 in back taxes. For both total taxes owed and the amount owed on each of the various taxes, an overwhelming proportion of the sampled delinquent owners owe relatively small amounts of money. As indicated in Chapter 6, *delinquency in Pittsburgh appears to be comprised largely of a substantial number of properties each of which has accumulated a small amount of back taxes.*

A primary concern of the remainder of this analysis will be to differentiate between two sets of factors that result in the accumulation of this large number of small delinquent tax bills. On the one hand, a low level of taxes owed might result when an owner of a sound, economically viable property misses tax payments over a short period either inadvertently or because of a temporary lack of funds. Owners of this type are committed to maintaining ownership of their property and can be expected to pay their back taxes prior to accumulation of a large delinquent tax bill.

On the other hand, owners of poor-quality, low-value housing might accrue a low level of delinquency simply because of the low assessed value of the property. Even long-term delinquency in such cases would result in a relatively small cumulative tax bill since the amount due in any one tax period would be relatively low. Owners of this latter type of property tend to be among those least committed to property maintenance and most likely to relinquish title to the City after "milking" the property for the longest possible period.

Initial evidence that the pattern of chronic nonpayment of taxes on low-value property is likely to be a significant part of the problem of tax delinquency in Pittsburgh is demonstrated by the data in Exhibit 7-3 which summarizes owners' plans regarding payment of back taxes tabulated by the total amount of taxes owed. Owners who declared their intention to pay in full and those who said that they would pay as much as possible whenever possible are roughly evenly divided according to the size of their total tax

EXHIBIT 7-2

DISTRIBUTION OF TOTAL TAXES OWED ON SAMPLED PROPERTIES ON DECEMBER 31, 1973,
BY STRUCTURE TYPE

Dollars Owed Per Property	Structure Type											Total Delinquent Properties	
	Single-Family		Duplex		Apartment		Rooming House		Other				
	Number	Percent	Number	Percent	Number	Percent	Number	Percent	Number	Percent		Number	Percent
Less than $500	65	55.6	17	70.8	4	36.4	2	66.7	1	33.3		89	56.3
$500-999	32	27.4	3	12.5	4	36.4	1	33.3	1	33.3		41	25.9
$1,000 or more	20	17.1	4	16.7	3	27.3	0	0.0	1	33.3		28	17.7
TOTAL	117	100.0	24	100.0	11	100.0	3	100.0	3	100.0		158	100.0

Sources: Tax Delinquency File: CUPR Pittsburgh Delinquency Survey, Summer 1974.

EXHIBIT 7-3

OWNER'S PLANS REGARDING PAYMENT OF BACK TAXES, BY SIZE OF
TOTAL TAX BILL, PITTSBURGH (percents)[a]

Owner's plans regarding payment of back taxes	Size of Total Tax Bill		
	Less Than $500	*$500-999*	*⩾ $1,000*
Pay in full	52.5 (31)	62.5 (20)	45.5 (10)
Pay as much as possible whenever possible	15.3 (9)	15.6 (5)	22.7 (5)
Minimum payment	5.1 (3)	12.5 (4)	27.3 (6)
No payment	27.1 (16)	9.4 (3)	4.5 (1)

Note: a. Absolute numbers are in parentheses.

Source: CUPR Pittsburgh Delinquency Survey, Summer 1974.

bills. Owners who claimed they woud pay only the minimum amount required to keep title to the property are disproportionately represented among those with the highest tax bills: 27 percent of owners owing $1,000 or more are in this category, compared to only 5 percent of those owing less than $500. Most significantly, the distribution is exactly reversed for owners claiming their intention to make no further tax payments on their property: 27 percent of those owing less than $500 are in this category compared to only 5 percent of owners owing $1,000 or more. Thus, over a fourth of those owners with relatively low absolute levels of delinquency state an intention to discontinue tax payments. These owners are likely to comprise that subgroup of delinquent owners who account for chronic tax delinquency in Pittsburgh and who furnish the stock of low-value, poor-quality housing that the City is likely to acquire through tax sale.

The distinction between owners with low levels of delinquency because of a short-term, temporary inability to pay, and those associated with chronic delinquency on low-value properties will be pursued in detail throughout the remainder of this discussion.

CHARACTERISTICS OF DELINQUENT OWNERS AND THEIR PROPERTIES

A full description of the characteristics of delinquent property owners and their properties can be gleaned from the distributions of all 325 survey

EXHIBIT 7-4

SUMMARY CHARACTERISTICS OF DELINQUENT HOMEOWNERS AND LANDLORDS, PITTSBURGH (percents)[a]

	Homeowners	Landlords	Total
A. Race:			
White	56.3	68.9	62.3
	(45)	(51)	(96)
Black	43.8	31.1	37.7
	(35)	(23)	(58)
B. Age:			
< 40 Years	13.0	16.2	14.6
	(10)	(12)	(22)
40-59 Years	46.8	54.1	50.3
	(36)	(40)	(76)
≥60 Years	40.3	29.7	35.1
	(31)	(22)	(53)
C. Income:			
< $10,000	71.8	44.8	58.7
	(51)	(30)	(81)
$10,000-14,999	22.5	28.4	25.4
	(16)	(19)	(35)
≥ $15,000	5.6	26.9	15.9
	(4)	(18)	(22)
D. Occupation:			
Professional or Technical	9.2	8.5	8.8
	(7)	(6)	(13)
Managers or Proprietors	6.6	23.9	14.9
	(5)	(17)	(22)
Sales	6.6	14.1	10.2
	(5)	(10)	(15)
Clerical	0.0	7.0	3.4
	(0)	(5)	(5)
Craftsmen, Foremen	7.9	5.6	6.8
	(6)	(4)	(10)
Service	9.2	2.8	6.1
	(7)	(2)	(9)
Operatives	10.5	8.5	9.5
	(8)	(6)	(14)
Laborers	11.8	2.8	7.5
	(9)	(2)	(11)

EXHIBIT 7-4 (cont'd)

SUMMARY CHARACTERISTICS OF DELINQUENT HOMEOWNERS AND
LANDLORDS, PITTSBURGH (percents)[a]

	Homeowners	Landlords	Total
Retired	22.4	21.1	21.8
	(17)	(15)	(32)
Student	3.9	0.0	2.0
	(3)	(0)	(3)
Housewife	9.2	2.8	6.1
	(7)	(2)	(9)
Unemployed	2.6	2.8	2.7
	(2)	(2)	(4)

Note: a. Absolute numbers are in parentheses.

Source: CUPR Pittsburgh Delinquency Survey, Summer 1974.

variables tabulated in Appendix B. Several salient aspects of the sample, however, deserve additional highlighting and it is these that we focus on in the following discussion.

Exhibit 7-4 presents basic socioeconomic data for homeowners and landlords in the sample. Homeowners are defined as those respondents who own a single-family house in which they live and do not rent out any part of the structure. Landlords are those respondents who either rent out part of their own homes or own property which they rent out in entirety.

Almost two-thirds of our total sample of delinquent property owners are white and slightly over a third are black (see Exhibit 7-4A). More landlords than homeowners are white, while exactly the reverse is true for blacks. This pattern quite likely reflects the suburbanization and out-migration of white homeowners from Pittsburgh and also reflects the relative inability of lower income blacks to engage in entrepreneurial ownership of rental properties.

Slightly over a third of the total sample was sixty years old or over at the time of the interview (see Exhibit 7-4B). Landlords tend to be younger than homeowners: 40 percent of homeowners, compared to 30 percent of landlords, were sixty years old or over.

Well over half of all respondents make less than $10,000 a year, reflecting the City's 1970 median annual income of $8,800. Delinquent landlords in our sample, however, tend to have annual incomes disproportionately higher than those of delinquent homeowners: 72 percent of homeowners compared to 45 percent of landlords have incomes below $10,000; 27 percent of landlords but only 6 percent of homeowners reported incomes equal to or greater than $15,000 a year (see Exhibit 7-4C).

By far the greatest proportion of the sample arranged by occupation are retired — 22 percent (see Exhibit 7-4D). Commensurate with the data on race, age, and income, delinquent landlords tend to be concentrated in the higher- and middle-class occupations — managers or proprietors, sales, and clerical — while homeowners in the sample are strongly represented among blue-collar occupations: service workers, operatives, and laborers.

EXHIBIT 7-5

SUMMARY CHARACTERISTICS OF PROPERTIES OWNED BY DELINQUENT
HOMEOWNERS AND LANDLORDS, PITTSBURGH
(percents)[a]

	Homeowners	Landlords	Total
A. Total Assessed Value:			
< $2,500	19.5	30.3	24.7
	(16)	(23)	(39)
$2,500-4,999	51.2	35.5	43.7
	(42)	(27)	(69)
⩾ $5,000	29.3	34.2	31.6
	(24)	(26)	(50)
B. Building Condition:			
Poor	14.8	28.0	21.1
	(12)	(21)	(33)
Average	29.6	26.7	28.2
	(24)	(20)	(44)
Good	55.6	45.3	50.6
	(45)	(34)	(79)
C. Property Maintenance Pattern:			
Maintain in Good Condition	68.3	52.6	60.8
	(56)	(40)	(96)
Maintain in Fair Condition	23.2	28.9	25.9
	(19)	(22)	(41)
Make No Repairs or Emergency Repairs Only	8.5	18.4	13.3
	(7)	(14)	(21)

Note: a. Absolute numbers are in parentheses.

Source: CUPR Pittsburgh Delinquency Survey, Summer 1974.

Turning to selected characteristics of the properties owned by the delinquent homeowners and landlords in our sample, fully 68 percent of all properties have assessed values of less than $5,000 (see Exhibit 7-5A). Somewhat surprisingly, a considerably greater proportion of the properties owned by landlords (30 percent) have assessed values of less than $2,500 than is true for properties owned by homeowners (20 percent). These low-value rental units can be expected to figure largely in Pittsburgh's tax delinquency problem. At the same time, 34 percent of the landlord-owned properties are assessed at $5,000 or more compared to 29 percent of the single-family nonrental units.

As might be expected, buildings owned by homeowners tend to be in better condition than those owned by landlords (see Exhibit 7-5B): almost twice as many landlord-owned buildings (28 percent) were in poor condition compared to 15 percent of buildings owned by homeowners. Simultaneously, 10 percent more homeowner-occupied buildings than landlord-owned buildings were in good condition.

Paralleling the data on building condition, homeowners appear to be considerably more committed to maintaining their property in good condition than are landlords (see Exhibit 7-5C). Approximately 15 percent more homeowners than landlords maintain their buildings in good condition, while twice the proportion of landlords as homeowners make no repairs at all or make repairs only in emergency situations.

THE CHARACTER OF TAX DELINQUENCY

The data derived from the survey of delinquent property owners in Pittsburgh provide six separate but interrelated measures of the character of real estate tax delinquency. These measures are:

1. The absolute dollar amount of total taxes owed

2. The delinquency-to-assessment (D/A) ratio: the absolute dollar amount of total taxes owed expressed as a proportion of the total assessed value of the property

3. Tabulation of the owner's reasons for initially missing tax payments

4. A measure of short-term versus chronic delinquency: comparison of the dollar value of taxes owed per sampled owner on December 31, 1973 with the amount of taxes owed six months later in July 1974; an indication of the actual repayment of back taxes over the six-month period

5. Specification of the owner's stated plans for the payment of back taxes

6. Specification of the owner's stated intention to let the City take title to the property

Each of these various measures provides insight to a slightly different component of the picture of tax delinquency in Pittsburgh. The first two measures provide a numerical index of the severity of tax delinquency; when tabulated against selected characteristics of owners and their properties, they can be used to identify the correlates of high levels of delinquency.

A similar process cross-classifying the owner's stated reasons for initially missing tax payments by characteristics of the owners and their properties contributes to the crucial differentiation between temporary delinquency and the chronic nonpayment of taxes that is preliminary to abandonment.

This critical dichotomization is further reinforced by examination of actual payments made over the first six months of 1974. Owners who have paid some or all of their back taxes during the period can be considered to have been temporarily delinquent and should clearly be differentiated from owners for whom delinquency is more persistent. Each of these two types of delinquency poses a vastly different set of problems to the City, and each requires a different set of policy responses.

The data on actual payment of back taxes are further complemented by an examination of owners' stated plans for the payment of their delinquent tax bills. While these responses are probably to some degree hypothetical, they have the advantage of extending further into the future the time period being considered rather than having it restricted to a six-month period. Those owners who clearly state their intention to discontinue tax payments can be identified and their characteristics can be described in great detail.

Finally, the analysis can be extended to a description of owners who state their intention to let title to their property pass to the City. These owners have reached the point in the cycle of delinquency where abandonment is imminent or has already occurred. Identification of these owners serves two important purposes. First, examination of the characteristics of these owners contributes to identification of the "hard core" of delinquent property owners. Secondly, examination of the characteristics of the properties of these owners provides an important preview of the type of properties that the City is most likely to gain under a program of public acquisition. Planning for the eventual sale and/or reuse of acquired properties can thus proceed with a detailed knowledge of the characteristics and potential value of the properties that are most likely to fall into the City's hands.

SUMMARY CHARACTERISTICS OF DELINQUENCY

Exhibits 7-6 and 7-7 present basic summary data on absolute levels of tax delinquency of homeowners and landlords in the Pittsburgh sample.

Considering total taxes owed by age of homeowners and landlords, landlords in the forty to fifty-nine and the sixty-or-over age groups are more likely to have accumulated very large bills for back taxes than are the

EXHIBIT 7-6

TOTAL TAXES OWED BY AGE OF HOMEOWNERS AND LANDLORDS, PITTSBURGH

(percents)[a]

Total Taxes Owed	Age of Property Owner					
	Less than 40 Years		40-59 Years		60 Years or Older	
	Homeowners	Landlords	Homeowners	Landlords	Homeowners	Landlords
< $500	70.0	58.3	55.6	52.5	61.3	54.5
	(7)	(7)	(20)	(21)	(19)	(12)
$500-999	20.0	33.3	27.8	20.0	29.0	22.7
	(2)	(4)	(10)	(8)	(9)	(5)
≥ $1,000	10.0	8.3	16.7	27.5	9.7	22.7
	(1)	(1)	(6)	(11)	(3)	(5)

Note: a. Absolute numbers are in parentheses.

Source: CUPR Pittsburgh Delinquency Survey, Summer 1974.

EXHIBIT 7-7

TOTAL TAXES OWED BY ANNUAL INCOME OF HOMEOWNERS AND LANDLORDS, PITTSBURGH

(percents)[a]

Total Taxes Owed	Annual Income of Property Owner					
	Less than $10,000		$10,000-14,999		$15,000 or More	
	Homeowners	Landlords	Homeowners	Landlords	Homeowners	Landlords
< $500	58.8	40.0	62.5	68.4	75.0	72.2
	(30)	(12)	(10)	(13)	(3)	(13)
$500-999	33.3	26.7	12.5	21.1	0.0	5.6
	(17)	(8)	(2)	(4)	(0)	(1)
≥$1,000	7.8	33.3	25.0	10.5	25.0	22.2
	(4)	(10)	(4)	(2)	(1)	(4)

Note: a. Absolute numbers are in parentheses.

Source: CUPR Pittsburgh Delinquency Survey, Summer 1974.

homeowners in the same age groups. For owners under forty years old, the proportion of homeowners who owe $1,000 or more in back taxes is slightly higher than the proportion of landlords who owe the same. To the extent that age of owner is correlated with age of building, building condition, and consequent assessed value, it is possible that the slighty higher absolute level of delinquency among relatively young homeowners reflects the higher assessed value of their properties.

In general, however, *landlords tend to be disproportionately represented among owners at all age levels who owe large tax bills.*

An interesting pattern emerges in Exhibit 7-7 which tabulates total taxes owed by income of homeowners and landlords. The expected pattern of landlords exceeding homeowners in the amount of taxes owed holds only among owners in the lowest income group — those reporting an annual income of less than $10,000. Within this low-income group, a proportion of landlords substantially larger than that of homeowners owe more than $1,000 in back taxes. Among middle-income owners, with incomes between $10,000 and $15,000, 25 percent of homeowners compared to only 11 percent of landlords owe $1,000 or more in back taxes. For the highest income group, the proportions of landlords and homeowners with the highest delinquency level are almost equal at 25 percent and 22 percent, respectively. Again, to the extent that income reflects property value, upper-income homeowners and landlords are likely to own properties at relatively high levels of assessed values and are thus likely to incur equally high delinquent tax bills measured in absolute terms. *The data in the exhibit, however, call attention to the subpopulation of low-income landlords who are likely to own*

EXHIBIT 7-8

USUAL TIMING OF TAX BILL PAYMENTS BY HOMEOWNERS AND
LANDLORDS, PITTSBURGH
(percents)[a]

	Homeowners	Landlords
Pay Before Due	27.8	27.1
	(10)	(13)
Pay After Due	69.4	41.7
	(25)	(20)
No Payment	2.8	31.3
	(1)	(15)

Note: a. Absolute numbers are in parentheses.

Source: CUPR Pittsburgh Delinquency Survey, Summer 1974.

low-value, marginally-viable rental properties and who incur high levels of delinquency through prolonged nonpayment of taxes.

A further indication of the different character of delinquency for landlords and homeowners is gained from a comparison of reported usual timing of tax bill payments for the two groups. The data for owners who responded to this question in the interview are presented in Exhibit 7-8. Roughly the same proportion of homeowners and landlords claim to habitually pay their property taxes before the due date; a proportion of homeowners somewhat higher than that of landlords report payment of their tax bills after they fall due. Most significantly, 31 percent of landlords but only 3 percent of homeowners claim they make or will make no payments on their properties. To the extent that our sample is representative of delinquency in Pittsburgh, *these data furnish initial support for the conclusion that chronic delinquency in the City is a product of rental properties that have been written off by their landlord owners.* This hypothesis will be examined in greater detail in a later section.

Total dollar amount of taxes owed provides a sensitive measure of the severity and persistence of delinquency of a given owner when expressed as a proportion of the total assessed value of the property. Several characteristics of this measure (the D/A ratio) deserve particular attention.

First, the ratio of taxes owed to assessed value indicates the severity of delinquency "controlling for" the assessed value of the property. As evidenced in the top half of Exhibit 7-9, the simple dollar amount of taxes owed is a direct function of assessed valuation: the proportion of properties assessed at less than $2,500 that owe less than $500 in back taxes is substantially higher than the proportion of properties assessed at $5,000 or more owing the same amount of taxes. Likewise, the proportion of high-value properties owing $1,000 or more in taxes is three times the proportion of low-value properties that owe taxes in the same category.

In contrast, the relationship is reversed in the bottom half of the Exhibit in which the D/A ratio is categorized by assessed value of properties. Fully half of all properties assessed at $5,000 or more have very *low* D/A ratios and exactly the same proportion of the properties assessed below $2,500 have very *high* ratios.

One implication of these findings is that delinquency extends over a longer period for owners of low-value properties. A higher ratio of taxes owed to assessed value is attained as delinquency continues over a prolonged period and the cumulative dollar value of taxes owed approaches the assessed value of the property. The presence of a strong positive relationship between the D/A ratio and the length of the delinquency period is demonstrated in Exhibit 7-10. Quite clearly, the ratio increases as the number of years since the owner stopped paying taxes increases. While 50 percent of owners who first

EXHIBIT 7-9

TOTAL TAXES OWED AND RATIO OF TOTAL TAXES OWED TO TOTAL
ASSESSED VALUE OF PROPERTY, BY TOTAL ASSESSED VALUE OF
PROPERTY, PITTSBURGH (percents)[a]

Total Taxes Owed	Total Assessed Value of Property		
	< $2,500	$2,500-4,999	⩾ $5,000
< $500	71.8 (28)	52.2 (36)	50.0 (25)
$500-999	17.9 (7)	34.8 (24)	20.0 (10)
⩾ $1,000	10.3 (4)	13.0 (9)	30.0 (15)
Ratio of Total Taxes Owed to Total Assessed Value of Property			
⩽.060	12.8 (5)	29.0 (20)	51.0 (25)
.061-.199	38.5 (15)	33.3 (23)	32.7 (16)
⩾.200	48.7 (19)	37.7 (26)	16.3 (8)

Note: a. Absolute numbers are in parentheses.

Source: CUPR Pittsburgh Delinquency Survey, Summer 1974.

EXHIBIT 7-10

RATIO OF TOTAL TAXES OWED TO TOTAL ASSESSED VALUE OF PROPERTY,
BY YEAR OWNER STOPPED PAYING TAXES, PITTSBURGH
(percents)[a]

Ratio of Total Taxes Owed to Total Assessed Value of Property	Year Owner Stopped Paying Taxes				
	1970 or Before	1971	1972	1973	1974
⩽.060	8.0 (2)	0.0 (0)	11.8 (2)	20.8 (5)	50.0 (7)
.061-.199	36.0 (9)	47.1 (8)	41.2 (7)	45.8 (11)	21.4 (3)
⩾.200	56.0 (14)	52.9 (9)	47.1 (8)	33.3 (8)	28.6 (4)

Note: a. Absolute numbers are in parentheses.

Source: CUPR Pittsburgh Delinquency Survey, Summer 1974.

missed tax payments within the present year have a ratio of .06 or less, this low ratio is maintained by only 8 percent of those owners who have been delinquent for five years or more. Similarly, 56 percent of long-term delinquents have attained the highest ratio level compared to 29 percent of current year delinquents at this level. The D/A ratio not only provides an indication of the severity of tax delinquency but also constitutes a measure of the persistence of delinquency over time. Thus, the ratio presents an additional means of separating chronic long-term delinquency from the temporary nonpayment of taxes because of lack of funds.

The significance of the difference between resident and absentee owners is highlighted by the comparison of taxes owed and the D/A ratio for these two subgroups of the sample. The data are presented in Exhibit 7-11. Considering the absolute dollar amount of taxes owed, 22 percent of absentee owners compared to 16 percent of resident owners have tax bills of $1,000 or more. The disparity between the two groups is even greater when consider-

EXHIBIT 7-11

TOTAL TAXES OWED AND RATIO OF TOTAL TAXES OWED TO TOTAL ASSESSED VALUE OF PROPERTY, BY OWNER'S PLACE OF RESIDENCE, PITTSBURGH
(percents)[a]

| | Owner's Place of Residence | |
| | In the Building | Not in the Building |
Total Taxes Owed	*(resident owner)*	*(absentee owner)*
< $500	58.8	53.3
	(57)	(32)
$500-999	25.8	25.0
	(25)	(15)
⩾ $1,000	15.5	21.7
	(15)	(13)
Ratio of Total Taxes Owed to Total Assessed Value of Property		
⩽ .060	35.1	26.7
	(34)	(16)
.061-.199	35.1	33.3
	(34)	(20)
⩾ .200	29.9	40.0
	(29)	(24)

Note: a. Absolute numbers are in parentheses.

Source: CUPR Pittsburgh Delinquency Survey, Summer 1974.

ing the D/A ratio. *A larger proportion of resident owners than absentee owners exhibit relatively low ratios, and 40 percent of absentee owners compared to 30 percent of resident owners fall into the highest ratio category. In addition to the strong influence of rental ownership on delinquency, these data further indicate the importance of absentee ownership of rental properties as a factor associated with substantial and prolonged tax delinquency.*

REASONS FOR MISSING TAX PAYMENTS

Responses to a survey question soliciting an explanation of why the owner began to miss tax payments reveal a broad range of rationales for delinquency. *Substantially all of the reasons, however, reflected some aspect of the owner's immediate financial situation or financial considerations related to operating costs of the property.* The range of reasons given by owners for nonpayment of taxes has been summarized and cross-tabulated by selected characteristics of delinquent owners and their properties (see Exhibit 7-12); these cross-tabulations indicate the basic lines of division within which different types of owners give different reasons for their delinquency.

Exhibit 7-12A differentiates between the reasons given for nonpayment of property taxes by homeowners and by landlords in the sample. For both groups, a general and unspecified lack of funds figured significantly in the decision not to pay property taxes — 23 percent of homeowners and 19 percent of landlords gave this blanket response in explaining their delinquency. For those respondents who specified the source of their financial difficulties, however, a substantially larger proportion of homeowners than landlords cited personal emergencies, while the proportion of landlords who cited a lack of funds due to financial problems with the building was far larger than the proportion of homeowners who cited the same reason. Since landlords presumably view their property as a financial investment rather than a home, larger expenditure requirements or an inadequate cash flow from the building are likely to be seen in a different light for this group than for homeowners. Significantly, *22 percent of the landlords but none of the homeowners indicated that their decision to discontinue tax payments derived from the conclusion that the property was of no value and therefore warranted no further expenditures.*

As would be expected, a lack of funds due to personal emergencies is experienced most often by lower-income owners. As indicated in Exhibit 7-12B, 26 percent of owners with incomes below $10,000 gave this as the reason for their delinquency, while none of the owners with incomes of $15,000 or more offered this as a reason for their nonpayment of taxes. On the other hand, a higher proportion of upper-income owners (19 percent) than those with lower incomes (7 percent) declared that their property was of no value.

OWNER'S REASONS FOR INITIALLY MISSING TAX PAYMENTS BY CHARACTERISTICS OF OWNERS AND PROPERTIES, PITTSBURGH (percents)[a]

	A. Ownership Status		B. Owner Income			C. Condition of Building			D. Current Market Value[b]			E. Change in the Vacancy Rate[c]	
	Homeowners	Landlords	<$10,000	$10,000-14,999	≥$15,000	Poor	Average	Good	<$10,000	$10,000-19,999	≥$20,000	Lower or No Change	Higher
Owner Denies Delinquency or Claims Bills Paid in Full	4.2 (3)	11.1 (7)	5.6 (4)	6.7 (2)	25.0 (4)	0.0 (0)	10.8 (4)	9.4 (6)	6.8 (4)	10.5 (4)	10.5 (2)	11.1 (4)	7.7 (1)
General Lack of Money	22.5 (16)	19.0 (12)	23.6 (17)	20.0 (6)	18.8 (3)	12.9 (4)	18.9 (7)	26.6 (17)	18.6 (11)	26.3 (10)	10.5 (2)	25.0 (9)	7.7 (1)
Lack of Money, Personal Reasons	35.2 (25)	4.8 (3)	26.4 (19)	23.3 (7)	0.0 (0)	12.9 (4)	21.6 (8)	25.0 (16)	20.3 (12)	21.1 (8)	21.1 (4)	11.1 (4)	0.0 (0)
Lack of Money for Reasons Related to the Building	5.6 (4)	19.0 (12)	9.7 (7)	13.3 (4)	12.5 (2)	22.6 (7)	13.5 (5)	4.7 (3)	15.3 (9)	5.3 (2)	15.8 (3)	19.4 (7)	23.1 (3)
Property of No Value	0.0 (0)	22.2 (14)	6.9 (5)	10.0 (3)	18.8 (3)	32.3 (10)	2.7 (1)	3.1 (2)	20.3 (12)	0.0 (0)	0.0 (0)	8.3 (3)	53.8 (7)
Administrative Problems with Mortgage Holder or Estate	16.9 (12)	6.3 (4)	11.1 (8)	10.0 (3)	6.3 (1)	9.7 (3)	16.2 (6)	10.9 (7)	11.9 (7)	15.8 (6)	10.5 (2)	0.0 (0)	0.0 (0)
Habitual Late Payment Related to Potential Interest Income	5.6 (4)	1.6 (1)	4.2 (3)	3.3 (1)	6.3 (1)	0.0 (0)	2.7 (1)	6.3 (4)	0.0 (0)	2.6 (1)	15.8 (3)	2.8 (1)	0.0 (0)
General Conflict with the City, and misc.	9.9 (7)	15.9 (10)	12.5 (9)	13.3 (4)	12.5 (2)	9.7 (3)	13.5 (5)	14.1 (9)	6.8 (4)	18.4 (7)	15.8 (3)	22.2 (8)	7.7 (1)

Notes: a. Absolute numbers are in parentheses.
b. Owner's estimate of current market value of building.
c. Owner's perception of change in the vacancy rate in the building in the last six years.

Source: CUPR Pittsburgh Delinquency Survey, Summer - 1974.

The data on building condition, current market value, and vacancy rate conform exactly to expectations. *The poorer the condition of the building, the lower its market value, and the higher the vacancy rate, the higher the proportion of owners who stipulate the unsatisfactory financial position of the property as their reason for delinquency. Even higher proportions of owners who describe their properties in these terms have decided that the value of their property is so low that no further tax payments are warranted.*

At the same time as different reasons for nonpayment are given by different types of owners, each of these reasons is associated with a different owner's reason for missing tax payments in Exhibit 7-13. Owners who claim to have paid their bills in full or claim no delinquency tend to have relatively low D/A ratios. Similarly, owners who cite administrative problems with mortgage holders or estates and owners who habitually pay their taxes late with the expectation of earning a larger amount of interest on their capital also have relatively low levels of taxes owed in relation to the assessed value of their property. In the same vein, more than twice the proportion of owners citing a lack of money due to personal reasons as owners citing a lack of money due to reasons related to the building have a low D/A ratio. Finally, only 7 percent of owners who stopped paying taxes because they felt their property was of no value have low ratios of taxes owed to assessed value. At the other extreme, *close to 70 percent of owners claiming lack of money for reasons related to the building and fully half of those who feel that their property is of no value fall in the highest D/A ratio category.*

SHORT-TERM VERSUS CHRONIC DELINQUENCY

Of the 158 owners delinquent on December 31, 1973, eleven owners, or 7 percent of the sample had made full payment of back taxes by July 1974, and an additional twenty-three owners, 15 percent of the total, made partial payment during the six-month period. Thus 22 percent or slightly over one-fifth of the sample of 158 delinquent owners paid at least some of the taxes owed on December 31, 1973 within the first six months of 1974. A comparison of this 22 percent with the remainder of the sample which made no payments during the six-month period furnishes some insight into the differences between short-term and chronic delinquency.

Twenty-two percent of the total sample owed only municipal and/or school district property taxes on December 31, 1973. The pattern of full and partial payments appears to differ for property taxes and for water and sewer charges (see Exhibit 7-14). Eleven percent of the sample had paid their property taxes in full by July 1974, compared to only 4 percent who had made full payment on water and sewer charges. On the other hand the proportion of the sample who made partial payments on their sewer and

EXHIBIT 7-13

RATIO OF TOTAL TAXES OWED TO TOTAL ASSESSED VALUE OF PROPERTY, BY OWNER'S REASON
FOR INITIALLY MISSING TAX PAYMENTS, PITTSBURGH
(percents)[a]

Ratio of total taxes owed to total assessed value of property	Owner claims no delinquency or bills paid in full	General lack of money	Lack of money, personal reasons	Lack of money, for reasons related to the building	Property of no value	Administrative problems with mortgage holder or estate	Habitual late payment related to potential interest income	General conflict with city and misc.
≤.060	50.0 (5)	25.9 (7)	28.6 (8)	12.5 (2)	7.1 (1)	43.8 (7)	80.0 (4)	23.5 (4)
.061-.199	40.0 (4)	29.6 (8)	28.6 (8)	18.8 (3)	42.9 (6)	43.8 (7)	20.0 (1)	41.2 (7)
≥.200	10.0 (1)	44.4 (12)	42.9 (12)	68.8 (11)	50.0 (7)	12.5 (2)	0.0 (0)	35.3 (6)

Note: a. Absolute numbers are in parentheses.
Source: CUPR Pittsburgh Delinquency Survey, Summer 1974.

water bills (25 percent) was much larger than the proportion who made partial payments (10 percent).

Several interpretations of these data appear equally plausible. It is likely that at least some of the owners who paid their property taxes in full were among the 22 percent of the sample who were not delinquent in water and sewer charges. The short-term duration of their delinquency prior to payment of taxes in full suggests that owners in this group were only temporarily and perhaps inadvertently delinquent in their accounts. Payments by these owners would thus explain the higher rate of full payment made on property taxes compared to full payment made on sewer and water charges.

At the same time, the higher overall rate of at least some payment of water and sewer bills suggests that owners might perceive greater sanctions against delinquency on these services as compared to sanctions against delinquency on property taxes. To the extent that water and sewer charges are grouped together with charges for other utilities by owners, the perceived threat of disruption of services might result in a higher level of at least partial payment in an effort to ensure continued service. No similar immediate incentive exists at present in regard to property tax payments.

Analyses of the distribution of full and partial tax payments by characteristics of owners in the sample provide insight into the durability of the delinquency problem. First, the pattern of payments of back taxes is related to the size of the total tax bill and the D/A ratio in Exhibits 7-15 and 7-16. Again, an interesting differentiation emerges in viewing payment patterns of property taxes versus water and sewer charges. For water and sewer taxes, the higher the total tax bill, the lower the proportion of owners who made either full or partial payment, and the higher the proportion who made no payments during the first six months of 1974. This pattern does not hold, however, for payments made on municipal and school district property taxes. Considering payment of property taxes, full or partial payment was made by proportionally more owners with very small or very large tax bills than by owners in the intermediate group. A slightly larger proportion of owners owing less than $500 in property taxes paid their bills in full than did owners owing $1,000 or more; a somewhat larger proportion of owners in the high tax bill category made partial payment of their property taxes than did owners in the lowest delinquency category. Thus, of owners who made any tax payments by July 1974, those owing smaller absolute amounts tended to pay in full while owners owing $1,000 or more tended to make partial payments.

The distribution of payments made, categorized by D/A ratio, conforms to the expected pattern. With only minor exceptions, for both types of taxes and for all charges combined, *the higher the ratio of taxes owed to assessment, the lower the proportion of owners who paid in full and the higher the*

EXHIBIT 7-14

PAYMENT OF TAXES DELINQUENT ON DECEMBER 31, 1973, AS OF JULY 1974, PITTSBURGH

	Not Delinquent		Full Payment Made		Partial Payment Made		No Payment Made		Total	
	Number	Percent	Number	Percent	Number	Percent	Number	Percent	Number	Percent
Municipal and school district property taxes	0	0.0	17	10.8	15	9.5	126	79.7	158	100.0
City water bills and sewer tax	34	21.5	7	4.4	39	24.7	78	49.4	158	100.0
All taxes	0	0.0	11	6.9	23	14.6	124	78.5	158	100.0

Source: Tax Delinquency File, City Treasury Records.

EXHIBIT 7-15

PAYMENT OF TAXES DELINQUENT ON DECEMBER 31, 1973, AS OF JULY 1974, BY SIZE OF TOTAL TAX BILL, FOR PROPERTY TAX BILL, SERVICE BILL, AND ALL BILLS COMBINED, PITTSBURGH

(percents)[a]

| | Municipal and School District Property Tax | | | Water and Sewer Charges | | | All Charges Combined | | |
	<500	500-999	≥1,000	<500	500-999	≥1,000	<500	500-999	≥1,000
				Total Taxes Owed (in dollars)					
Full Payment Made	12.4 (11)	7.3 (3)	10.7 (3)	8.5 (5)	2.6 (1)	3.8 (1)	9.0 (8)	4.9 (2)	3.6 (1)
Partial Payment Made	10.1 (9)	2.4 (1)	17.9 (5)	40.7 (24)	28.2 (11)	15.4 (4)	11.2 (10)	9.8 (4)	32.1 (9)
No Payment Made	77.5 (69)	90.2 (37)	71.4 (20)	50.8 (30)	69.2 (27)	80.8 (21)	79.8 (71)	85.4 (35)	64.3 (18)

Note: a.   Absolute numbers are in parentheses.

Source: Tax Delinquency File; CUPR Pittsburgh Delinquency Survey, Summer 1974.

EXHIBIT 7-16

PAYMENT OF TAXES DELINQUENT ON DECEMBER 31, 1973, AS OF JULY 1974, BY RATIO OF TAXES OWED TO ASSESSED VALUE, FOR PROPERTY TAX BILL, SERVICE BILL, AND ALL BILLS COMBINED, PITTSBURGH

(percents)[a]

	Municipal and School District Property Tax			Water and Sewer Charges			All Charges Combined		
	≤.060	.061-.199	≥.200	≤.060	.061-.199	≥.200	≤.060	.061-.199	≥.200
Full Payment Made	14.0 (7)	18.5 (10)	0.0 (0)	13.0 (3)	6.4 (3)	1.9 (1)	14.0 (7)	7.4 (4)	0.0 (0)
Partial Payment Made	18.0 (9)	3.7 (2)	7.5 (4)	43.5 (10)	31.9 (15)	26.4 (14)	8.0 (4)	22.2 (12)	13.2 (7)
No Payment Made	68.0 (34)	77.8 (42)	92.5 (49)	43.5 (10)	61.7 (29)	71.7 (38)	78.0 (39)	70.4 (38)	86.8 (46)

Notes: a. Absolute numbers are in parentheses.
Sources: Tax Delinquency File; CUPR Pittsburgh Delinquency Survey, Summer 1974.

EXHIBIT 7-17

PAYMENT OF TAXES DELINQUENT ON DECEMBER 31, 1973, AS OF JULY 1974,
BY TOTAL ASSESSED VALUE OF PROPERTY, FOR PROPERTY TAX BILL, SERVICE BILL, AND
ALL BILLS COMBINED, PITTSBURGH

(percents)[a]

| | Total Assessed Value of Property | | | | | | | | |
| | Municipal and School District Property Tax | | | Water and Sewer Charges | | | All Charges Combined | | |
	<2500	2500-4999	≥5000	<2500	2500-4999	≥5000	<2500	2500-4999	≥5000
Full Payment Made	5.1 (2)	10.1 (7)	16.0 (8)	0.0 (0)	6.9 (4)	8.6 (3)	0.0 (0)	8.7 (6)	10.0 (5)
Partial Payment Made	0.0 (0)	8.7 (6)	18.0 (9)	51.6 (16)	22.4 (13)	28.6 (10)	10.3 (4)	14.5 (10)	18.0 (9)
No Payment Made	94.9 (37)	81.2 (56)	66.0 (33)	48.4 (15)	70.7 (41)	62.9 (22)	89.7 (35)	76.8 (53)	72.0 (36)

Note: a. Absolute numbers are in parentheses.
Sources: Tax Delinquency File: CUPR Pittsburgh Delinquency Survey, Summer 1974.

EXHIBIT 7-18

PAYMENT OF TAXES DELINQUENT ON DECEMBER 31, 1973, AS OF JULY 1974, BY OWNER'S ANNUAL INCOME, FOR PROPERTY TAX BILL, SERVICE BILL, AND ALL BILLS COMBINED, PITTSBURGH

(percents)[a]

| | Owner's Annual Income | | | | | | | | |
| | Municipal and School District Property Tax | | | Water and Sewer Charges | | | All Charges Combined | | |
	<10,000	10,000-14,999	≥15,000	<10,000	10,000-14,999	≥15,000	<10,000	10,000-14,999	≥15,000
Full Payment Made	8.6 (7)	14.3 (5)	18.2 (4)	4.5 (3)	8.0 (2)	14.3 (2)	4.9 (4)	11.4 (4)	13.6 (3)
Partial Payment Made	7.4 (6)	11.4 (4)	18.2 (4)	30.3 (20)	28.0 (7)	35.7 (5)	11.1 (9)	17.1 (6)	18.2 (4)
No Payment Made	84.0 (68)	74.3 (26)	63.6 (14)	65.2 (43)	64.0 (16)	50.0 (7)	84.0 (68)	71.4 (25)	68.2 (15)

Note: a. Absolute numbers are in parentheses.
Sources: Tax Delinquency File; CUPR Pittsburgh Delinquency Survey, Summer 1974.

EXHIBIT 7-19

PAYMENT OF TAXES DELINQUENT ON DECEMBER 31, 1973, AS OF JULY 1974. BY OWNER'S REASON FOR MISSING TAX PAYMENTS, PITTSBURGH
(percents)[a]

	Owner denies delinquency or claims bills paid in full	General lack of money	Lack of money due to personal reasons	Lack of money for reasons related to the building	Property of no value: no reason to pay taxes	Administrative problems with mortgage holder or estate	Habitual late payment related to potential interest income	General conflict with the city
A. Municipal and School District Property Taxes								
Full Payment Made	30.0 (3)	7.1 (2)	3.6 (1)	12.5 (2)	0.0 (0)	25.0 (4)	0.0 (0)	0.0 (0)
Partial Payment Made	20.0 (2)	7.1 (2)	3.6 (1)	6.3 (1)	0.0 (0)	12.5 (2)	0.0 (0)	11.8 (2)
No Payment Made	50.0 (5)	85.7 (24)	92.9 (26)	81.3 (13)	100.0 (14)	62.5 (10)	100.0 (5)	88.2 (15)
B. City Water and Sewer Charges								
Full Payment Made	33.3 (2)	0.0 (0)	0.0 (0)	6.7 (1)	0.0 (0)	0.0 (0)	25.0 (1)	0.0 (0)
Partial Payment Made	0.0 (0)	33.3 (8)	27.3 (6)	46.7 (7)	57.1 (8)	27.3 (3)	25.0 (1)	30.8 (4)
No Payment Made	66.7 (4)	66.7 (16)	72.7 (16)	46.7 (7)	42.9 (6)	72.7 (8)	50.0 (2)	69.2 (9)
C. All Charges Combined								
Full Payment Made	20.0 (2)	3.6 (1)	3.6 (1)	6.3 (1)	0.0 (0)	18.8 (3)	0.0 (0)	0.0 (0)
Partial Payment Made	20.0 (2)	17.9 (5)	10.7 (3)	25.0 (4)	0.0 (0)	12.5 (2)	20.0 (1)	5.9 (1)
No Payment Made	60.0 (6)	78.6 (22)	85.7 (24)	68.8 (11)	100.0 (14)	68.8 (11)	80.0 (4)	94.1 (16)

Note: a. Absolute numbers are in parentheses.

Sources: Tax Delinquency File; CUPR Pittsburgh Delinquency Survey, Summer 1974.

proportion who made no payment. No owner with a ratio of .2 or more made full payment on property taxes owed; a very small proportion (2 percent) of owers in this category paid their delinquent water and sewer bills.

Exhibits 7-17 and 7-18 present data on the distribution of payments made tabulated against two closely related measures: total assessed value of the property and owner's income. Both of these Exhibits present similar findings: the higher the owner's annual income and the higher the assessed value, the greater the proportion of owners who paid their bills in full. No owner of property assessed at under $2,500 made full payment of back taxes. Only 5 percent of owners with incomes less than $10,000 made full payment of all tax bills while 14 percent of owners with incomes of $15,000 or more made full payments. The data provide yet additional evidence for the finding that continued delinquency is largely a function of the un-availability of funds to meet tax payments.

While the simple availability of funds is clearly important, an adequate in-terpretation of the data requires the further specification of the reason for this financial shortage. The distribution of payments made between January and July of 1974 is tabulated in Exhibit 7-19 by the owner's reason for in-itially missing tax payments. Focusing on payments for all taxes and charges summarized in Exhibit 7-19C, full payment was made predominantly by owners who had experienced administrative problems with mortgage holders or whose properties were involved in estate difficulties. At the other extreme, fully 100 percent of the owners who reported a belief that their property was of no value followed suit with their actions and paid none of their outstanding taxes during the six-month period.

Significantly, some or all of their back taxes were paid by more owners whose lack of funds derived from conditions related to the building than by owners whose financial difficulties derived from personal reasons. *A lack of funds due to personal emergencies such as sickness appears to be a compelling factor for a significant proportion of delinquent owners. In contrast, a lack of funds associated with a deficit in a property owner's balance sheet might pre-sent a situation more amenable to pressure exerted by the City for payment of delinquent taxes.* In this regard, stricter enforcement and higher interest and penalty charges on back taxes are likely to influence a substantial propor-tion of owners — such as landlords who view their property as a source of income — to pay back taxes. On the other hand, increased penalties and in-terest on back taxes would tend to exacerbate the problem of limited finances for lower-income groups, the elderly, and others whose property provides them with a home rather than a source of income. A substantial ef-fort would be warranted on the part of the City to differentiate between in-terest and penalty charges levied on homeowners as opposed to those levied on landlords, since only the latter group could be expected to respond to the incentive of higher penalties.

OWNER'S PLANS FOR TAX PAYMENT

The data on actual payments of taxes owed are paralleled by owners' *plans* for the payment of back taxes. In response to a survey question, owners stated whether they intended to pay their back taxes in full, pay as much as possible whenever possible, make minimum payments, or make no further payments of real estate taxes. An owner's avowal that he intends to pay no more taxes on his property can be taken as a firm indication of continued delinquency.

Cross-classification of owners' payment plans by owners' characteristics reveals the expected relationships. Exhibit 7-20 compares plans for payment by homeowners and landlords, resident and absentee owners, and by ownership of other real estate in addition to the sampled property. The results are striking. Sixty-two percent of homeowners but only 46 percent of landlords declared their intention to pay in full; *the proportion of landlords who stated an intention to pay none of their back taxes was six times the proportion of homeowners who stated the same — 31 percent compared to 5 percent* (see Exhibit 7-20A).

Focusing on place of residence, 61 percent of resident owners said they intended to pay in full while only 43 percent of absentee landlords gave the same response. The 7 percent of resident owners who said they would make no further tax payments is substantially below the 34 percent of nonresident owners who made the same decision (see Exhibit 7-20B). Finally, ownership of other real estate, indicating a financial interest in property ownership, follows the same pattern. Ten percent more owners who owned no other real estate than owners who did own other real estate said they intended to pay in full; the proportion of owners of other real estate who said they would make no payments on their tax bills was two and a half times the proportion of owners who owned no additional property and stated an intention to make no payments on their tax bills (see Exhibit 7-20C).

An important implication of these findings is summarized in the cross-tabulation of plans for payment of back taxes by the type of structure owned (see Exhibit 7-21). As would be expected from the foregoing analysis, a *substantially larger proportion of owners of single-family homes intend to pay their taxes in full than do owners of all other types of housing structures* (i.e., duplex and multifamily structures). Similarly, the proportion of owners of single-family homes who will make no payments is only half as large as the proportion of owners of all other type structures who intend no further payments. Structure type therefore appears to serve as a suitable proxy for the characteristics of owners described in Exhibits 7-20A to 7-20C.

Yet additional information is available on the characteristics of owners planning various levels of tax payment. As indicated in Exhibit 7-22, lower-income owners appear to intend full or at least partial payment, while upper-income owners (those with incomes of $15,000 or more) are disproportionately found in the category of owners who intend no payments of back taxes. These upper-income owners are most likely to be in a position to

EXHIBIT 7-20

OWNER'S PLANS FOR PAYMENT OF BACK TAXES, BY
OWNER STATUS, PLACE OF RESIDENCE, AND OWNERSHIP
OF OTHER REAL ESTATE, PITTSBURGH
(percents)[a]

	A. Owner Status:	
	Homeowners	*Landlords*
Pay in Full	62.1	45.5
	(36)	(25)
Pay as Much as Possible Whenever Possible	22.4	10.9
	(13)	(6)
Minimum Payment	10.3	12.7
	(6)	(7)
No Payment	5.2	30.9
	(3)	(17)

	B. Owner's Place of Residence:	
	In Building (resident owner)	*Not in Building (absentee owner)*
Pay in Full	60.9	43.2
	(42)	(19)
Pay as Much as Possible Whenever Possible	21.7	9.1
	(15)	(4)
Minimum Payment	10.1	13.6
	(7)	(6)
No Payment	7.2	34.1
	(5)	(15)

	C. Ownership of Other Real Estate:	
	Owns No Other Real Estate	*Owns Other Real Estate*
Pay in Full	57.8	47.8
	(37)	(22)
Pay as Much as Possible Whenever Possible	20.3	10.9
	(13)	(5)
Minimum Payment	10.9	13.0
	(7)	(6)
No Payment	10.9	28.3
	(7)	(13)

Note: a. Absolute numbers are in parentheses.

Source: CUPR Pittsburgh Delinquency Survey, Summer 1974.

write off property as no longer profitable, while lower-income owners are likely to require the property as a home and shelter.

OWNER'S INTENTION TO RELINQUISH TITLE TO THE CITY

The final descriptive measure of the character of tax delinquency pertains to the owner's stated intention to let title to his property pass to the City. This statement reflects the owner's decision to abandon ownership of his property. Properties falling into this category constitute the core of chronic delinquency, since owners have ceased tax payments and will merely wait until the process of tax sale and acquisition has run its course. The current lengthy time period required for this to occur ensures that delinquency of this type will be prolonged. As demonstrated in Exhibit 7-23, owners who have decided to give up title to their property tend to have been delinquent in payments over a considerable period. Only 13 percent of those owners who first became delinquent within the past year have decided to give up title; the proportion of owners who have been delinquent since 1971 and have decided to give up title is almost three times as great, and the proportion of owners who have been delinquent for five years or more and have made the decision to surrender title is twice as large.

As would be expected from the foregoing analysis, *26 percent of landlords but only 1 percent of homeowners intend to let title to the property pass to the*

EXHIBIT 7-21

OWNER'S PLANS REGARDING PAYMENT OF BACK TAXES BY STRUCTURE TYPE, PITTSBURGH

(percents)[a]

Owner's Plans Regarding Payment of Back Taxes	Structure Type	
	Single-Family House	Other
Pay in full	58.0	37.5
	(51)	(9)
Pay as Much as Possible Whenever Possible	18.2	12.5
	(16)	(3)
Minimum Payment	9.1	20.8
	(8)	(5)
No Payment	14.8	29.2
	(13)	(7)

Note: a. Absolute numbers are in parentheses.

Source: CUPR Pittsburgh Delinquency Survey, Summer 1974.

City (see Exhibit 7-24). Since these properties constitute the stock of housing that the City will acquire through tax sale, a detailed examination of the structure characteristics will provide the City with the information necessary to plan constructively for reuse of the properties.

Selected characteristics of these properties are presented in Exhibit 7-25. Focusing on the top row of each section, it is possible to distinguish the overall characteristics of properties that owners have decided to abandon to the City. Proportionally, owners of these structures have accrued high delinquency/assessment ratios. The proportion of these properties with D/A ratios of .2 or more is nearly four times larger than the proportion of structures with low ratios. As expected, these properties have very low assessed values. Thirty-two percent of properties assessed at under $2,500 have been written-off by owners, while none of the sample properties with assessed values of $5,000 or more are in this category. The proportion of multifamily structures is nearly twice the proportion of single-family structures, and the proportion of absentee owners is overwhelmingly larger than the proportion of resident owners. *Only 6 percent of those owners who purchased the property as a home state a readiness to abandon title, while 28 percent of those for whom rental income was the motivating factor in purchasing the property and 23 percent who obtained the property through inheritance or foreclosure now claim a willingness to relinquish the property to the City.*

Buildings in poor condition are much more likely to be passed on to the City than are buildings in good condition, and the proportion of buildings

EXHIBIT 7-22

OWNER'S PLANS REGARDING PAYMENT OF BACK TAXES, BY ANNUAL INCOME OF OWNER, PITTSBURGH
(percents)[a]

Owner's Plans Regarding Payment of Back Taxes	Owner's Annual Income		
	<$10,000	$10,000-14,999	≥$15,000
Pay in Full	54.8	57.7	41.7
	(34)	(15)	(5)
Pay as Much as Possible Whenever Possible	21.0	11.5	8.3
	(13)	(3)	(1)
Minimum Payment	14.5	3.8	8.3
	(9)	(1)	(1)
No Payment	9.7	26.9	41.7
	(6)	(7)	(5)

Note: a. Absolute numbers are in parentheses.

Source: CUPR Pittsburgh Delinquency Survey, Summer 1974.

in need of major repairs is two and half times the proportion of buildings that do not need such repairs. Disproportionately more owners feel that the property will be worth less in five years than those who feel that in five years it will be worth the same or more than it is today. *In summary, the City can expect to obtain the worst of its housing stock through tax sale and acquistion.*

EXHIBIT 7-23

OWNER'S INTENT TO LET THE CITY TAKE TITLE TO HIS PROPERTY, BY YEAR OWNER STOPPED PAYING TAXES, PITTSBURGH
(percents)[a]

Owner's Intent to Let the City Take Title	Year Owner Stopped Paying Taxes				
	1970 or Before	1971	1972	1973	1974
Yes	26.1 (6)	35.3 (6)	16.7 (3)	12.5 (3)	0.0 (0)
No	73.9 (17)	64.7 (11)	83.3 (15)	87.5 (21)	100.0 (14)

Note: a. Absolute numbers are in parentheses.

Source: CUPR Pittsburgh Delinquency Survey, Summer 1974.

EXHIBIT 7-24

OWNER'S INTENT TO LET THE CITY TAKE TITLE TO HIS PROPERTY, FOR HOMEOWNERS AND LANDLORDS, PITTSBURGH
(percents)[a]

Owner's Intent to Let the City Take Title	Homeowners	Landlords
Yes	1.4 (1)	26.2 (17)
No	98.6 (71)	73.8 (48)

Note: a. Absolute numbers are in parentheses.

Source: CUPR Pittsburgh Delinquency Survey, Summer 1974.

EXHIBIT 7-25

OWNER'S INTENT TO LET THE CITY TAKE TITLE TO HIS PROPERTY BY SELECTED CHARACTERISTICS OF OWNER AND STRUCTURES, PITTSBURGH
(percents)[a]

Owner's intention to let city take title			
A. Ratio of Total Taxes Owed to Total Assessed Value			
	<.060	*.061-199*	*≥.200*
Yes	4.8 (2)	16.3 (7)	17.6 (9)
No	95.2 (40)	83.7 (36)	82.4 (42)
B. Total Assessed Value of Property			
	<$2,500	*$2,500-4,999*	*≥$5,000*
Yes	32.4 (11)	11.3 (7)	0.0 (0)
No	67.6 (23)	88.7 (55)	100.0 (41)
C. Structure Type			
	Single-Family House	*Other*	
Yes	11.4 (12)	20.0 (6)	
No	88.6 (93)	80.0 (24)	
D. Owner's Place of Residence			
	In Building (Resident Owner)	*Not In Building (Absentee Owner)*	
Yes	2.4 (2)	30.8 (16)	
No	97.6 (83)	69.2 (36)	
E. Owner's Reason For Purchasing Property			
	Home	*Rental Return*	*Inheritance, Debt or Mortgage Foreclosure*
Yes	6.4 (5)	28.0 (7)	23.1 (6)
No	93.6 (73)	72.0 (18)	76.9 (20)

EXHIBIT 7-25 (cont'd)

OWNER'S INTENT TO LET THE CITY TAKE TITLE TO HIS PROPERTY BY
SELECTED CHARACTERISTICS OF OWNERS AND STRUCTURES,
PITTSBURGH
(percents)[a]

	F. Building Condition		
	Poor	*Good*	*Excellent*
Yes	43.8	2.8	3.0
	(14)	(1)	(2)
No	56.3	97.2	97.0
	(18)	(35)	(65)

	G. Need For Major Repairs	
	Yes	*No*
Yes	13.7	5.3
	(10)	(3)
No	86.3	94.7
	(63)	(54)

	H. Owner's Evaluation of Value of the Property in Five Years		
	More than Today	*Same as Today*	*Less than Today*
Yes	4.3	10.0	25.9
	(3)	(2)	(7)
No	95.7	90.0	74.1
	(67)	(18)	(20)

Note: a. Absolute numbers are in parentheses.

Source: CUPR Pittsburgh Delinquency Survey, Summer 1974.

The Cycle of Delinquency: Property Maintenance, Property Value, and Vacancy Rates

INTRODUCTION

The macro analysis reported in Chapters 4 and 6 served to narrow the focus of analytic attention to the related elements of property maintenance, property value, and vacancy as the basic factors associated with a high delinquency rate. A high vacancy rate, for instance, was found to be one of the factors most strongly associated with a high level of tax delinquency. It can be hypothesized on the basis of this finding that a high vacancy rate contributes to tax delinquency by reducing an owner's cash flow from his property. This loss of revenue is hypothesized in turn to result in lower expenditures and consequently in even greater difficulty in finding tenants. As the cycle is continued, prolonged vacancy eventually results in depreciation of the value of the property, a growing delinquency-to-assessment ratio, chronic delinquency and ultimate abandonment of the structure.

PROPERTY MAINTENANCE AND DELINQUENCY

Evidence for the actual operation of this cycle is provided by the survey data on delinquent owners. The data graphically portray the interaction between (1) the owner's pattern of property maintenance; (2) the condition of the structure; (3) the inability to attract tenants and the consequent vacancy rate; and, coming full circle, (4) the effect of the vacancy rate on the owner's ability to maintain the structure and on the value of the property. The following series of Exhibits summarizes the components of this process.

Exhibit 8-1 relates the level of total expenditures on the property, the owner's pattern of property maintenance, and the ultimate condition of the building, to the owner's place of residence. Within our sample of delinquent property owners, resident owners as a group clearly maintain a higher level of expenditures on their properties than do absentee owners (see Exhibit 8-1A. Almost three times as many absentee owners as resident owners scored at the low extreme on an index of total expenditures. This index summarizes variables measuring expenditures for insurance, maintenance, heating, utilities, mortgage and debt payments, and all taxes on the property: a score of "0", attained by 22 percent of the sample, indicates an extremely low relative level of expenditures while a score of "3", attained by 11 percent of the sample, signifies the highest relative level of total expenditures on the property. While the 11 percent of the total sample with an extremely high expenditure level is evenly divided between resident and nonresident owners, the proportion of owners who live in their buildings and attain the next highest expenditure level is almost four times the proportion of absentee owners who are in the same expenditure category.

The distribution of expenditures is reproduced in the distribution of property maintenance activity summarized in Exhibit 8-1B. As would be expected from the foregoing discussion of total expenditures, while approximately the same proportion of resident and absentee owners claim to keep their properties in "good as new condition," 56 percent of resident owners compared to only 37 percent of nonresident owners claim to maintain their properties in "good" condition. Absentee owners who characterize their maintenance pattern as designed to keep their property in only "fair" condition lead by 10 percentage points the resident owners who claim the same. Most significantly, while only 8 percent of owners who live in their buildings admit to making emergency repairs only or none at all, fully 22 percent of absentee owners fall into this category of self-reported maintenance behavior.

Exhibit 8-1C summarizes these data by relating the condition of the building to the owner's place of residence. The building condition index summarizes an owner's responses to questions concerning the condition of the heating equipment, plumbing, wiring, building exterior, and roof, and an additional question on the condition of the building as a whole. The worse the condition of each of these items and the building as a whole, the higher the respondent's score on the index.

Quite clearly, absentee owners score higher on the index of building condition, indicating a higher incidence of problems in their buildings. The proportion of resident owners scoring low on the index is nearly 12 percentage points higher than the corresponding proportion of absentee owners, while the proportion of absentee owners who attained the highest score (i.e.,

EXHIBIT 8-1

TOTAL EXPENDITURES, MAINTENANCE PATTERN, AND BUILDING
CONDITION, BY OWNER'S PLACE OF RESIDENCE, PITTSBURGH
(percents)[a]

	Owner's Place of Residence	
	In the Building (Resident Owner)	Not in the Building (Absentee Owner)
A. Level of Total Expenditures on the Property: Total Expenditures Index[b]:		
0 Low Expenditures	13.3 (13)	35.0 (21)
1 Medium-low	44.9 (44)	46.7 (28)
2 Medium-high	30.6 (30)	8.3 (5)
3 High Expenditures	11.2 (11)	10.0 (6)
B. Pattern of Property Maintenance:		
Maintain in "Good as New" Condition	13.3 (13)	10.0 (6)
Maintain in Good Condition	56.1 (55)	36.7 (22)
Maintain in Fair Condition	22.4 (22)	31.7 (19)
Make No Repairs or Emergency Repairs Only	8.2 (8)	21.7 (13)
C. Building Condition: Building Condition Index[b]:		
0 Excellent Condition	31.6 (31)	20.0 (12)
1 Good	27.6 (27)	25.0 (15)
2 Fair	31.6 (31)	36.7 (22)
3 Poor Condition	9.2 (9)	18.3 (11)

Notes: a. Absolute numbers are in parentheses.
b. See Appendix A for discussion of index construction.

Source: CUPR Pittsburgh Delinquency Survey, Summer 1974.

poorest condition) on the index is twice the proportion of resident owners in the same category. The relatively low levels of total expenditures and the less stringent pattern of maintenance practiced by nonresident property owners in the sample are evidenced in the measure of the condition of the buildings owned by the two groups.

While it may appear to be a truism that building condition is a direct function of the level of expenditures on the property, the significance of this relationship for the cycle of tax delinquency warrants its explicit empirical substantiation. Exhibit 8-2 summarized this relationship by arraying scores on the index of building condition against scores on the index of total expenditures, for the entire sample of delinquent owners. Almost two and a half times the proportion of owners at the highest expenditure level than those at the lowest level own buildings that are in the best relative condition. Similarly, for buildings in the worst condition, 23.5 percent of the owners scored low in total expenditures while only 5.9 percent scored high.

Given the relationship between maintenance levels and total expenditures, further insight can be gained by examining selected additional factors contributing to an owner's pattern of maintenance. For instance, a clear relationship exists between the extent of property maintenance undertaken by the delinquent owners in our sample and the age of the building: older buildings in general have much lower maintenance levels than buildings constructed in the postwar period (see Exhibit 8-3).

An equally important relationship exists between an owner's pattern of property maintenance and his original reason for purchasing the property. This relationship is particularly important in light of the role that vacancy rates and the owner's ability to find tenants play in influencing the owner's decision not to pay property taxes. Exhibit 8-4 relates the level of property maintenance to whether the owner purchased the property as a home or with the expectation of earning rental income. Fully 56 percent of owners who purchased the property for a home keep the property in good condition, compared to the 32 percent of owners who purchased the property for rental purposes and keep it in good condition. While only 8 percent of those who intended to make the property their home make repairs in emergency situations only or not at all, 29 percent of owners who intended to rent out the property — almost four times the former proportion — admit to this extremely low level of maintenance. Owners who obtained their properties through inheritance or foreclosure on a debt or a mortgage fall into the intermediate categories of maintenance level. Quite clearly, within our sample of delinquent property owners, respondents who purchased their properties in hopes of rental return undertake relatively less property maintenance than do those respondents who purchased their property as a home.

Finally, the extent of property maintenance is directly related to the

EXHIBIT 8-2

CONDITION OF BUILDING BY LEVEL OF TOTAL EXPENDITURES ON
PROPERTY, PITTSBURGH
(percents)[a]

| | Total Expenditures Index[b] | | | |
Building Condition Index[b]	0 *Low*	1	2	3 *High*
0 Excellent	14.7 (5)	27.8 (20)	34.3 (12)	35.3 (6)
1 Good	32.4 (11)	26.4 (19)	17.1 (6)	35.3 (6)
2 Fair	29.4 (10)	36.1 (26)	37.1 (13)	23.5 (4)
3 Poor	23.5 (8)	9.7 (7)	11.4 (4)	5.9 (1)

Notes: a. Absolute numbers are in parentheses.
         b. See Appendix A for discussion of index construction.

Source: CUPR Pittsburgh Delinquency Survey, Summer 1974.

EXHIBIT 8-3

OWNER'S PATTERN OF PROPERTY MAINTENANCE, BY AGE OF BUILDING,
PITTSBURGH
(percents)[a]

| | Age of Building | | |
Owner's *Pattern of* *Maintenance*	<30 years *(Post-W.W. II)*	30-74 years *(Post-1900)*	>74 years *(Pre-1900)*
Maintain in "good as new" condition	41.7 (5)	12.0 (10)	2.3 (1)
Maintain in good condition	41.7 (5)	53.0 (44)	41.9 (18)
Maintain in fair condition	16.7 (2)	20.5 (17)	39.5 (17)
Make no repairs or emergency repairs only	0.0 (0)	14.5 (12)	16.3 (7)

Note: a. Absolute numbers are in parentheses.

Source: CUPR Pittsburgh Delinquency Survey, Summer 1974.

EXHIBIT 8-4

PATTERN OF PROPERTY MAINTENANCE, BY OWNER'S REASON FOR
PURCHASING PROPERTY, PITTSBURGH
(percents)[a]

Owner's Pattern of Property Maintenance	Owner's Reason for Purchasing Property		
	Home	Rental Return	Inheritance or Debt or Mortgage Foreclosure
Maintain in "good as new" condition	12.4 (11)	12.9 (4)	3.7 (1)
Maintain in good condition	56.2 (50)	32.3 (10)	44.4 (12)
Maintain in fair condition	23.6 (21)	25.8 (8)	37.0 (10)
Make no repairs or emergency repairs only	7.9 (7)	29.0 (9)	14.8 (4)

Note: a. Absolute numbers are in parentheses.

Source: CUPR Pittsburgh Delinquency Survey, Summer 1974.

EXHIBIT 8-5

OWNER'S PATTERN OF PROPERTY MAINTENANCE, BY OWNER'S
PERCEPTION OF CHANGE IN THE VALUE OF HIS PROPERTY, PITTSBURGH
(percents)[a]

Owner's Pattern of Property Maintenance	Owner's Perception of Change in the Value of His Property	
	Increasing	Same or Decreasing
Maintain in "good as new" condition	18.9 (17)	0.0 (0)
Maintain in good condition	52.2 (47)	38.1 (16)
Maintain in fair condition	23.3 (21)	33.3 (14)
Make no repairs or emergency repairs only	5.6 (5)	28.6 (12)

Note: a. Absolute numbers are in parentheses.

Source: CUPR Pittsburgh Delinquency Survey, Summer 1974.

owner's perception of change in the value of his property. As indicated in Exhibit 8-5, no respondent who felt the value of his property was stable or decreasing claimed to keep his property in "good as new" condition; at the same time, almost 20 percent of the owners who perceived an increase in their property value fell into this maintenance category. In contrast, the proportion of owners who made no repairs on their property and felt that the value of the property was falling was five times larger — 29 percent compared to 6 percent — than the proportion of owners who made no repairs but felt that their property was increasing in value. Clearly, perception of a drop in property value serves as a powerful deterrent to investment of further expenditures in the property in the form of maintenance or improvements.

The emphasis on levels of property maintenance warrants presentation of additional data on the maintenance behavior of the sample of delinquent owners. While fully 60 percent of sampled owners claimed to keep their buildings in "good" or "good as new" condition and an additional 26 percent kept their buildings in at least "fair" shape, over half of the sample felt that their building was in need of major repairs.

Lack of financing is cited most frequently by owners as a major problem in property maintenance. Exhibit 8-6 summarized owners' identification of up to four significant factors that constitute problems in maintaining their properties. Almost a third of those owners who responded to the question listed lack of finances as the most important problem hindering their maintenance efforts.

Improvements and repairs have been undertaken by a considerable proportion of owners despite these difficulties. Approximately half of the sample delinquent owners have completed repairs or improvements in plumbing facilities, plaster and paneling, roof and/or building exterior in the last ten years. Forty percent have improved or repaired the heating plant and/or the wiring in their buildings in the same period. The entire sample of 158 owners accounted for some 472 property improvements in the last ten years (see Exhibit 8-7). This same exhibit documents the number, type, and average cost of improvements made by owners in the sample. The average cost of all improvements for which cost data were reported amounts to $758.

Forty-one owners in the sample, representing over a fourth of the total, believe that their property was reassessed by the city as a result of improvements they made. At the same time, only nine respondents reported having increased the rents they charged as a result of improvements. While Pittsburgh and other cities are experimenting with tax abatement programs associated with property improvements, a greater effort aimed at publicizing such a program might help to alleviate owners' fears that the expenditure of

EXHIBIT 8-6

FACTORS CONTRIBUTING TO PROBLEMS IN PROPERTY MAINTENANCE, PITTSBURGH

Problem	Most Important Problem		Second Most Important Problem		Third Most Important Problem		Fourth Most Important Problem		Total	
	Number	Percent	Number	Percent	Number	Percent	Number	Percent	Number	Percent
Lack of financing	42	28.2	8	9.5	7	13.5	2	11.1	59	19.5
Neighborhood deterioration	23	15.4	20	23.8	10	19.2	0	0.0	53	17.5
Neighborhood vandalism	9	6.0	24	28.6	6	11.5	1	5.6	40	13.2
Reassessment and tax increases	2	1.3	4	4.8	4	7.7	2	11.1	12	3.9
Level of property tax payment	3	2.0	7	8.3	2	3.8	1	5.6	13	4.3
Insurance costs	5	3.4	3	3.6	8	15.4	2	11.1	18	5.9
Tenant vandalism or unconcern	14	9.4	9	10.7	8	15.4	7	38.9	38	12.5
Unavailability of labor	1	0.7	3	3.6	1	1.9	1	5.6	6	1.9
Other	17	11.4	0	0.0	3	5.8	1	5.6	21	6.9
No problems	33	22.1	6	7.1	3	5.8	1	5.6	43	14.2
Total	149	100.0	84	100.0	52	100.0	18	100.0	303	100.0

Source: CUPR Pittsburgh Delinquency Survey, Summer 1974.

limited resources on improvements will incur yet additional costs in the form of increased tax payments.

The discussion thus far has demonstrated the close interrelationships among the value of the property, the owner's expenditures on the property, his level of maintenance, the age and condition of the building, the owner's residence in the building, and the function of the property as a home or rental structure. This cycle of interrelationships comes full circle to a consideration of vacancy rates.

A low maintenance level, poor condition of the building, and falling value of the structure are likely to exacerbate the problem of finding tenants at rental levels high enough to furnish a sufficient cash flow from the structure to maintain the viability of the property. Exhibit 8-8 summarizes the relationship between vacancy level and property value for our sample. The vacancy index summarizes responses to several questions designed to measure the extent and persistence of vacancy as a problem for owners. Of

EXHIBIT 8-7

PROPERTY IMPROVEMENTS AND REPAIRS MADE BY OWNERS IN THE LAST TEN YEARS, PITTSBURGH

Improvement or Repair	Number[a]	Frequency[b] (Percent)	Percent of all respondents[c]	Average cost of improvement[d]
Plumbing	83	17.6	52.5	$ 790
Plaster, paneling	80	16.9	50.6	746
Roof work	76	16.1	48.1	660
Exterior paint and/or siding	73	15.5	46.2	940
Heating plant	63	13.3	39.9	800
Wiring	60	12.7	38.0	386
Apartment size	16	3.4	10.1	713
Building lobby or entrance	12	2.5	7.6	718
Expanded livable space	9	1.9	5.7	2,225
Total	472	100.0		$ 758

Notes: a. Number of respondents who reported each improvement or repair made in the last ten years.

b. Frequency with which each improvement or repair was made in the last ten years.

c. Percent of all 158 respondents who reported having made each improvement or repair in the last ten years.

d. Average costs are computed for the 355 reported improvements and repairs for which cost data are available. The average cost for all improvements represents a weighted average of individual improvements.

Source: CUPR Pittsburgh Delinquency Survey, Summer 1974.

EXHIBIT 8-8

VACANCY LEVEL BY CHANGE IN VALUE OF OWNER'S PROPERTY, PITTSBURGH
(percents)[a]

Vacany Index[b]	Owner's Perception of Change in Value of His Property	
	Increasing	Same or Decreasing
0 Low vacancy	74.4	47.6
	(67)	(20)
1	18.9	26.2
	(17)	(11)
2	5.6	9.5
	(5)	(4)
3 High vacancy	1.1	16.7
	(1)	(7)

Notes: a. Absolute numbers are in parentheses.
    b. See Appendix A for a discussion of index construction.

Source: CUPR Pittsburgh Delinquency Survey, Summer 1974.

EXHIBIT 8-9

OWNER'S PERCEPTION OF CHANGE IN PROPERTY VALUE, BY CHANGE IN THE BUILDING VACANCY RATE AND CHANGE IN THE AVERAGE PERIOD OF VACANCY, PITTSBURGH
(percents)[a]

Owner's perception of change in property value	Change in Building Vacancy Rate	
	Lower or no change	Higher
Increasing	64.1	41.7
	(25)	(5)
Same or decreasing	35.9	58.3
	(14)	(7)

	Change in Average Period of Vacancy	
	Shorter or no change	Longer
Increasing	60.5	28.6
	(23)	(2)
Same or decreasing	39.5	71.4
	(15)	(5)

Note: a. Absolute numbers are in parentheses.

Source: CUPR Pittsburgh Delinquency Survey, Summer 1974.

the owners who scored lowest on this index, suggesting that vacancy was a very minor problem for them, those who felt their properties were increasing in value led by 30 percent those who felt their properties were decreasing or unchanged in value. At the same time, 17 percent of those who noted a drop in the property value reported vacancy to be a significant problem, compared to the 1 percent of owners who perceived an increase in the value of their property but felt vacancy to be a major problem. In sum, vacancy is considerably more of a problem in properties that are falling in value.

The circle of causation is finally completed when we consider the reverse relationship: a high vacancy rate and owner's inability to find tenants are reflected in the owner's perception of a decrease in the value of his property. The data for this final component of the cycle are presented in Exhibit 8-9. Of those owners who felt the value of their property was increasing, the proportion of those who reported that the vacancy in their building was decreasing was substantially greater than the proportion of those owners who felt vacancy was increasing. This relationship holds whether we consider change in the building vacancy rate or change in the average period of vacancy. And of course the converse also holds: more owners who felt vacancy was a growing problem than those who felt vacancy was decreasing also perceived a decline in the value of their property. The inability to find tenants clearly detracts from the owner's evaluation of his property.

PROPERTY VALUE, VACANCY, AND DELINQUENCY

The complex set of interrelationships discussed in the preceding section summarizes the basic parameters of the cycle of tax delinquency. It remains only to examine the explicit link among high vacancy rates, falling property values, and the owner's decision to discontinue tax payments.

An initial appreciation of this relationship is obtained by relating owners' responses to a question concerning the usual timing of tax bill payments to the extent to which owners consider vacancy to be a problem. Respondents described their habitual payment pattern in terms of payment prior to the due date, payment after the due date, or no payment at all. The data are summarized in Exhibit 8-10. Substantially more owners scoring low on the vacancy in his building in Exhibit 8-11. For both change in the building owners scoring high on the index. Most significantly, *only 8 percent of those owners scoring low in the index state that they have discontinued tax payments, compared to the 56 percent of owners for whom vacancy is a major problem who have decided not to pay their property taxes.* These data take on added significance when considering the likelihood that owners who are willing to state to an interviewer that they no longer pay taxes on their property are definite in their decision.

The relationship between vacancy rates and delinquency can be examined further through several additional measures of delinquency. As we have seen, the D/A ratio—the total dollar amount of taxes owed expressed as a proportion of the total assessed value of the property—provides a highly significant measure of the severity of delinquency. The higher this ratio, the more serious the level of delinquency, for as the amount of taxes owed approaches the value of the property the owner is more likely to decide to "sell" the property to the City for the value of back taxes.

The D/A ratio is tabulated against owners' perception of change in vacancy in his building in Exhibit 8-11. For both change in the building vacancy rate and change in the average period of vacancy, owners who report an increase in vacancy exhibit higher ratios of taxes owed to assessed value than do owners who report a decrease or no change in vacancy. The identical relationship is reflected by the data in Exhibit 8-11C, relating the D/A ratio to the owner's appraisal of the difficulty of finding good tenants. Finally, considering neighborhood-wide vacancy levels, the relationship between higher vacancy rates and higher ratios of taxes owed to assessed value still pertains (see Exhibit 8-11D).

The correspondence between vacancy and property values demonstrated earlier suggests that tax delinquency should relate to both variables in a similar fashion. Exhibits 8-12 and 8-13 summarize the data for the relationship between the level of tax delinquency and (1) the owner's estimate of the current market value of the parcel, and (2) owner's perception of change in the value of his property.

EXHIBIT 8-10

USUAL TIMING OF TAX BILL PAYMENTS, BY VACANCY LEVEL, PITTSBURGH
(percents)[a]

Timing of tax bill payments	Vacancy Index[b]			
	0 Low Vacancy	1	2	3 High Vacancy
Pay before due	36.5 (19)	16.7 (3)	0.0 (0)	11.1 (1)
Pay after due	55.8 (29)	61.1 (11)	40.0 (2)	33.3 (3)
No payment	7.7 (4)	22.2 (4)	60.0 (3)	55.6 (5)

Note: a. Absolute numbers are in parentheses.
           b. See Appendix A for a discussion of index construction.

Source: CUPR Pittsburgh Delinquency Survey, Summer 1974.

EXHIBIT 8-11

D/A RATIO BY CHANGE IN THE VACANCY RATE, CHANGE IN THE AVERAGE PERIOD OF VACANCY, DIFFICULTY OF FINDING GOOD TENANTS, AND CHANGE IN THE NEIGHBORHOOD VACANCY RATE, PITTSBURGH
(percents)[a]

Ratio of taxes owed to assessed value of property	A. Owner's Perception of Change in the Building Vacancy Rate in the Last Six Years	
	Lower now or no change	*Higher now*
⩽ .060	32.6 (14)	7.1 (1)
.061-.199	23.3 (10)	42.9 (6)
⩾ .200	44.2 (19)	50.0 (7)

	B. Change in the Average Period of Vacancy	
	Lower now or no change	*Higher now*
⩽ .060	26.8 (11)	11.1 (1)
.061-.199	29.3 (12)	33.3 (3)
⩾ .200	43.9 (18)	55.6 (5)

	C. Owner's Appraisal of the Difficulty of Finding Good Tenants	
	More difficult now	*Easier now or no change*
⩽ .060	12.0 (3)	44.4 (8)
.061-.199	44.0 (11)	27.8 (5)
⩾ .200	44.0 (11)	27.8 (5)

	D. Owner's Perception of Change in the Neighborhood Vacancy Rate		
	Increasing	*Same*	*Decreasing*
⩽ .060	15.8 (6)	36.0 (36)	54.5 (6)
.061-.199	39.5 (15)	32.0 (32)	27.3 (3)
⩾ .200	44.7 (17)	32.0 (32)	18.2 (2)

Note: a. Absolute numbers are in parentheses.

Source: CUPR Pittsburgh Delinquency Survey, Summer 1974.

In Exhibit 8-12, the total dollar value of taxes owed is seen to be positively related to the estimated value of the parcel. Parcels of higher value, in other words, have accrued higher absolute levels of taxes owed. Since parcels of higher value pay larger tax bills, this relationship is hardly surprising. In the bottom half of the exhibit, the D/A ratio is used as the measure of delinquency tabulated against parcel market value. Considering the dollar value of taxes owed expressed as a proportion of property assessed value, it is seen that lower value properties have accrued the highest levels of delinquency.

Exhibit 8-13 expands the analysis to consider delinquency related to changing property values for all levels of assessed value. For both total taxes owed and the D/A ratio as the measures of delinquency, more properties decreasing in value have attained a high level delinquency than have properties increasing in value, at all levels of assessed value. Regardless of the value of the property, in other words, decreasing property value is associated with high levels of tax delinquency.

EXHIBIT 8-12

TOTAL TAXES OWED AND D/A RATIO, BY OWNER'S ESTIMATE OF CURRENT
MARKET VALUE OF PARCEL, PITTSBURGH
(percents)[a]

Total Taxes Owed	Owner's Estimate of Current Market Value of Parcel		
	< $10,000	$10,000-19,999	≥ $20,000
< $500	55.6	55.8	46.4
	(35)	(24)	(13)
$500-999	31.7	25.6	21.4
	(20)	(11)	(6)
≥ $1,000	12.7	18.6	32.1
	(8)	(8)	(9)
Ratio of Taxes Owed to Assessed Value			
≤ .060	11.1	39.5	51.9
	(7)	(17)	(14)
.061-.199	47.6	20.9	33.3
	(30)	(9)	(9)
≥ .200	41.3	39.5	14.8[a]
	(26)	(17)	(4)

Note: a. Absolute numbers are in parentheses.

Source: CUPR Pittsburg Delinquency Survey, Summer 1974.

These relationships coalesce in the owner's final decision to discontinue tax payments and eventually let title to the property pass to the City. The distribution of owner's stated plans regarding payment of back taxes and the owner's intent to let the City take title to his property are both related to property maintenance, building condition, vacancy level, and property value in a highly striking fashion. The data are presented in the final set of Exhibits 8-14 to 8-19.

Focusing on those owners who state they will make no payment of back taxes on their properties: the proportion of owners who make repairs only in emergencies or make no repairs at all is three times greater than the proportion of owners who maintain their property in good condition; the proportion of buildings in poor condition is five times greater than the proportion in good condition; the proportion of owners who have a serious problem

EXHIBIT 8-13

TOTAL TAXES OWED AND D/A RATIO, BY OWNER'S PERCEPTION OF CHANGE IN THE VALUE OF HIS PROPERTY, FOR ALL LEVELS OF ASSESSED VALUE, PITTSBURGH

(percents)[a]

| | Perception of Change in Property Value | | | | | |
| | Assessed Value <$2,500 | | Assessed Value $2,500-4,999 | | Assessed Value ≥ $5,000 | |
Total Taxes Owed	Increasing	Same or Decreasing	Increasing	Same or Decreasing	Increasing	Same or Decreasing
< $500	61.1	73.3	58.5	23.5	58.1	30.0
	(11)	(11)	(24)	(4)	(18)	(3)
$500-999	27.8	13.3	31.7	47.1	16.1	30.0
	(5)	(2)	(13)	(8)	(5)	(3)
≥ $1,000	11.1	13.3	9.8	29.4	25.8	40.0
	(2)	(2)	(4)	(5)	(8)	(4)
Ratio of Taxes Owed to Assessed Value						
≤.060	5.6	13.3	36.6	11.8	66.7	30.0
	(1)	(2)	(15)	(2)	(20)	(3)
.061-.199	44.4	33.3	34.1	23.5	16.7	50.0
	(8)	(5)	(14)	(4)	(5)	(5)
≥.200	50.0	53.3	29.3	64.7	16.7	20.0
	(9)	(8)	(12)	(11)	(5)	(2)

Note: a. Absolute numbers are in parentheses.

Source: CUPR Pittsburgh Delinquency Survey, Summer 1974.

with vacancy is eleven times greater than the proportion with minimal or no vacancy problems; and the proportion of owners who estimate the market value of their property to be $10,000 or more is exceeded four times by the proportion who estimate their property value to be less than $5,000.

The ultimate decision to let the City take title to the property follows the same pattern. By way of illustration, for those owners who declared their intention to give up title to the City, the 2 percent of owners scoring low in the vacancy index can be compared to the 64 percent for whom vacancy is a significant problem.

Finally, an interesting finding emerges when relating the owner's intention to relinquish title to his perception of change in the value of his property, for all levels of assessed value. For properties with very low and middle-range levels of assessed value, a substantially greater proportion of owners who feel their properties are decreasing in value intend to let the City take over title than do the proportion of owners who feel their property value is increasing. At the highest level of assessed value, however, all owners respond that they have no intention of giving up title. Thus, the relationship between the owner's decision to relinquish title and his perception of change in the value of his property is particularly strong not only for those properties that are low in value but also for those the value of which the owner feels is decreasing yet further.

EXHIBIT 8-14

OWNER'S PLANS REGARDING PAYMENT OF BACK TAXES, BY PATTERN OF PROPERTY MAINTENANCE, PITTSBURGH

(percents)[a]

Owner's Plans Regarding Payment of Back Taxes	Pattern of Property Maintenance		
	Maintain in Good Condition	Maintain in Fair Condition	Make No Repairs or Emergency Repairs Only
Pay in full	67.7 (42)	39.4 (13)	33.3 (6)
Pay as much as possible whenever possible	14.5 (9)	24.2 (8)	11.1 (2)
Minimum payment	4.8 (3)	21.2 (7)	16.7 (3)
No payment	12.9 (8)	15.2 (5)	38.9 (7)

Note: a. Absolute numbers are in parentheses.

Source: CUPR Pittsburgh Delinquency Survey, Summer 1974.

EXHIBIT 8-15

OWNER'S PLANS REGARDING PAYMENT OF BACK TAXES, BY CONDITION
OF BUILDING, PITTSBURGH
(percents)[a]

Owner's Plans Regarding Payment of Back Taxes	*Condition of Building*		
	Poor	*Average*	*Good*
Pay in full	17.9	62.5	68.6
	(5)	(20)	(35)
Pay as much as possible whenever possible	17.9	12.5	19.6
	(5)	(4)	(10)
Minimum payment	17.9	18.8	2.0
	(5)	(6)	(1)
No payment	46.4	6.3	9.8
	(13)	(2)	(5)

Note: a. Absolute numbers are in parentheses.

Source: CUPR Pittsburgh Delinquency Survey, Summer 1974.

EXHIBIT 8-16

OWNER'S PLANS REGARDING PAYMENT OF BACK TAXES, BY VACANCY
LEVEL, PITTSBURGH
(percent)[a]

Owner's Plans Regarding Payment of Back Taxes	*Vacancy Index*[b]			
	0 *Low Vacancy*	*1*	*2*	*3* *High Vacancy*
Pay in full	67.1	42.3	16.7	0.0
	(49)	(11)	(1)	(0)
Pay as much as possible whenever possible	15.1	26.9	16.7	0.0
	(11)	(7)	(1)	(0)
Minimum payment	11.0	7.7	16.7	25.0
	(8)	(2)	(1)	(2)
No payment	6.8	23.1	50.0	75.0
	(5)	(6)	(3)	(6)

Notes: a. Absolute numbers are in parentheses.
b. See Appendix A for a discussion of index construction.

Source: CUPR Pittsburgh Delinquency Survey, Summer 1974.

EXHIBIT 8-17

OWNER'S PLANS REGARDING PAYMENT OF BACK TAXES, BY OWNER'S
EVALUATION OF CURRENT MARKET VALUE OF THE PROPERTY,
PITTSBURGH
(percents) [a]

Owner's Plans Regarding Payment of Back Taxes	Owner's Evaluation of Current Market Value		
	<$5,000	$5,000-9,999	≥$10,000
Pay in full	42.6 (23)	64.3 (18)	75.0 (12)
Pay as much as possible whenever possible	16.7 (9)	17.9 (5)	12.5 (2)
Minimum payment	14.8 (8)	10.7 (3)	6.3 (1)
No payment	25.9 (14)	7.1 (2)	6.3 (1)

Note: a. Absolute numbers are in parentheses.

Source: CUPR Pittsburgh Delinquency Survey, Summer 1974.

EXHIBIT 8-18

OWNER'S INTENTION TO LET THE CITY TAKE TITLE TO HIS PROPERTY, BY
VACANCY LEVEL, PITTSBURGH
(percents) [a]

Owner's Intention To Let City Take Title	Vacancy Index [b]			
	0 Low Vacancy	1	2	3 High Vacancy
Yes	2.2 (2)	21.4 (6)	37.5 (3)	63.6 (7)
No	97.8 (88)	78.6 (22)	62.5 (5)	36.4 (4)

Notes: a. Absolute numbers are in parentheses.
         b. See Appendix A for a discussion of index construction.

Source: CUPR Pittsburgh Delinquency Survey, Summer 1974.

EXHIBIT 8-19

OWNER'S INTENTION TO LET CITY TAKE TITLE TO HIS PROPERTY, BY
OWNER'S PERCEPTION OF CHANGE IN THE VALUE OF HIS PROPERTY, FOR
ALL LEVELS OF ASSESSED VALUE, PITTSBURGH
(percents) [a]

Owner's Intention To Let the City Take Title	*Perception of Change in Property Value*					
	Assessed Value < $2,500		*Assessed Value $2,500-4,999*		*Assessed Value ≥ $5,000*	
	Increasing	*Same or Decreasing*	*Increasing*	*Same or Decreasing*	*Increasing*	*Same or Decreasing*
Yes	14.3 (2)	53.3 (8)	8.1 (3)	11.8 (2)	0.0 (0)	0.0 (0)
No	85.7 (12)	46.7 (7)	91.9 (34)	88.2 (15)	100.0 (26)	100.0 (7)

Note: a. Absolute numbers are in parentheses.

Source: CUPR Pittsburgh Delinquency Survey, Summer 1974.

Chapter 9

The Public Response

INTRODUCTION

Our discussion has examined the complex linkages between tax delinquency and the withdrawal of central city private investment. The remaining question is that of identifying an appropriate public response.

Two issues arise immediately from our analysis. The first issue is identification of the appropriate levels of government from which action is required. Traditionally, responsibility for ameliorative public action has been limited to the local municipal government directly effected. Evidence that delinquency in a particular city has national system-wide rather than merely local origins, however, indicates the need for involvement of broader levels of government in designing a workable response strategy. Specific aspects of Federal responsibility in countering local delinquency are outlined below.

Secondly, the question of public response again raises the nature of the traditional public-private sector relationship described in Chapter 2. A realistic public response strategy must encompass both a recognition of the terms of the traditional relationship as well as the necessity of altering this pattern in light of unprecedented developments in the evolution of the nation's urban system.

Our analysis suggests the need for a greatly expanded scope of public involvement in central city land management, extending the public role considerably beyond that legitimized in traditional institutional structures.
Municipal governments, aided by State and Federal funding initiatives,
must be empowered to manage, develop, and retain the large (and growing)
segments of urban realty abandoned by private sector interests. Central to
an expanded public role is the retention of public control over acquired
parcels and direct return of social investment to the public fisc.

The question may fairly be raised as to why such an expansion of public
initiative is warranted. The decline and abandonment of urban centers
resulting from the waning of private investment interest is a basic theme underlying American urban history: the demise of market towns by-passed by
the railroads and the eclipse of communities resting on depleted natural
resource beds are two of many examples of the decline dimension of urban
history. Why should the well-established precedent of public nonintervention be overturned in this latest case? At least two compelling arguments come to mind. First, the unprecedented scale of social investment
already expended in the nation's major urban centers represents an un-
disputable public stake in the future of these areas. While the beneficiary of
public investment has traditionally been the private sector, the massive scale
of prior social investment validates a continued public claim even as private
interests have moved elsewhere. Secondly, the United States has become
committed to socialization of the costs of decline. In an earlier era, the resident population would be left to shift for itself following withdrawal of the
venture capitalists. More recently, however, the experience of the Depression and the more recent reminder of civil disorders of the 1960s have
resulted in public subsidies for the working class population left behind in
the central cities. Rather than taking the form of non-productive unemployment compensation and welfare payments, however, such subsidies would
be far more effective if based on the productive re-use of what may be the
central city's greatest asset: direct control over its own real estate.

This approach represents a considerable extension of current philosophy
underlying municipal treatment of real estate tax delinquency. In this
chapter, we briefly assess the standard strategy adopted by most cities facing
a tax delinquency problem, and then examine the limitations of the policy
assumptions underlying this strategy. We then set forth a number of exten-
sions of standard policy suggested by the empirical findings of our analysis.

STANDARD STRATEGY

Standard municipal policy (abetted by State enabling legislation) for
countering the tax delinquency problem commonly takes three forms: (1)
disincentives and sanctions against non-payment of taxes; (2) incentives for

continued owner commitment to the property; and (3) public acquisition of title to the property as a last recourse upon failure of (1) and (2).

DISINCENTIVES TO NON-PAYMENT

Sanctions against the non-payment of real estate taxes generally take the form of penalty fees and interest charged on unpaid taxes. Most municipalities have recognized the futility of such charges when set below market interest rates: low fees simply afford owners a cheap way of borrowing money. While owners may know they will be charged for late payment, this cost will be lower than the market cost of borrowing. An increasingly common practice is therefore to either fix a uniformly high penalty and interest rate or to allow the rate to float at some fixed number of percentage points above the prime lending rate. A further refinement escalates penalty and interest charges with the length of delinquency. For example, 8 percent interest might be charged on accounts overdue up to three months, 12 percent on accounts delinquent between four and twelve months, and 18 percent on taxes overdue a year or more. This policy imposes a relatively mild penalty on short term delinquency due to an unanticipated personal emergency, while imposing the heaviest burden on the most flagrant chronic delinquents .

INCENTIVES FOR CONTINUED OWNERSHIP

Encouragement of continued owner commitment to the property takes several forms. These typically involve various tax abatement or exemption schemes for specified classes of owners and/or properties, and various modes of owner assistance for property maintenance, home repair, or neighborhood renewal. As an example of the former, New York City's J-51 program is perhaps one of the best-known programs of tax exemptions for structural rehabilitation of properties.[1] The program provides for an abatement in annual tax payments equal to a portion of rehabilitation costs, and an exemption in property taxes for twelve years on any increase in assessed value resulting directly from improvements to the property. In the same category of tax incentives are the numerous programs of tax rebates for the elderly. As is the case in New York City, Pittsburgh, Wisconsin, and elsewhere, tax payments up to a fixed amount are either abated or refunded for persons meeting minimum age requirements with incomes (usually including Social Security) below a set figure.

Direct assistance to property owners for maintenance, repair, or rehabilitation has flourished in many cities. By decreasing maintenance costs through provision of low-interest home repair or rehabilitation loans, local governments assist owners in extending the life of the property, thereby extending in turn the attractiveness of ownership. As an example,

Baltimore's Structural Improvement Revolving Loan Fund allows homeowners wanting to make property improvements to borrow directly from the municipal government at a 7 percent interest rate. Loans must be used to bring a unit up to specified standards, and may also be used to finance general improvements such as the remodelling of a room or installation of central air conditioning. Similar programs are operating in Trenton (Property Improvement Assistance Program), Pittsburgh (Neighborhood Housing Services), and elsewhere.[2]

PUBLIC ACQUISITION

The strongest sanction available to local municipalities in countering delinquency is the acquisition of title in the event of non-payment of property taxes. Traditionally, both municipal intent as well as the sense of State enabling legislation have viewed title acquistion within an extremely limited framework. The objectives of acquisition have been to terminate the ownership claims of the delinquent party, recoup taxes owed on the parcel, and return the property to the tax rolls under a new private owner. As described in Chapter 3, much of the extant State law governing the terms of the acquisition process stems from the Depression years, when the emphasis was on the protection of private ownership under extremely straitened circumstances. Recent years have seen a rash of adoptions of "fast take" procedures, allowing municipalities to acquire title in a far shorter time period than was formerly possible. This is accomplished by reducing the required waiting period (the "redemption period") between sale of the tax lien and final foreclosure on the property. As a legacy of the 1930s, this period, during which owners can regain clear title by paying taxes owed plus accumulated fees and interest, commonly extended as long as four years. The municipality was barred from foreclosing on the property during the redemption period, while the owner was effectively excused from tax payments but was free to continue collecting rents or otherwise deriving income from the property. As a result of recent legislative changes adopted in several states, municipalities empowered to pursue "fast-take" procedures may foreclose on the property as early as six months after sale of the tax title lien.

The record of acquisitions in Pittsburgh is indicative of the experience of many cities facing a growing tax delinquency problem. As of December 1973, a total of 10,837 parcels had been obtained by the City through treasury sales. The rate of municipal acquisitions has increased over time as a result of more stringent enforcement practices. Between 1950 and 1964, the City acquired an average of 232 parcels a year; between 1965 and 1969, average acquisitions amounted to 340 a year; and by the 1970-72 period, the City acquired 470 parcels a year on average. Recent years have shown a significant increase in the proportion of improved parcels acquired: with an increase in the *magnitude* of acquisitions, it is correspondingly more difficult to select predominantly vacant parcels for public taking. In total, over 1,800 acres of land have been acquired by the City of Pittsburgh through Treasury sale, with a high proportion of this land concentrated in relatively few wards in the city.

A record of acquisition of this magnitude immediately raises the corollary issue of disposition. The available options commonly pursued are relatively few: (1) sale to a private purchaser in public auction; (2) transfer to private ownership at a nominal fee under an "urban homesteading" program; (3) combination of contiguous acquired parcels for joint sale to a private owner; (4) sale to owners of adjacent parcels at a reduced cost; (5) rental management; and (6) reservation for public use. *All but the last two are in accord with the premise that the objective of public acquisition is to return the parcel to private ownership.*

Institutional mechanisms presently available in most cities for administering rental management or public re-use programs are largely inadequate given the scale of operations required. Reflecting the paucity of administrative structures and in line with the dominant ideology of limited public initiative, most municipal officials are understandably reluctant to embark on large-scale programs involving the development and re-use of acquired parcels.

Recognizing the absence of private interest in purchasing acquired parcels, several municipalities have recently initiated "land banking" programs which allow the city to retain title. As implemented to date, such programs provide a means of holding acquired parcels until such time as private investment interest should reappear. Under Cleveland's "land bank" program, for instance, no plans have been developed for direct municipal utilization of acquired parcels, and only vacant land or parcels with abandoned structures can be acquired.[3] The land bank concept represents an important first step in moving away from the traditional concept of private market dominance and towards an increasing legitimation of municipal land management. The city's role has thus far been a passive one, however, bred more from an absence of private demand than from a commitment to municipal control.

In sum, all three components of the standard strategy for countering delinquency are in accord with the basic tenets of the private-public sector relationship outlined in Chapter 2. Underlying all three components is a simple assumption: private ownership is preferable to public ownership. Disincentives are aimed at encouraging ownership responsibility; incentives are provided to facilitate private ownership and offset negative externalities; and the thrust of foreclosure and acquisition policy is to return parcels to private ownership at any expense, or to hold parcels until private ownership interest reemerges.

INADEQUACY OF STANDARD STRATEGY

In a context of diminishing private interest in central city property ownership, a strategy premised on facilitating private investment must be seriously questioned. The shortcomings of standard delinquency strategy involve inadequate mechanisms, opportunity costs, speculator involvement, market weakness, and outmoded assumptions.

INADEQUATE MECHANISMS

It is questionable whether the disincentives to nonpayment have much impact. For example, it is the cities with the highest delinquency rates that have instituted the highest interest and penalty charges and implemented the most stringent fast-take mechanisms. Adoption of these measures *may* have kept delinquency rates from climbing higher than they have; it has not, however, brought the non-payment rate down below the highest level nationwide. The comparative data reported in Chapter 4 indicate the consistently high level of delinquency reported by these cities over a twenty-five year period - a span of years which encompasses implementation of these procedures.

OPPORTUNITY COSTS

Simply stated, the administrative costs of tax lien, foreclosure, and resale often exceed revenues lost through unpaid taxes. In this case, the foreclosure process becomes an extremely expensive rear-guard action. Acquisition is pursued not to recoup lost revenues (since a net loss ensues) but rather to forestall owner interpretation of municipal inaction as leniency, a perception likely to generate an increase in the non-payment rate.

SPECULATOR INVOLVEMENT

The sale of tax title liens to private buyers creates a class of property transactions with the characteristics of "distressed merchandise." The proliferation of non-arm's length transactions attracts speculator involvement and a resulting instability of ownership.[4] A high proportion of purchases by speculators increases the likelihood that acquired parcels will reappear on the list of delinquent properties, even though these parcels have nominally been returned to the tax rolls in private ownership.

MARKET WEAKNESS

A strategy based on resale of acquired parcels to private purchasers must founder if it is the absence of a viable market that accounts for the original delinquency. A land banking program designed to await a resurgence of private market activity engenders the likelihood of a prolonged period of stagnant land holding in a municipality unwilling to expand the public sector's traditionally passive role.

BASIC ASSUMPTIONS

The greatest drawback of standard delinquency strategy is the underlying assumption that the primary goal of public action is to maintain and support private ownership. Most significantly, this shortcoming holds even if the city should succeed in rekindling private investment interest. Limitation of the municipal role to that of facilitating private ownership leaves the city, as a social collectivity, vulnerable to the negative impact of a cyclical decline in private investment interest. Today's boom cities of the South and Southwest can expect to experience a similar decline when the investment interest currently focused there moves elsewhere to take advantage of yet another round of technological innovation which can more profitably be exploited in another locale.

TOWARDS GREATER PUBLIC CONTROL

A policy limited to abetting private ownership is thus open to serious debate. At the same time, significant and substantive positive reasons exist which justify the retention of public control of acquired parcels. Principal among these are the massive direct and indirect public investment already made in the parcel and the potential for public benefit derived from future increases in value.

Prior public investment. Direct public investment already made in acquired parcels includes: (1) unpaid taxes; (2) administrative costs pertaining to delinquency, foreclosure, and acquisition proceedings; and (3) services provided to the parcel in the past, such as police and fire protection, water, sewage disposal, and the like. In addition, indirect prior public investment in the parcel includes services and infrastructure provided to the parcel and the surrounding area which contribute significantly to the use-value of the parcel. Land economists have argued persuasively that public spending in services and infrastructure is one of the prime contributors of land value and of the land rent extracted from any given parcel.[5] While in private ownership, the component of land rent generated by public expenditures accrues to the private owner. Public recapture of this prior investment is a reasonable objective.

Future increase in value. The potential for future increase in use-value is a further argument for retaining acquired parcels in public ownership. Ownership and maintenance responsibilities devolve on the public sector by default in the absence of private investment interest. Public ownership must then be equally valid in periods of revival of such private market interest/ There is little to commend a policy which condones public ownership when a parcel is valueless but requires the public to relinquish control when value increases.

BREAKING THE DELINQUENCY CYCLE

Municipal ownership of tax delinquent parcels is a resource rather than a liability. Large-scale municipal land holdings resulting from private abandonment provide an incentive for a new policy initiative aimed at breaking the cycle of delinquency resulting from the ebb and flow of private investment interest. To break this cycle of delinquency, the basic objective of public policy must move from facilitating private ownership to maximizing the efficiency of public ownership. The city must have the ability to manage and develop its real estate holdings to benefit itself directly as a social collectivity, rather than indirectly through support of private ownership.

Progress toward the goal of breaking the tax delinquency cycle requires a comprehensive program focusing on four key issues. These issues involve (1) consolidating municipal land holdings; (2) maximizing the value and attractiveness of these holdings; (3) ensuring that public investment in acquired parcels is returned to the public purse; and (4) retaining municipal control over city-owned land in the event of a resurgence of private demand.

CONSOLIDATING MUNICIPAL LAND HOLDINGS

Municipal acquisition of tax delinquent parcels has been hampered by legislative restraints (i.e., length of the mandated redemption period) and municipal inability to administer large land holdings. Implementation of fast-take acquisition procedures has remedied the former constraint but not the latter. The inadequacy of administrative mechanisms, however, is not an inherent trait but rather a legacy of traditional and outmoded ideology. Legislative mandate of fast-take capability is a meaningless gesture in the absence of municipal capacity to administer parcels so acquired. Without such capacity, municipal taking of delinquent parcels is reduced to a haphazard process characterized by expediency rather than sound planning principles. One factor restraining state legislatures from granting unfettered fast-take capacity is the politically unpalatable prospect of municipal taking of delinquent owner-occupied residential units. A selective acquisition strategy is therefore necessary.

Municipal land holdings can be augmented, consolidated, and rationalized through selective fast-take acquisition of all delinquent property other than owner-occupied residential structures of three units or less. This differentiation follows directly from our documentation of two divergent delinquency scenarios. First-order delinquency involves income producing real estate in which delinquency results from the owner's perception of inadequate return on investment. Second-order or derivative delinquency involves owner-occupied residential units in which delinquency stems from a temporary financial emergency intensified by the housing market degeneration which is engendered in part by the former group's disinvestment. Our analysis in Chapter 7 showed a strong correlation between the two delinquency scenarios and owner occupancy of small residential structures. Owner-occupancy of small residential structures therefore serves as an operational proxy for delinquency type. Exemption of such structures from fast-take procedures both recognizes the involuntary nature of derivative delinquency and relieves the municipality of the burden of unwarranted taking.

The impact of a selective fast-take policy would be accelerated municipal acquisition of delinquent multi-family, commercial, industrial, and vacant (unimproved) parcels. Focusing acquisition efforts on these parcels maximizes the city's ability to consolidate its holdings in selected areas and plan for the creative re-use of acquired parcels.

Selective acquisition has substantial precedent in both law and practice. In light of severe limitations on both funds and administrative personnel for extensive property management, most municipalities have largely restricted their actual acquisitions to unimproved parcels and vacant structures. Improved parcels of any sort have been acquired in appreciable numbers in Pittsburgh only in the most recent period. Similarly, occupied structures are specifically excluded from the fast-take acquisition and land-banking program recently enacted in Cleveland.[6] While selectivity in acquisitions is thus well established in practice, the nature of the selection has been dictated by expediency and the traditional ideology of limited municipal initiative. In contrast, the basis of selection proposed here derives directly from the nature of the delinquency process and reflects a new municipal commitment to actively shape local land use patterns.

MAXIMIZING THE VALUE OF PUBLIC HOLDINGS

Acquisition of tax delinquent parcels is only the first step towards breaking the delinquency cycle. *A major federal and local commitment is required to up-grade the value and re-use potential of acquired parcels. A substantial funding effort must be devoted to demolition, rehabilitation, and capital improvements on city-owned parcels.* The emphasis should be on deriving the maximum direct public benefit from acquired parcels. Urban waterfront areas can be reclaimed from outmoded industrial uses and transformed into parks and open space. Off-street parking facilities can be developed to ease congested streets. Pedestrian malls, covered markets, neighborhood play space, office complexes, cultural centers, and the like can be developed. In short, large-scale municipal acquisition provides a means for a major transformation of the urban landscape by maximizing environmental amenities and regenerating the attractiveness of urban areas.

Three factors can be cited to justify a renewal of public funding for upgrading municipally acquired property. First, massive social investment in urban infrastructure has been traditionally legitimated when to the benefit of private sector investment; a similar scale of expenditures is now justified to ensure continued viability of the city itself. Secondly, the urban renewal programs of the 1960s serve as a precedent for substantial federal involvement in transforming urban land use. A new form of "urban renewal" is now required, with the city itself rather than private interests within the city as the direct beneficiary. Thirdly, public spending to offset the effects of delinquency is justified since to some extent public policy contributes to the delinquency problem. The longitudinal data in Chapter 4 suggest that delinquency increases in periods of uncertainty generated by both rapid urban growth and decline. A potential policy conflict exists between regional development strategies spurring growth in one area while undermining stability (thereby engendering delinquency) in other areas: federal growth policies which alter relationships between cities appear to contribute to uncertainty and higher delinquency within cities. Regional development programs at the federal level should therefore include an allocation of funds to help offset the disruption of revenue collections at the local level.

MAXIMIZING PUBLIC BENEFIT AND RETAINING PUBLIC CONTROL

A major commitment of public funds in city-owned land dictates two final inter-related objectives: maximizing the direct public benefit of such investment, and maintaining the legitimacy of public ownership given a resurgence of private market demand. *This two-fold objective can be approached through state enabling legislation allowing municipalities to lease rather than re-sell acquired parcels to private owners.* Under a leasehold system, the municipal government retains ownership of the land and, in accordance with a development plan, subdivides and prepares building sites which are leased to private or governmental developers. The municipality retains the interest in the land while the developer's rights rest with the building. As R.W. Archer has noted in a thorough review of leasehold tenure:

> This would provide a leasehold system of urban development (and redevelopment) in which the land development stage. . .is unified in a single organization while the building development stage is carried out by a large number of private and government developers.[7]

Leasehold tenure has been widespread in both historical time and geographic extent. Central governments serve the land ownership function through leasehold arrangements in Israel, Kenya, and the Sudan, in city states such Hong Kong and Singapore, and in federal capital cities including New Delhi (India) and Canberra (Australia). Municipal leasehold systems are in operation in Amsterdam, the Hague, and other cities in the Netherlands; in Stockholm, Sweden; in Liverpool, Birmingham, and elsewhere in England; and in cities in Germany and Norway. Private leasehold estates constitute an important tenure system in England, Ireland, and the State of Hawaii.[8] A series of national and city ordinances providing for compulsory (public) purchase, massive public investment in urban infrastructure, and the institution of a leasehold system has been credited with revitalizing the nearly defunct City of Amsterdam at the end of the nineteenth century.[9] Similarities between the over-built Dutch commercial centers of the 1890s and American industrial cities of the 1970s are striking, with the notable exception that the scale of private abandonment in the latter makes compulsory public purchase superfluous.

The lease, rather than sale, of land acquired by the city would allow necessary municipal control over the direction and speed of the redevelopment process. It would further avoid the problems inherent in fragmentation of the development process among many small-scale individual landowners. It would prevent land speculation by eliminating speculative dealing in building sites. Finally, it would provide a means whereby the municipality could be repaid for social investment expenditures which contribute to the value of the property. Under the terms of the lease, periodic rent adjustments would allow increases in land value over time due to public action to accrue to the public fisc. The effect would be similar to (but perhaps more politically palatable than) a program of site value taxation, with all of the benefits that have been widely attributed to such a system.[10]

CONCLUSION

Real estate tax delinquency is but a surface manifestation of deep-rooted antagonisms inherent in the way we have proceeded with the task of urban development. Left unadjusted, these strains will continue to exact their toll in uncompensated investment, under-utilized resources, and mounting dissatisfaction among the underclass relegated to the deteriorating cities. These costs cannot and should not be sustained. In an era of rapidly diminishing open space, continuing disfigurement of fringe areas through low density development, and a growing concern with the preservation of agricultural land, it appears counter to national objectives to leave acres of land under-utilized in the already developed central cities. Delinquency and abandon-ment in the central cities are national, not local, problems. As a symptom of the breakdown of long-standing institutional structures, tax delinquency provides an incentive to initiate new institutional relationships in the land use and development process which show promise of avoiding the pitfalls of earlier outmoded forms.

NOTES

1. For a useful description of New York City's J-51 program, see George Sternlieb, Elizabeth Roistacher, and James Hughes, *Tax Subsidies and Housing Investment* (New Brunswick: Center for Urban Policy Research, 1976).

2. U.S. Department of Housing and Urban Development, *Neighborhood Preservation, A Catalog of Local Programs* (Washington, D.C.: U.S. Government Printing Office, 1975).

3. John Linner, "Cleveland is Banking Tax Delinquent Land," *Practicing Planner*, 7 (June 1977): 9-13.

4. See for example, John Kifner, "Tax-Delinquent Realty Group Buys More Property at Municipal Auction, Though Law Bars the Sales," *New York Times,* 2 March 1978.

5. Mason Gaffney, "Land Rent, Taxation, and Public Policy," *Papers of the Regional Science Association,* 23 (1969): 141-153.

6. Susan Olson and M. Leanne Lachman, *Tax Delinquency in the Inner City* (Lexington, Mass.: D.C. Heath, 1976).

7. R.W. Archer, "The Leasehold System of Urban Development: Land Tenure, Decision-Making and the Land Market in Urban Development and Land Use," *Regional Studies,* 8 (Nov. 1974): 225-238.

8. R.W. Archer, "The Leasehold System of Urban Development," p. 230. See also Ian J. McDonald, "The Leasehold System: Towards a Balanced Land Tenure for Urban Development," *Urban Studies,* 6 (June 1969): 179-195, and I.J. Rutgers, "Municipal Land Policy in the Netherlands," *Journal of the Town Planning Institute,* 46 (1960).

9. George Carey, "Land Tenure, Speculation, and the State of the Aging Metropolis," *Geographical Review,* 66 (July 1976): 253-265.

10. Dick Netzer, among many others, has argued for the benefits of land value taxation from numerous perspectives. See, for example, Dick Netzer, *Economics of the Property Tax* (Washington, D.C.: The Brookings Institution, 1966): esp. 197-212; *Economics and Urban Problems* (N.Y.: Basic Books, 1970): esp. 196-199; "Tax Structures and their Impact on the Poor," in *Financing the Metropolis* (John P. Crecine, ed.) *Urban Affairs Annual Reviews,* 4 (Beverly Hills: Sage Publications): 459-479; "Impact of the Property Tax: Effect on Housing, Urban Land Use, and Local Government Finance," in *Municipal Needs, Services and Financing: Readings on Municipal Expenditures* W. Patrick Beaton, ed. (New Brunswick: Center for Urban Policy Research, 1968): 151-178. See also, Arthur P. Becker, "Arguments for Changing the Real Estate Tax to a Land Value Tax," *Tax Policy* 37 (1970): 15-31; Colin Clark, "Land Taxation: Lessons from International Experience," in *Land Values* Peter Hall, ed. (London: Sweet and Maxwell, 1965): 126-146; and Edward Neuner, et al., "The Impact of a Transition to Site-Value Taxation on Various Classes of Property in San Diego," *Land Economics,* 50 (May 1974): 181-185.

Appendix A

Notes on Methodology

DATA PROCESSING METHODS - PITTSBURGH DELINQUENCY
FILES

No one source was sufficient to supply all the information necessary to adequately quantify the scale and nature of tax delinquency in Pittsburgh. Four separate data sources were merged in carrying out the analysis.

(1) *The Tax Delinquency File of the Pittsburgh Treasurer's Office.* This computerized file includes data describing the tax bills owed on individual parcels of real property in Pittsburgh. Identifying data are recorded for each property, such as block and lot number and the owner's name and address. No information is provided on the use or other characteristics of the property.

(2) *The Real Property File of the Pittsburgh Planning Department.* This source records information on every parcel of real property in Pittsburgh, including public and tax-exempt properties. Parcel census tract, ward, block and lot number, zoning, and assessed values of both land and improvements are provided. In addition, the name and address of the owner or owners, information characterizing the owner, and sale price and year of most recent sale are reported. No information on the use of the parcel is included in this file, aside from the assessed value of improvements to the property and its zoning.

(3) *The Public Property File of the Pittsburgh Planning Department.* This computer file contains extensive information on publicly owned properties in Pittsburgh. Information on the method and year of acquisition of the property is also recorded, so it is possible using this file to identify parcels acquired by the City, the County, and the school district, via treasury sale. The use of the property prior to public acquisition, the type of structure on the land, the assessed value of the land and its acquisition are also recorded in the file. Records of all properties procured by the City are permanently maintained in this file. For properties sold from public ownership to private purchasers, it is possible in many cases to determine sale price. When the City Planning Commission has made formal decisions regarding the use or disposition of properties, these decisions are recorded in the Public Property File.

(4) *The Land Use Survey of the Southwestern Pennsylvania Regional Planning Commission.* This computer file records the findings of a major survey of the uses of individual land parcels in the Pittsburgh metropolitan area, undertaken in 1967. For each property in the City of Pittsburgh, this file provides block and lot numbers comparable to those in the three city files described above, plus a four-digit land use code describing the use of the land in 1967. These codes identify many types of residential and non-residential land uses.

The basic data processing step undertaken in this study was the computer matching of records in the Tax Delinquency File with records in the Real Property File and the Land Use Survey. This matching provided all the information contained in these latter two files for each of the delinquent parcels. Matching between the Real Property File and the Tax Delinquency File was virtually perfect: only a negligible number of properties in the Tax Delinquency File could not be matched with records in the Real Property File. However, approximately one in ten properties in the Tax Delinquency File could not be matched with properties in the Land Use Survey. Thus, land use information was available for approximately 90 percent of delinquent parcels.

SURVEY DESIGN AND ANALYSIS

SAMPLE SELECTION

The objective of the survey was to contact and interview the owners of a representative sample of privately owned residential properties in Pittsburgh, which according to Treasury Department records owed the City real estate taxes, water bills assumed by the City, and/or sewer charges on December 31, 1973. Three prerequisites conditioned a property's inclusion in the universe of structures from which the sample was to be selected:

(1) only residential properties were included:
(2) real estate taxes were delinquent on the property on December 31, 1973; and
(3) title to the property was in private hands according to city records current in June 1974.

Three primary data files were used in the definition of this universe of properties: the Real Property File; the Tax Delinquency File; and the Southwestern Pennsylvania Regional Planning Commission's 1967 Land Use Survey. Using Pittsburgh block and lot numbers, parcels included in the Tax Delinquency File were matched with property records in the Real Property File and in the Land Use Survey. Residential properties were defined using three criteria:

(1) the assessed value of improvements to the land was greater than zero in 1974 and either
(2) land use zoning permitted only residential uses or
(3) the land Use Survey reported residential land uses on the property. It was anticipated that in some cases non-residential properties would be found on residentially zoned land, and as a result the sampling universe would overestimate the actual universe of residential delinquent properties. In addition, because some properties in non-residentially zoned areas could not be assigned land use codes, undoubtedly some delinquent residential

properties were lost from the universe. However, these difficulties would tend to offset each other.

Privately owned parcels were identified using title and sale information from the Real Property File. Approximately 3 percent of the residential tax delinquent parcels were found to be owned by public agencies such as the Urban Redevelopment Authority, and these properties were deleted from the group of properties to be sampled. Properties were selected from this universe using systematic sampling without replacement.

SURVEY MANAGEMENT

Two objectives governed the methods used to contact and interview owners. First, the number of completed interviews had to be sufficiently large for reliable statistical analysis. Second, a representative sample of properties was required. Property owners were in some cases difficult to locate and contact. A lengthy search process, repeated call-backs, and on-site visits were utilized so that fugitive owners would be included as well as owners who were easy to locate.

Property owners were contacted in three ways. First, an introductory letter was mailed to the owner at the address recorded in the Real Property File. This letter described the study and the nature of the desired interview. The letter was followed up immediately by a telephone call in those cases where a telephone number could be determined using regular or reverse telephone directories. The purpose of this call was to further explain the study and to schedule an interview. In those cases where a working

EXHIBIT A-1

SUMMARY OF INTERVIEW RESULTS,
CUPR PITTSBURGH TAX DELINQUENCY SURVEY

	Number	Percent
Total sample	465	100.0
Out-of-state owner [a]	10	2.2
Ineligible or no contact [b]	208	44.7
Refused	64	13.8
Interview cancelled by owner and not rescheduled	19	4.1
Completed	164	35.3
Useable [c]	158	34.0

Notes: a. No attempt was made to contact these owners.
   b. Includes properties which were found to be non-residential or vacant lots or properties whose owners could not be located.
   c. Useable interviews were those determined to be sufficiently complete to warrant inclusion in the analysis.

telephone number could not be found, a door-to-door search for the owner was undertaken. Owners were approached with great flexibility, in order to guarantee the highest possible degree of cooperation.

The work was done using three consecutive samples of owners to be sought for interviews. Each sample was exhausted before continuing on with the next. Exhibit A-1 summarizes the distribution of successful and unsuccessful interviews.

Interviews were conducted at whatever site respondents indicated as convenient. In most cases, these included either the respondent's home or workplace location. The actual job of locating respondents, arranging appointments, and completing interviews was conducted by representatives of Arthur Young and Company, a management consultant firm with offices in Pittsburgh.

REPRESENTATIVENESS OF THE SAMPLE

There is no way to determine whether the *owners* who could be located and interviewed differ in any systematic way from those who could not be found. Properties whose owners were interviewed, however, appear to reflect the universe of delinquent residential structures, in terms of available characteristics of the buildings. There is thus strong reason to believe that our sample is representative of the universe of delinquent residential structures. Exhibits A-2 to A-5 present tabular comparisons of the characteristics of three groups of privately owned delinquent residential structures in Pittsburgh. The first group comprises all such structures in the city which could be assigned land use codes using the Southwestern Pennsylvania Regional Planning Commission Land Use Survey. Parcels in residentially zoned areas which could not be assigned land use codes were included in the overall sampling, but not in these summary statistics. This latter group of structures was relatively small, and would not materially affect the results. The second group comprises the 465 structures we selected for interview attempts. The third is the 158 parcels whose owners we successfully interviewed.

The exhibits present distributions of these groups of parcels among wards in the city, among ranges of assessed values, among ranges of taxes owed and among classes denoting the ratio of taxes owed to assessed values of properties. Characteristics of sampled and interviewed properties are essentially identical to those of the universe of structures in terms of each of these measures. A small degree of apparently systematic bias does exist in only one of these four measures of property characteristics. The assessments of the interviewed parcels are somewhat higher than those of sampled parcels or the universe of parcels as a whole. The difference is concentrated in the parcels assessed for less than $2,000 and undoubtedly results from the deletion of demolished structures from consideration in the door-to-door searches for property owners.

EXHIBIT A-2

DISTRIBUTION AMONG PITTSBURGH WARDS OF THE SAMPLE UNIVERSE
OF DELINQUENT RESIDENTIAL STRUCTURES, SAMPLED STRUCTURES AND
STRUCTURES FOR WHICH USEABLE OWNER INTERVIEWS WERE
COMPLETED

Ward	Total Delinquent Structures[a]		Selected for Interviews		Interviewed	
	Number	Percent	Number	Percent	Number	Percent
1	31	0.5	0	0.0	0	0.0
2	19	0.3	2	0.4	0	0.0
3	227	3.7	19	4.1	2	1.3
4	174	2.8	13	2.8	5	3.2
5	534	8.6	46	9.9	19	12.0
6	120	1.9	8	1.7	6	3.8
7	115	1.9	7	1.5	5	3.2
8	88	1.4	7	1.5	1	0.6
9	79	1.3	6	1.3	4	2.5
10	300	4.8	25	5.4	7	4.4
11	108	1.7	8	1.7	6	3.8
12	406	6.6	29	6.2	8	5.1
13	712	11.5	55	11.8	18	11.3
14	257	4.1	19	4.1	8	5.1
15	251	4.0	19	4.1	5	3.2
16	190	3.1	11	2.4	5	3.2
17	150	2.4	11	2.4	2	1.3
18	265	4.3	20	4.3	2	1.3
19	331	5.3	23	4.9	6	3.8
20	253	4.1	16	3.4	9	5.7
21	266	4.3	25	5.4	11	7.0
22	62	1.0	3	0.6	1	0.6
23	9	0.1	1	0.2	0	0.0
24	155	2.5	11	2.4	2	1.3
25	248	4.0	20	4.3	7	4.4
26	311	5.0	20	4.3	7	4.4
27	177	2.9	13	2.8	4	2.5
28	64	1.0	6	1.3	3	1.3
29	102	1.6	8	1.7	2	1.3
30	65	1.0	4	0.9	2	1.3
31	80	1.3	8	1.7	1	0.6
32	49	0.8	2	0.4	1	0.6
Total	6,198	100.0	465	100.0	158	100.0

Note: a. This total includes all delinquent privately owned residential structures which could be assigned land use codes using the 1967 Land Use Survey of the Southwestern Pennsylvania
Regional Planning Commission. See text for a discussion of discrepancies between this group
of buildings and the sampled population.

EXHIBIT A-3

ASSESSED VALUES OF THE UNIVERSE OF DELINQUENT RESIDENTIAL
STRUCTURES, SAMPLE STRUCTURES, AND STRUCTURES FOR WHICH A
USEABLE OWNER INTERVIEW WAS COMPLETED

Real Property Assessment	Total[a]		Selected for Interviews		Interviewed	
	Number	Percent	Number	Percent	Number	Percent
Less than $2,000	1,173	19.0	96	20.7	21	13.3
$2,000-4,999	3,343	54.1	233	50.2	87	55.1
$5,000-9,999	1,240	20.1	98	21.1	34	21.5
$10,000 or more	420	6.8	37	8.0	16	10.1
Total	6,176[b]	100.0	464[c]	100.0	158	100.0

Notes: a. This total includes all delinquent privately owned residential structures which could be assigned land use codes using the 1967 Land Use Survey of the Southwestern Pennsylvania Regional Planning Commission. See text for a discussion of discrepancies between this group of buildings and the sampled population.
  b. Assessment data were missing for 22 structures.
  c. Assessment information was missing for one structure.

EXHIBIT A-4

BACK TAXES OWED ON THE UNIVERSE OF DELINQUENT RESIDENTIAL
STRUCTURES, SAMPLED STRUCTURES, AND STRUCTURES FOR WHICH A
USEABLE OWNER INTERVIEW WAS COMPLETED

Delinquent Taxes	Total[a]		Selected for Interviews		Interviewed	
	Number	Percent	Number	Percent	Number	Percent
Less than $500	3,598	58.1	267	57.4	89	56.3
$500-999	1,672	27.0	130	28.0	40	25.3
$1,000 or more	928	15.0	68	14.6	29	18.4
Total	6,198	100.0	465	100.0	158	100.0

Note: a. This total includes all delinquent privately owned residential structures which could be assigned land use codes using the 1967 Land Use Survey of the Southwestern Pennsylvania Regional Planning Commission. See text for a discussion of discrepancies between this group of buildings and the sampled population.

EXHIBIT A-5

RATIO OF BACK TAXES TO CURRENT ASSESSMENTS OF THE UNIVERSE OF DELINQUENT RESIDENTIAL STRUCTURES, SAMPLE STRUCTURES, AND STRUCTURES FOR WHICH USEABLE OWNER INTERVIEWS WERE COMPLETED

Ratio of Delinquent Taxes to Total Assessment	Total[a]		Selected for Interviews		Interviewed	
	Number	Percent	Number	Percent	Number	Percent
Less than 0.25	4,880	78.7	375	80.6	126	79.7
0.25-0.49	1,030	16.6	69	14.8	25	15.8
0.50 or more	288	4.6	21	4.5	7	4.4
Total	6,198	100.0	465	100.0	158	100.0

Note: a. This total includes all delinquent privately owned residential structures which could be assigned land use codes using the 1967 Land Use Survey of the Southwestern Pennsylvania
Regional Planning Commission. See text for a discussion of discrepancies between this group
of buildings and the sampled population.

STATISTICAL ANALYSIS

A few words are in order about the basic statistical methods utilized in our analysis. Those well versed in these techniques can easily skip over this section; for those less imbued with the details of statistical mystification, we hope this brief discussion will clarify more than it confuses.

REGRESSION ANALYSIS

The principal statistical procedure whereby it is possible to simultaneously assess the relative significance of one or a large number of causative factors is known as regression analysis. Regression analysis specifies the amount and direction of influence that each of a list of characteristics (e.g. total population, vacancy rate, tax rate, etc.) has on the item under scrutiny (e.g. the rate of tax delinquency). The causative factors are known as independent variables and the item under study is known as the dependent variable. In light of possible interaction among causative factors, regression analysis permits the evaluation of the impact of each of the independent variables on the dependent variable *after* all the other independent variables have explained all the variation in the dependent variable associated with them.

The objective of regression analysis is to identify the smallest number of independent variables which together explain the greatest possible amount of variation in the dependent variable. Specifically the regression technique produces an equation which specifies the nature and direction of the relationship between each independent variable and the dependent variable. This equation takes the form:

$$Y = a + b_1x_1 + b_2x_2 + b_3x_3 + \ldots + b_nx_n$$

where Y = the dependent variable (in this case the rate of tax delinquency)

a = a constant generated by the regression equation

$x_1, x_2, x_3 \ldots x_n$ are the names of the independent variables which are found to explain some portion of the variation in the dependent variable "Y"

$b_1, b_2, b_3 \ldots b_n$ are regression coefficients which indicate the rate of change in the dependent variable associated with a unit change (change of ± 1) in each independent variable after all the other independent variables have explained all the variation associated with them.

The sign $(+)$ or $(-)$ of the coefficient indicates the *direction* of the relationship between the dependent and the independent variable. A $(+)$ before a coefficient indicates a positive relationship; the greater the increase in the independent variable, the greater the *increase* in the dependent variable. A $(-)$ before a coefficient indicates a negative relationship; the greater the increase in the independent variable, the greater the *decrease* in the dependent variable.

The regression model of this form is used to test specific hypotheses concerning the strength and the direction of relationships between combinations of independent variables and tax delinquency. Selection of appropriate independent variables to enter into the regression equation is made on the basis of previous experience, a review of the relevant literature, a preliminary examination of the data, and specification of hypotheses derived from the theoretical underpinning of the analysis.

The regression technique tests the resulting hypotheses by substituting data for combinations of independent variables in the right side of the equation and observing the magnitude and direction (signs) of the resulting coefficients, the size of the "standard errors" of the coefficients, and the level of statistical significance attributed to each coefficient. The "standard error" provides a measure of the likelihood that the coefficient generated by the regression equation to indicate the relationship betweeen the independent and dependent variables within the *sample* of observations utilized, (e.g., a sample of cities), in fact is the same as the "true" coefficient which summarizes the relationship between dependent and independent variables within the entire universe of observations (i.e., all cities). The coefficients $(b_1, b_2, b_3 \ldots b_n)$ generated by the regression equation are estimates of the "true" coefficients that would be generated for the universe (of all cities), and should be read as $b \pm$ the standard error. Thus, when the standard error is much smaller than the coefficient estimate, the likelihood is increased that the estimate produced from the sample data is very close (in magnitude and sign) to the coefficient which summarizes the relationship between the independent and dependent variables for the universe of observations.

Finally, significance levels indicate the probability with which the predicted relationship summarized in the coefficient estimate ± the standard error could have resulted from chance rather than from a systematic relationship between the dependent and independent variables. A significance level of .05, for instance, indicates a 5 percent probability that the relationship predicted by the regression coefficient could have occurred by random chance, and a 95 percent probability that the predicted relationship is due to systematic interaction between the variables. A .01 significance level then, suggests that there is only a 1 percent probability - or one chance in a hundred - that the predicted relationship could be due to chance alone. Thus, the significance level is important in determining whether to accept or reject a given hypothesis: the higher the probability that a predicted relationship might be due to random effects, the more difficult it is to accept the hypotheses embodying that particular relationship.

FACTOR ANALYSIS

Factor analysis was used in Chapter 5 to identify the basic dimensions underlying the distribution of 50 different population and housing characteristics across Pittsburgh's 182 census tracts. The general objective of factor analysis is to reduce a large set of such descriptive characteristics or variables, into a much smaller number of "factors" which summarize important clusters of interrelationships among the variables.

Typically, a data set comprised of a large number of variables all measured over the same census tracts will exhibit strong correlations among particular clusters of these variables. The factor analysis technique searches through this pattern of correlations to statistically identify the most important of these clusters, or "factors."

Each factor delineated in the analysis can be described in terms of its correlation with the original set of variables. These correlations are known as the "factor loadings." Some variables will be highly correlated with a given factor; others will be uncorrelated. Each factor can then be assigned a name which summarizes or reflects the particular cluster of variables with high loadings on that factor. In the analysis reported in Chapter 5, nine factors were identified by the factor analysis routine, and then named on the basis of our interpretation of the clusters of variables associated with each factor.

INDEX CONSTRUCTION

In several cases, related groups of data items obtained from the survey of delinquent owners in Pittsburgh were combined in the analysis to form indexes. Indexes computed on the basis of respondent's replies to several closely related questions are often more reliable than responses to a single question since they tend to minimize the potential effect of the sources of error-respondent bias, misunderstanding, interviewer error, etc. - that might limit the validity of single responses.

The indexes constructed for the analysis of the survey are simple additive summations of responses to related questions, with constituent variables recoded where necessary to ensure congruence in the direction of responses.

BUILDING CONDITION INDEX

The building condition index was composed of answers to questions concerning the owner's evaluation of the condition of the heating equipment, plumbing, wiring, the roof, the building exterior, and the building as a whole, plus the availability of piped water, hot water, toilets, and private bathtub or shower. The index is a simple additive combination of the following values:

	Variable		Code
V97	Condition of building as a whole	1	if very poor, poor, or average
V98	Condition of heating equipment	0	if good or very good
V100	Condition of plumbing		
V103	Condition of wiring		
V106	Condition of building exterior		
V107	Does the roof leak?	1	if yes
V92	Units lacking piped water	0	if no
V93	Units lacking hot water		
V94	Units lacking toilets		
V95	Units lacking private bathtub or shower		

Values on these variables were summed yielding an index ranging between 0 and 10, with 10 indicating the worst condition. These index scores were in turn recoded into four roughly equal categories. The final building condition index ranges between 0 and 3 with a mean of 1.32.

TOTAL EXPENDITURES INDEX

The index of total expenditures summarizes owners' reported annual expenditures for mortgage payments, taxes, water and sewer charges, maintenance and repairs, utilities, heating, and insurance. The index was constructed by coding these expenditures as above or below the mean for that category, and then summing the result. The components of the total expenditures index are as follows:

Variable		Code
V172	Annual expenditures on insurance	1 if $>$ mean
V173	Annual expenditures on maintenance and repairs	0 if $\leqslant$ mean
V174	Annual expenditures on heating	
V175	Annual expenditures on utilities	
V290	Annual municipal tax bill	
V291	Annual school tax bill	
V292	Annual sewer tax bill	
V294	Annual water bill	
V162	Monthly mortgage payments	
V167	Monthly payments-second mortgage	
V170	Monthly payments on other debts	

These variables were coded 1 if the respondent's reported expenditures was greater than the mean expenditure for that item, and 0 if reported expenditures were less than or equal to the mean. The results were then summed and recoded into roughly equal categories, yielding a final index of total expenditures ranging between 0 and 3 with a mean of 1.22. A high score on the index indicates a high frequency of above average expenditures on the building.

VACANCY INDEX

The vacancy index is composed of answers to four questions which summarize the owner's evaluation of the relative severity of vacancy as a problem over the six year period prior to and at the time of the interview. The component questions and codes comprising the vacancy index are:

Variable		Code
V249	Change in building vacancy rate over last six years	1 if higher now
V250	Change in average period of vacancy over last six years	0 if lower now or no change
V123	Change in area vacancy rate over last six years	
V281	Difficulty in finding "good tenants" today compared to last six years	1 if more difficult now
		0 if easier or no change

Values on these four variables were summed and recoded to yield four categories ranging between 0 and 3 with a mean of 0.53. A high score on the vacancy index reflects an owner's evaluation of vacancy as a serious problem.

Appendix B

Summary of Results
(Marginals) of the
CUPR Pittsburgh
Delinquency Survey

EXHIBIT B-1

SIZE DISTRIBUTIONS OF TAXES OWED, PITTSBURGH DELINQUENCY SURVEY
(percents)[a]

A. Total Taxes Owed, July 1974 (V10)

0	<$500	$500-999	≥$1,000	N
6.9	53.8	24.1	15.2	
(11)	(85)	(38)	(24)	(158)

B. Total Taxes Owed, December 31, 1973 (V11)

	<$500	$500-999	≥$1,000	N
	56.3	25.9	17.7	
	(89)	(41)	(28)	(158)

C. Municipal Property Taxes Owed, July 1974 (V12)

0	<$250	$250-499	≥$500	N
15.2	60.1	18.4	6.3	
(24)	(95)	(29)	(10)	(158)

D. Municipal Property Taxes Owed, December 31, 1973 (V13)

0	<$250	$250-499	≥$500	N
5.1	66.5	20.3	8.2	
(8)	(105)	(32)	(13)	(158)

E. School District Property Taxes Owed, July 1974 (V14)

0	<$250	$250-499	≥$500	N
12.0	71.5	13.3	3.2	
(19)	(113)	(21)	(5)	(158)

F. School District Property Taxes Owed, December 31, 1973 (V15)

0	<$250	$250-499	≥$500	N
1.3	78.5	16.5	3.8	
(2)	(124)	(26)	(6)	(158)

G. Pittsburgh Water Bills Owed, July 1974 (V16)

0	<$250	$250-499	≥$500	N
32.3	52.5	10.8	4.4	
(51)	(83)	(17)	(7)	(158)

H. Pittsburgh Water Bills Owed, December 31, 1973 (V17)

0	<$250	$250-499	≥$500	N
27.8	55.7	11.4	5.1	
(44)	(88)	(18)	(8)	(158)

I. Pittsburgh Sewer Bills Owed, July 1974 (V18)

0	<$250	$250-499	≥$500	N
40.5	51.3	5.1	3.2	
(64)	(81)	(8)	(5)	(158)

J. Pittsburgh Sewer Bills Owed, December 31, 1973 (V19)

0	<$250	$250-499	≥$500	N
34.8	57.6	5.1	2.5	
(55)	(91)	(8)	(4)	(158)

Note: a. Absolute numbers are in parentheses.

EXHIBIT B-2

OWNER CHARACTERISTICS, PITTSBURGH DELINQUENCY SURVEY
(percents)[a]

A. Owner Age (V27)

<40 Years	40-59 Years	≥60 Years	N
14.6	50.3	35.1	
(22)	(76)	(53)	(151)

B. Owner Ethnicity (V25)

White	Black	N
62.3	37.7	
(96)	(58)	(154)

C. Owner Occupation (V50C)

Professional or Technical	Manager or Proprietor	Sales	Clerical	Craftsman, Foreman
8.8	14.9	10.2	3.4	6.8
(13)	(22)	(15)	(5)	(10)

Service	Operatives	Laborers	Retired	Student
6.1	9.5	7.5	21.8	2.0
(9)	(14)	(11)	(32)	(3)

Housewife	Unemployed	N
6.1	2.7	
(9)	(4)	(147)

D. Owner Income (V52)

<5,000	5,000- 9,999	10,000- 14,999	15,000- 24,999	≥25,000	N
25.4	33.3	25.4	10.1	5.8	
(35)	(46)	(35)	(14)	(8)	(138)

E. Major Source of Income (V51)

Salaries and Wages	Social Security and Public Assistance	Self- Employed	Real Estate	N
55.3	27.7	12.1	4.9	
(78)	(39)	(17)	(7)	(141)

Note: a. Absolute numbers are in parentheses.

EXHIBIT B-3

OWNERS' LENGTH OF RESIDENCE AND PLANS TO MOVE, PITTSBURGH DELINQUENCY SURVEY
(percents)[a]

A. Owners' Length of Residence in Building (V282)

<10 Years	10-24 Years	25-49 Years	≥50 Years	N
23.7	43.3	25.8	7.2	
(23)	(42)	(25)	(7)	(97)

B. "Have You Any Plans to Move?" (V283)

Yes	No	N
15.8	84.2	
(15)	(80)	(95)

C. "If You Moved, What Would You Plan to Do With This Property?" (V285)

Keep	Sell	Abandon	Other	N
43.8	43.8	6.3	6.3	
(7)	(7)	(1)	(1)	(16)

D. "Where Would You Move To?" (V286)

Same Neighborhood	Different Neighborhood in Pittsburgh	Outside Pittsburgh in Metropolitan Area	Outside Metropolitan Area	N
35.0	15.0	20.0	30.0	
(7)	(3)	(4)	(6)	(20)

E. "Did You Ever Live in the Building?" (V287)

Yes	No	N
32.7	67.3	
(18)	(37)	(55)

F. When Moved From Building (V288)

Before 1955	1955-1965	Since 1965	N
33.3	38.9	27.8	
(6)	(7)	(5)	(18)

G. Why Moved From Building (V289)

Housing Related	Personal	Job Related	Nieghborhood Related	N
46.7	40.0	0.0	13.3	
(7)	(6)	(0)	(2)	(15)

Note: a. Absolute numbers are in parentheses.

EXHIBIT B-4

PROPERTY OWNERSHIP CHARACTERISTICS, PITTSBURGH DELINQUENCY SURVEY
(percents)[a]

A. Ownership Status

Homeowner	Landlord	N
51.9	48.1	
(82)	(76)	(158)

B. Location of Owner's Residence (V24)

Outside Pittsburgh	Inside Pittsburgh	N
26.7	73.3	
(36)	(99)	(135)

C. Residence Status (V34)

Owner Occupant	Absentee Owner	N
62.0	38.0	
(98)	(60)	(158)

D. Sole or Joint Ownership (V41)

Sole Owner	Partnership	Corporation	Other	N
93.0	5.1	0.6	1.3	
(146)	(8)	(1)	(2)	(157)

E. Year First Owned Real Estate (V30)

Before 1954	1954-1963	1964-1974	N
43.8	23.5	32.7	
(67)	(36)	(50)	(153)

F. Year First Owned Rental Real Estate (V31)

None Owned	Before 1954	1954-1963	1964-1974	N
54.5	11.9	15.4	18.2	
(78)	(17)	(22)	(26)	(143)

G. Year Acquired Sample Property (V32)

Before 1954	1954-1963	1964-1974	N
34.2	22.1	43.6	
(51)	(33)	(65)	(149)

H. Reason for Purchase of Sample Property (V38)

Home	Rent	Inheritance	Other	N
57.1	15.6	21.1	6.1	
(84)	(23)	(31)	(9)	(147)

I. Is This Still Owner's Reason for Keeping Property? (V39)

Yes	No	N
78.5	21.8	
(115)	(32)	(147)

EXHIBIT B-4 (continued)
PROPERTY OWNERSHIP CHARACTERISTICS,
PITTSBURGH DELINQUENCY SURVEY
(percents)[a]

J. (If No) What Is Owner's Reason for Keeping Property? (V40)

Rental Return	Unable To Sell	Actively Trying To Sell	No Interest In Property	N
34.4	25.0	21.9	18.8	
(11)	(8)	(7)	(6)	(32)

K. Ownership of Other Real Estate (V42)

Owns Other Real Estate	Owns No Other Real Estate	N
38.3	61.7	
(59)	(95)	(154)

L. Number of Other Commercial Structures Owned (V43)

None	One	Two or More	N
88.3	6.8	4.9	
(91)	(7)	(5)	(103)

M. Number of Other One-Family Homes Owned (V44)

None	One	Two or More	N
57.3	22.3	20.4	
(59)	(23)	(21)	(103)

N. Number of Other Duplex Structures Owned (V45)

None	One	Two or More	N
80.6	9.7	9.7	
(83)	(10)	(10)	(103)

O. Number of Other Apartment Structures Owned (V46)

None	One	Two or More	N
89.3	4.9	5.8	
(92)	(5)	(6)	(103)

P. Total Number of Other Structures Owned (V47)

None	One	Two/Three	Four or More	N
43.7	23.3	16.5	16.5	
(45)	(24)	(17)	(17)	(103)

Q. Location of Other Properties (V48)

Owns No Other	Same Area of Pittsburgh	Other Areas of Pittsburgh	Outside Pittsburgh in Metropolitan Area	Outside Metropolitan Area	N
44.2	28.3	20.0	4.2	3.3	
(53)	(34)	(24)	(5)	(4)	(120)

Note: a. Absolute numbers are in parentheses.

EXHIBIT B-5

STRUCTURE CHARACTERISTICS, PITTSBURGH DELINQUENCY SURVEY
(percents)[a]

A. Structure Type (V33)

Single Family	Duplex	Apartment Building	Rooming House	Other	N
74.1	15.2	6.9	1.9	1.9	
(117)	(24)	(11)	(3)	(3)	(158)

B. Assessed Value of Land (V21)

< $500	$500-749	$750-999	· ⩾ $1,000	N
25.9	20.3	17.1	36.7	
(41)	(32)	(27)	(58)	(158)

C. Assessed Value of Improvements (V22)

< $2,000	$2,000-2,999	$3,000-4,999	⩾ $5,000	N
27.2	22.8	31.0	19.0	
(43)	(36)	(49)	(30)	(158)

D. Total Assessed Value of Property (V20)

< $2,500	$2,500-4,999	$5,000-7,499	⩾ $7,500	N
24.7	43.7	16.5	15.2	
(39)	(69)	(26)	(24)	(158)

E. Building Construction Material (V79)

Frame	Masonry	N
49.4	50.6	
(76)	(78)	(154)

F. Number of Stories (V80)

1	1½	2	2½	3	4	N
3.2	3.8	46.2	7.0	39.2	0.6	
(5)	(6)	(73)	(11)	(62)	(1)	(158)

G. Age of Building (V82)

Built 1945 or Later	1900 to 1945	Built Before 1900	N
8.7	60.1	31.2	
(12)	(83)	(43)	(138)

H. Structures Lacking Plumbing Facilities (V92 to V95)

Structures With All Plumbing Facilities	Structures Lacking Some Plumbing Facilities	N
96.8	3.2	
(120)	(4)	(124)

EXHIBIT B-5 (continued)

STRUCTURE CHARACTERISTICS, PITTSBURGH DELINQUENCY SURVEY
(percents)[a]

I. Structures with Mixed Commercial Uses (V96)

No Mixed Commercial Uses	With Mixed Commercial Uses	N
94.7	5.3	
(125)	(7)	(132)

J. Owner's Estimate of Current Market Value of Parcel (V124)

<$5,000	$5,000-9,999	$10,000-19,999	≥$20,000	N
12.7	34.3	32.1	20.9	
(17)	(46)	(43)	(28)	(134)

K. Owner's Method of Estimating Value (V125)

Guess	Sales of Comparable Properties	Recent Offers	Original Cost and Improvements	Other	N
52.4	20.6	11.1	8.7	7.1	
(66)	(26)	(14)	(11)	(9)	(126)

L. Amount Originally Paid for Property (V126)

<$5,000	$5,000-7,499	$7,500-9,999	≥ $10,000	N
30.3	21.0	20.2	28.5	
(36)	(25)	(24)	(34)	(119)

M. Owner's Perception of Change in Property Value (V127)

Increase	Same	Decrease	N
68.2	13.6	18.2	
(90)	(18)	(24)	(132)

N. Owner's Estimate of Property Value in Five Years (V153)

Much More Than Today	Somewhat More Than Today	Same	Somewhat Less Than Today	Much Less Than Today	N
6.6	52.9	19.9	12.5	8.1	
(9)	(72)	(27)	(17)	(11)	(136)

O. Factors Effecting Changes in Property Value (V154)

General City Trends	Aging of Buildings	Neighborhood Changes	Other	N
29.2	11.1	49.3	10.4	
(42)	(16)	(71)	(15)	(144)

Note: a. Absolute numbers are in parentheses.

EXHIBIT B-6

UNITS PER STRUCTURE AND ROOMS PER UNIT, PITTSBURGH DELINQUENCY SURVEY
(percents)[a]

A. Total Number of Dwelling Units Per Structure (V90)

One	*Two*	*Three or More*	*N*
74.1	15.2	10.8	
(117)	(24)	(17)	(158)

B. Number of Structures by Number of One-Room Units (V84)

None	*One*	*Two*	*Three or More*	*N*
98.1	0.6	0.0	1.2	
(152)	(1)	(0)	(2)	(155)

C. Number of Structures by Number of Two Room Units (V85)

None	*One*	*Two*	*Three or More*	*N*
96.1	3.9	0.0	0.0	
(149)	(6)	(0)	(0)	(155)

D. Number of Structures by Number of Three Room Units (V86)

None	*One*	*Two*	*Three or More*	*N*
88.4	7.1	3.2	1.2	
(137)	(11)	(5)	(2)	(155)

E. Number of Structures by Number of Four Room Units (V87)

None	*One*	*Two*	*Three or More*	*N*
83.9	11.0	3.2	1.9	
(130)	(17)	(5)	(3)	(155)

F. Number of Structures by Number of Five Room Units (V88)

None	*One*	*Two*	*Three or More*	*N*
80.0	17.4	2.6	0.0	
(124)	(27)	(4)	(0)	(155)

G. Number of Structures by Number of Units With Six or More Rooms (V89)

None	*One*	*Two*	*Three or More*	*N*
40.5	55.6	3.3	0.7	
(62)	(85)	(5)	(1)	(153)

Note: a. Absolute numbers are in parentheses.

EXHIBIT B-7

STRUCTURE CONDITION, PITTSBURGH DELINQUENCY SURVEY
(percents)[a]

A. Building Condition (V97)

Very Good	Good	Average	Poor	Very Poor	Boarded Up, Vacant	N
18.6	32.1	28.2	11.5	7.7	1.9	
(29)	(50)	(44)	(18)	(12)	(3)	(156)

B. Condition of Heating Equipment (V98)

Very Good	Good	Average	Poor	Very Poor	Boarded Up, Vacant	N
24.8	47.1	17.0	5.9	4.6	0.7	
(38)	(72)	(26)	(9)	(7)	(1)	(153)

C. Condition of Plumbing (V100)

Very Good	Good	Average	Poor	Very Poor	Boarded Up, Vacant	N
23.7	47.4	18.6	3.8	5.1	1.3	
(37)	(74)	(29)	(6)	(8)	(2)	(156)

D. Condition of Wiring (V103)

Very Good	Good	Average	Poor	Very Poor	Boarded Up, Vacant	N
25.0	45.4	20.4	4.6	4.6	0.0	
(38)	(69)	(31)	(7)	(7)	(0)	(152)

E. Condition of Building Exterior (V106)

Very Good	Good	Average	Poor	Very Poor	Boarded Up, Vacant	N
10.3	49.0	25.8	10.3	3.9	0.6	
(16)	(76)	(40)	(16)	(6)	(1)	(155)

F. Is All Wiring Concealed? (V105)

Yes	No	N
70.1	29.9	
(103)	(44)	(147)

G. Does The Roof Leak? (V107)

Yes	No	N
13.2	86.8	
(20)	(131)	(151)

Note: a. Absolute numbers are in parentheses.

EXHIBIT B-8

RACIAL AND ETHNIC CHARACTERISTICS OF NEIGHBORHOODS, PITTSBURGH DELINQUENCY SURVEY
(percents)[a]

A. Percent Non-White of Neighborhood Population (V109)

0%	*1-24%*	*25-89%*	*≥90*	*N*
24.2	21.5	21.5	32.9	
(36)	(32)	(32)	(49)	(149)

B. Change in Neighborhood Racial Composition in the Past Six Years (V108)

Black Increase	*Same*	*Black Decrease*	*N*
40.6	58.7	0.6	
(63)	(91)	(1)	(155)

C. Dominant Neighborhood Nationality (V110)

English	*Irish*	*German*	*Italian*	*Eastern European*	*Jewish*	*Spanish*	*Black*	*Mixed*	*N*
1.4	2.2	2.2	4.3	5.8	2.2	0.0	50.0	31.9	
(2)	(3)	(3)	(6)	(8)	(3)	(0)	(69)	(49)	(138)

Note: a. Absolute numbers are in parentheses.

EXHIBIT B-9

RESPONDENTS' PERCEPTIONS OF NEIGHBORHOOD PROPERTY VALUES, PITTSBURGH DELINQUENCY SURVEY
(percents)[a]

A. Current Land Value in the Neighborhood Compared to Those in the City as a Whole (V53)

Higher	Same	Lower	N
13.0	47.3	39.7	
(19)	(69)	(58)	(146)

B. Current Total Property Values in the Neighborhood Compared to Those in the City as a Whole (V54)

Higher	Same	Lower	N
12.2	44.2	43.5	
(18)	(65)	(64)	(147)

C. Change in Neighborhood Land Values in the Past Five or Six Years (V55)

Up	Same	Down	N
31.8	35.8	32.4	
(47)	(53)	(48)	(148)

D. Change in Neighborhood Total Property Values in the Past Five or Six Years (V56)

Up	Same	Down	N
31.3	33.3	35.4	
(46)	(49)	(52)	(147)

E. Change in Land Values in Neighborhood Compared to the City as a Whole (V57)

No Change	Increased More Rapidly	Increased As Rapidly	Increased Less Rapidly	Decreased More Rapidly	Decreased As Rapidly	Decreased Less Rapidly	N
5.2	12.9	31.0	8.6	28.4	12.9	0.9	
(6)	(15)	(36)	(10)	(33)	(15)	(1)	(116)

F. Change in Total Property Values in Neighborhood Compared to the City as a Whole (V58)

No Change	Increased More Rapidly	Increased As Rapidly	Increased Less Rapidly	Decreased More Rapidly	Decreased As Rapidly	Decreased Less Rapidly	N
5.2	12.2	28.7	48.7	31.3	13.9	0.9	
(6)	(14)	(33)	(9)	(36)	(16)	(1)	(115)

Note: a. Absolute numbers are in parentheses.

EVALUATION OF NEIGHBORHOOD AND IDENTIFICATION OF NEIGHBORHOOD PROBLEMS, PITTSBURGH DELINQUENCY SURVEY
(percents)[a]

A. Evaluation of Street As a Place to Live (V122)

Poor	Fair	Good	Excellent	N
15.5	24.5	38.1	21.9	
(24)	(38)	(59)	(34)	(155)

B. Street Noise (V111)

Problem	Not a Problem	N
39.7	60.2	
(60)	(91)	(151)

C. Aircraft Noise (V112)

Problem	Not a Problem	N
11.0	88.9	
(17)	(137)	(154)

D. Street Traffic (V113)

Problem	Not a Problem	N
39.6	60.3	
(61)	(93)	(154)

E. Odors or Smoke (V114)

Problem	Not a Problem	N
15.7	84.3	
(24)	(129)	(153)

F. Trash, Litter, or Junk (V115)

Problem	Not a Problem	N
34.6	65.3	
(53)	(100)	(153)

G. Abandoned Structures (V116)

Problem	Not a Problem	N
29.9	70.1	
(46)	(108)	(154)

H. Occupied Run-Down Housing (V117)

Problem	Not a Problem	N
25.2	74.8	
(38)	(113)	(151)

I. Non-Residential Nuisances (V118)

Problem	Not a Problem	N
12.4	87.6	
(19)	(134)	(153)

J. Street Disrepair (V119)

Problem	Not a Problem	N
28.9	71.1	
(44)	(108)	(152)

K. Inadequate Street Lighting (V120)

Problem	Not a Problem	N
9.9	90.0	
(15)	(136)	(151)

L. Street Crime (V121)

Problem	Not a Problem	N
34.9	65.1	
(52)	(97)	(149)

M. Change in Neighborhood Vacancy Rate in Past Six Years (V123)

Up	Down	No Change	N
26.0	7.3	66.7	
(39)	(11)	(100)	(150)

Note: a. Absolute numbers are in parentheses.

EVALUATIONS OF NEIGHBORHOOD SERVICES, PITTSBURGH DELINQUENCY SURVEY
(percents)[a]

A. Public Education (V59)

Very Poor	Poor	Neutral	Good	Very Good	N
5.8	13.1	23.4	51.1	6.6	
(8)	(18)	(32)	(70)	(9)	(137)

B. Police Protection (V60)

Very Poor	Poor	Neutral	Good	Very Good	N
11.0	14.5	21.4	48.3	4.8	
(16)	(21)	(31)	(70)	(7)	(145)

C. Fire Protection (V61)

Very Poor	Poor	Neutral	Good	Very Good	N
0.0	4.2	14.7	69.9	11.2	
(0)	(6)	(21)	(100)	(16)	(143)

D. Recreation Facilities (V62)

Very Poor	Poor	Neutral	Good	Very Good	N
6.8	29.5	17.8	37.0	8.9	
(10)	(43)	(26)	(54)	(13)	(146)

E. Sanitation (V63)

Very Poor	Poor	Neutral	Good	Very Good	N
6.9	11.7	17.2	53.8	10.3	
(10)	(17)	(25)	(78)	(15)	(145)

F. Public Health and Emergency Services (V64)

Very Poor	Poor	Neutral	Good	Very Good	N
3.0	15.9	14.4	56.1	10.6	
(4)	(21)	(19)	(74)	(14)	(132)

G. Public Transportation (V65)

Very Poor	Poor	Neutral	Good	Very Good	N
2.7	9.4	14.1	56.4	17.4	
(4)	(14)	(21)	(84)	(26)	(149)

H. Parking for Private Cars (V66)

Very Poor	Poor	Neutral	Good	Very Good	N
18.9	32.4	14.2	29.1	5.4	
(28)	(48)	(21)	(43)	(8)	(148)

I. Shopping Facilities (V67)

Very Poor	Poor	Neutral	Good	Very Good	N
9.9	23.7	12.5	42.1	11.8	
(15)	(36)	(19)	(64)	(18)	(152)

J. Most Needed Improvements (V77)

Police Protection	Public Education	Recreation	Parking	Shopping
21.2	16.8	16.8	15.3	9.5
(29)	(23)	(23)	(21)	(13)

Sanitation	Public Transportation	Public Health	Fire Protection	N
8.0	8.0	2.2	2.2	
(11)	(11)	(3)	(3)	(137)

K. Improvements That Would Most Affect Property Values (V78)

Police Protection	Education	Shopping	Recreation	Parking
24.4	19.7	14.2	12.6	11.0
(31)	(25)	(18)	(16)	(14)

Sanitation	Public Transportation	Public Health	Fire Protection	N
8.7	6.3	3.1	0.0	
(11)	(8)	(4)	(0)	(127)

Note: a. Absolute numbers are in parentheses.

EXHIBIT B-12

EVALUATIONS OF THE CHANGING QUALITY OF NEIGHBORHOOD SERVICES OVER THE LAST SIX YEARS, PITTSBURGH DELINQUENCY SURVEY
(percents)[a]

A. Change in Public Education (V68)

Much Worse	Worse	Same	Better	Much Better	N
3.8	23.3	45.9	26.3	0.8	
(5)	(31)	(61)	(35)	(1)	(133)

B. Change in Police Protection (V69)

Much Worse	Worse	Same	Better	Much Better	N
2.7	18.5	53.4	24.7	0.7	
(4)	(27)	(78)	(36)	(1)	(146)

C. Change in Fire Protection (V70)

Much Worse	Worse	Same	Better	Much Better	N
2.2	10.8	64.0	20.9	2.2	
(3)	(15)	(89)	(29)	(3)	(139)

D. Change in Recreation Facilities (V71)

Much Worse	Worse	Same	Better	Much Better	N
2.8	16.1	52.4	25.2	3.5	
(4)	(23)	(75)	(36)	(5)	(143)

E. Change in Sanitation (V72)

Much Worse	Worse	Same	Better	Much Better	N
4.9	15.3	56.3	21.5	2.1	
(7)	(22)	(81)	(31)	(3)	(144)

F. Change in Public Health and Emergency Services (V73)

Much Worse	Worse	Same	Better	Much Better	N
3.1	14.2	60.6	19.7	2.4	
(4)	(18)	(77)	(25)	(3)	(127)

G. Change in Public Transportation (V74)

Much Worse	Worse	Same	Better	Much Better	N
4.1	15.2	52.4	25.5	2.8	
(6)	(22)	(76)	(37)	(4)	(145)

H. Change in Parking for Private Cars (V75)

Much Worse	Worse	Same	Better	Much Better	N
4.7	29.3	58.0	8.0	0.0	
(7)	(44)	(87)	(12)	(0)	(150)

I. Change in Shopping Facilities (V76)

Much Worse	Worse	Same	Better	Much Better	N
4.6	24.3	50.7	18.4	2.0	
(7)	(37)	(77)	(28)	(3)	(152)

Note: a. Absolute numbers are in parentheses.

EXHIBIT B-13

PROPERTY MAINTENANCE FACTORS, PITTSBURGH DELINQUENCY SURVEY
(percents)[a]

A. Extent of Property Maintenance (V128)

Keep as Good as New	Keep in Good Condition	Keep in Fair Shape	Emergency Repairs Only	No Repairs	Boarded-Up, Vacant	N
12.0	48.7	25.9	8.9	1.9	2.5	
(19)	(77)	(41)	(14)	(3)	(4)	(158)

B. Has Building Been Inspected by the City in the Past Year or Two? (V129)

Yes — Violations Found	Yes — No Violations Found	No	N
17.0	21.8	61.2	
(25)	(32)	(90)	(147)

C. Building Violations Found in City Inspection (V130)

Heating	Wiring	Fire Hazards	Health	Plumbing	Vacant, Open to Entry
4.2	4.2	12.5	4.2	4.2	4.2
(1)	(1)	(3)	(1)	(1)	(1)

Multiple Violations	Miscellaneous	N
58.3	8.3	
(14)	(2)	(24)

D. Does Building Need Major Repairs? (V131)

Yes	No	N
53.3	46.7	
(80)	(70)	(150)

E. Types of Needed Repairs (V132)

Roof	Exterior	Heating	Plumbing	Modernization	Wiring
13.9	27.7	1.9	13.9	24.8	5.9
(14)	(28)	(2)	(14)	(25)	(6)

Foundation	Irreparable	N
6.9	4.9	
(7)	(5)	(101)

F. Cost of Needed Repairs (V133)

<500	500-2000	2001-5000	5001-10,000	>10,000	No Expenditure Required	N
9.4	30.2	20.8	9.4	4.7	25.4	
(10)	(32)	(22)	(10)	(5)	(27)	(106)

G. Owner's Return on Improvements Through Resale (V134)

Yes — Definitely	Yes — Maybe	Toss Up	Probably Not	Definitely Not	N
32.8	21.1	11.7	17.2	17.2	
(42)	(27)	(15)	(22)	(22)	(128)

EXHIBIT B-13 (continued)

PROPERTY MAINTENANCE FACTORS, PITTSBURGH DELINQUENCY SURVEY
(percents)[a]

H. Willingness to Improve Property if Given a Long-Term Mortgage (V135)

Yes	No	N
39.1	60.9	
(59)	(92)	(151)

I. Reasons For V135 (V136)

Not Needed	Capital Gains or Rental Profits	Personal Reasons	Owner Too Old	Improvements Not Reflected in Market Value	Bad Neighborhood
30.6	3.5	25.2	15.3	6.3	7.2
(34)	(4)	(28)	(17)	(7)	(8)

Terms Unacceptable	Intends To Sell	N
8.1	3.6	
(9)	(4)	(111)

J. Owner's Knowledge of Government Financial Programs for Improving Older Properties (V137)

Yes	No	N
43.8	56.2	
(67)	(86)	(153)

K. Known Titles of Government Programs (V138)

URA	FHA, General	HUD, General	Garfield Renewal Program	FHA 235, 236	Manchester Program
9.8	29.4	11.8	5.9	13.7	1.9
(5)	(15)	(6)	(3)	(7)	(1)

Community Economic Action Program	Neighborhood Housing Program	Homesteading	GI/VA Loans	Miscellaneous	N
1.9	5.9	3.9	3.9	11.8	
(1)	(3)	(2)	(2)	(6)	(51)

L. Owner's Knowledge of Tax Rebate Programs (V139)

Yes	No	N
25.0	75.0	
(34)	(102)	(136)

M. Known Types of Rebate Programs (V140)

Senior Citizen	Low Income	Homesteading	N
75.0	8.3	16.7	
(9)	(1)	(2)	(12)

EXHIBIT B-13 (continued)

PROPERTY MAINTENANCE FACTORS, PITTSBURGH DELINQUENCY SURVEY
(percents)[a]

N. Owners Considered Using Government Programs (V141)

Yes	No	N
19.6	80.4	
(27)	(111)	(138)

O. Why or Why Not? (V142)

Owner Not Eligible	Excessive Red Tape	Bad Neighborhood	Lack of Knowledge About Programs
39.1	2.9	2.9	24.6
(27)	(2)	(2)	(17)

Owner Too Old	Programs Not Needed	Improvements Not Needed	N
1.4	14.5	14.5	
(1)	(10)	(10)	(69)

P. Owner's Expectation of Interest Rates on Improvement Loans (V143)

$<7\%$	$7-9\%$	$10-12\%$	$>12\%$	N
9.9	55.0	27.9	7.2	
(11)	(61)	(31)	(8)	(111)

Q. Owner's Expectation of Term of Improvement Loans (V144)

<3 Years	3-4 Years	5-9 Years	10 Years	11-15 Years	15 Years	N
5.6	35.2	29.5	19.7	4.2	5.6	
(4)	(25)	(21)	(14)	(3)	(4)	(71)

R. Available Sources of Improvement Money (V145)

Mortgage-Savings Bank	Mortgage-Broker	Finance Company	Personal Loan-Commercial Bank	Personal Resources	Second Mortgage
21.4	1.5	5.3	19.8	10.7	0.8
(28)	(2)	(7)	(26)	(14)	(1)

Bank (No Details)	Government	N
32.8	7.6	
(43)	(10)	(131)

S. "Does It Make Sense to Improve Your Building?" (V184)

Yes	No	N
66.9	33.1	
(85)	(42)	(127)

Note: a. Absolute numbers are in parentheses.

EXHIBIT B-14

EXTENT AND COST OF MAINTENANCE AND PROPERTY IMPROVEMENTS, PITTSBURGH DELINQUENCY SURVEY
(percents)[a]

A. Year Improved/Repaired Heating Plant (V185)

No Improvement Made	Before 1965	1965- 1969	1970- 1974	Improvement Made Unknown Year	N
56.8	6.2	17.8	13.0	6.2	
(83)	(9)	(26)	(19)	(9)	(146)

B. Cost of Improving Heating Plant (V186)

< $500	$500-999	≥$1,000	N
35.9	23.4	40.6	
(23)	(15)	(26)	(64)

C. Year Improved/Repaired Wiring (V187)

No Improvement Made	Before 1965	1965- 1969	1970- 1974	Improvement Made Unknown Year	N
59.2	4.1	10.2	19.7	6.8	
(87)	(6)	(15)	(29)	(10)	(147)

D. Cost of Improving Wiring (V188)

<$200	$200-399	≥$400	N
33.9	33.9	32.1	
(19)	(19)	(18)	(56)

E. Year Improved/Repaired Lobby (V189)

No Improvement Made	Before 1965	1965- 1969	1970- 1974	Improvement Made Unknown Year	N
91.3	0.0	2.9	0.7	5.1	
(126)	(0)	(4)	(1)	(7)	(138)

F. Cost of Improving Lobby (V190)

< $500	$500-999	≥$1,000	N
20.0	60.0	20.0	
(1)	(3)	(1)	(5)

G. Year Improved/Repaired Plumbing (V191)

No Improvement Made	Before 1965	1965- 1969	1970- 1974	Improvement Made Unknown Year	N
43.2	7.5	8.9	25.3	15.1	
(63)	(11)	(13)	(37)	(22)	(146)

H. Cost of Improving Plumbing (V192)

< $300	$300-999	≥$1,000	N
34.3	35.7	30.0	
(24)	(25)	(21)	(70)

I. Year Changed Apartment Sizes, Partitions, Etc. (V193)

No Improvement Made	Before 1965	1965- 1969	1970- 1974	Improvement Made Unknown Year	N
88.7	0.7	0.0	4.9	5.7	
(125)	(1)	(0)	(7)	(8)	(141)

EXTENT AND COST OF MAINTENANCE AND PROPERTY IMPROVEMENTS, PITTSBURGH DELINQUENCY SURVEY
(percents)[a]

J. Cost of Changing Apartment Sizes (V194)

< $500	$500-999	≥$1,000	N
71.4	14.3	14.3	
(15)	(3)	(3)	(21)

K. Year Expanded Livable Space (V195)

No Improvement Made	Before 1965	1965-1969	1970-1974	Improvement Made Unknown Year	N
93.5	0.7	1.4	0.7	3.6	
(130)	(1)	(2)	(1)	(5)	(139)

L. Cost of Expanding Livable Space (V196)

< $1,000	$1,000-1,999	≥ $2,000	N
78.9	15.8	5.3	
(15)	(3)	(1)	(19)

M. Year Improved/Repaired Plaster, Paneling (V197)

No Improvement Made	Before 1965	1965-1969	1970-1974	Improvement Made Unknown Year	N
45.9	1.4	10.8	28.4	13.5	
(68)	(2)	(16)	(42)	(20)	(148)

N. Cost of Improving Plaster, Paneling (V198)

< $400	$200-499	≥ $500	N
23.1	30.8	46.2	
(15)	(20)	(30)	(65)

O. Year Improved/Repaired Building Exterior (V199)

No Improvement Made	Before 1965	1965-1969	1970-1974	Improvement Made Unknown Year	N
50.3	2.7	5.4	27.2	14.3	
(74)	(4)	(8)	(40)	(21)	(147)

P. Cost of Improving Exterior (V200)

< $200	$400-999	≥ $1,000	N
38.7	29.0	32.3	
(24)	(18)	(20)	(62)

Q. Year Improved/Repaired Roof (V201)

No Improvement Made	Before 1965	1965-1969	1970-1974	Improvement Made Unknown Year	N
46.5	6.3	8.5	25.4	13.4	
(66)	(9)	(12)	(36)	(19)	(142)

R. Cost of Improving Roof (V202)

< $250	$250-499	≥ $500	N
45.3	23.4	31.3	
(29)	(15)	(20)	(64)

S. Sum of Costs of All Indicated Improvements (V203)

< $1,000	$1,000-1,999	$2,000-2,999	≥ $3,000	N
25.6	25.6	23.1	25.6	
(30)	(30)	(27)	(30)	(117)

Note: a. Absolute numbers are in parentheses.

EXHIBIT B-15

EFFECTS OF PROPERTY IMPROVEMENT AND MAINTENANCE, PITTSBURGH DELINQUENCY SURVEY
(percents)[a]

A. Reasons for Improvements and Repairs (V204)

Replacement	Pride of Ownership	Get New Tenants	Keep Tenants
58.9	23.9	2.7	3.7
(86)	(35)	(4)	(5)

Correct Code Violations	Earn Higher Rents	Other	N
1.4	0.7	8.9	
(2)	(1)	(13)	(146)

B. Method of Financing Improvements (V205)

Not Financed	Personal Loan	Mortgage	Government Program	Other	N
70.7	23.3	2.0	1.3	2.7	
(106)	(35)	(3)	(2)	(4)	(150)

C. Effect of Improvements on Rents (V206)

Rents Much Higher	Rents Somewhat Higher	No Change	N
3.4	12.1	84.5	
(2)	(7)	(49)	(58)

D. Effect of Improvements on Rents, in Dollars Per Month (V207)

No Change	Increase < $25	Increase $25-99	Increase ≥ $100	N
28.6	28.6	28.6	14.3	
(4)	(4)	(4)	(2)	(14)

E. Effect of Improvements on Vacancies in the Building (V209)

Much Lower	Lower	No Change	N
13.6	4.5	81.8	
(6)	(2)	(36)	(44)

F. Most Important Problem in Maintaining the Building (V210)

Lack of Financing	Neighborhood Deterioration	Neighborhood Vandalism	Reassessment and Property Tax Increase	Level of Property Tax Payment
28.2	15.4	6.0	1.3	2.0
(42)	(23)	(9)	(2)	(3)

Insurance Costs	Tenant Vandalism or Unconcern	Unavailability of Labor	Other	No Problems	N
3.4	9.4	0.7	11.4	22.1	
(5)	(14)	(1)	(17)	(33)	(149)

EXHIBIT B-15 (continued)

EFFECTS OF PROPERTY IMPROVEMENT AND MAINTENANCE,
PITTSBURGH DELINQUENCY SURVEY
(percents)[a]

G. Second Most Important Problem in Maintaining the Building (V211)

Lack of Financing	Neighborhood Deterioration	Neighborhood Vandalism	Reassessment and Property Tax Increase	Level of Property Tax Payment
9.5	23.8	28.6	4.3	8.3
(8)	(20)	(24)	(4)	(7)

Insurance Costs	Tenant Vandalism or Unconcern	Unavailability of Labor	Other	No Problems	N
3.6	10.7	3.6	0.0	7.1	
(3)	(9)	(3)	(0)	(6)	(84)

H. Third Most Important Problem in Maintaining the Building (V212)

Lack of Financing	Neighborhood Deterioration	Neighborhood Vandalism	Reassessment and Property Tax Increase	Level of Property Tax Payment
13.5	19.2	11.5	7.7	3.8
(7)	(10)	(6)	(4)	(2)

Insurance Costs	Tenant Vandalism or Unconcern	Unavailability of Labor	Other	No Problems	N
15.4	15.4	1.9	5.8	5.8	
(8)	(8)	(1)	(3)	(3)	(52)

I. Fourth Most Important Problem in Maintaining the Building (V213)

Lack of Financing	Neighborhood Deterioration	Neighborhood Vandalism	Reassessment and Property Tax Increase	Level of Property Tax Payment
11.1	0.0	5.6	11.1	5.6
(2)	(0)	(1)	(2)	(1)

Insurance Costs	Tenant Vandalism or Unconcern	Unavailability of Labor	Other	No Problems	N
11.1	38.9	5.6	5.6	5.6	
(2)	(7)	(1)	(1)	(1)	(18)

J. Owner's Belief That Property Was Immediately Reassessed
as a Result of Property Improvements Made (V214)

Yes	No	N
18.1	81.9	
(23)	(104)	(127)

EXHIBIT B-15 (continued)

EFFECTS OF PROPERTY IMPROVEMENT AND MAINTENANCE,
PITTSBURGH DELINQUENCY SURVEY
(percents)[a]

K. Owner's Belief That Property Was Reassessed at Next General Reassessment
as a Result of Property Improvements Made (V215)

Yes	No	N
20.7	79.3	
(18)	(69)	(87)

L. Owner's Estimate of Assessment Increase Due to Property Improvements (V216)

No Increase	<$100	$100-999	⩾ $1,000	N
25.0	20.0	20.0	35.0	
(5)	(4)	(4)	(7)	(20)

M. Extent of Improvements Possible Without Tax Increase (V217A)

Major Improvements	Minor Improvements	N
16.7	83.3	
(7)	(35)	(42)

N. Location of Improvements Possible Without Tax Increase (V217B)

Interior	Exterior	N
91.7	8.3	
(22)	(2)	(24)

O. Type of Improvements Possible Without Tax Increase (V217C)

Plumbing	Cosmetic	Structural	Repairs and Replacement
1.1	7.7	3.3	36.3
(1)	(7)	(3)	(33)

Improvements, General	Anything	Nothing	N
18.7	6.6	26.4	
(17)	(6)	(24)	(91)

P. Does Owner Do General Repair Work on the Property? (V222)

All By Owner	Half By Owner	Little By Owner	None By Owner	N
43.1	13.9	7.6	35.4	
(62)	(20)	(11)	(51)	(144)

Q. Others Who Do Repair Work on the Property (V223)

Friends or Relatives	Permanent Employees	Hired Professionals	N
21.6	6.3	72.1	
(24)	(7)	(80)	(111)

Note: a. Absolute numbers are in parentheses.

EXHIBIT B-16

MORTGAGE AND HOME FINANCING DATA,
PITTSBURGH DELINQUENCY SURVEY
(percents)[a]

A. Mortgage Obtained to Purchase Property (V155)

Purchase Money Mortgage	Takeover or Assumption of Mortgage	No Mortgage	N
66.7	15.6	17.7	
(98)	(23)	(26)	(147)

B. Source of Mortgage (V156)

Savings and Loan Association	Commercial Bank	Credit Union	Insurance Company
35.7	30.0	2.9	5.7
(25)	(21)	(2)	(4)

Real Estate Broker	Seller	Personal or Individual	N
8.6	5.7	11.4	
(6)	(4)	(8)	(70)

C. Size of Downpayment (V157)

<$1,000	$1,000-1,999	≥$2,000	N
29.5	32.8	37.7	
(18)	(20)	(23)	(61)

D. Mortgage Interest Rate (V158)

≤5%	6%	≥7%	N
32.7	45.5	21.8	
(18)	(25)	(12)	(55)

E. Mortgage Term (V159)

≤10 Years	11-19 Years	≥20 Years	N
42.9	25.7	31.4	
(30)	(18)	(22)	(70)

F. Owner Still Paying on Mortgage? (V160)

Yes	Default or Delinquent	Paid Off	N
31.6	2.1	66.3	
(30)	(2)	(63)	(95)

G. Years Remaining on Mortgage (V161)

None	One to Five	Six or More	N
41.0	28.2	30.8	
(16)	(11)	(12)	(39)

H. Monthly Mortgage Payments (V162)

0	≤ $100	> $100	N
36.1	33.3	30.6	
(13)	(12)	(11)	(36)

EXHIBIT B-16 (continued)

MORTGAGE AND HOME FINANCING DATA, PITTSBURGH DELINQUENCY SURVEY
(percents)[a]

I. Year Arranged Second Mortgage (V163)

1960 or Earlier	1961-1965	1966-1970	Since 1970	N
30.0	20.0	30.0	20.0	
(3)	(2)	(3)	(2)	(10)

J. Term of Second Mortgage (V164)

≤5 Years	6-10 Years	>10 Years	N
30.0	50.0	20.0	
(3)	(5)	(2)	(10)

K. Years Remaining on Second Mortgage (V165)

None	One to Five	Six or More	N
33.3	55.6	11.1	
(3)	(5)	(1)	(9)

L. Source of Second Mortgage (V166)

Bank	Other	N
80.0	20.0	
(8)	(2)	(10)

M. Monthly Payments on Second Mortgage (V167)

0	≤ $100	> $100	N
14.3	28.6	57.2	
(1)	(2)	(4)	(7)

N. Any Other Debt on Property (V168)

Yes	No	N
14.3	85.7	
(20)	(120)	(140)

O. Year Other Debt Incurred (V169)

Before 1970	1970-1972	1973-1974	N
16.6	58.3	25.0	
(2)	(7)	(3)	(12)

P. Monthly Payments on Other Debt (V170)

≤$100	>$100	N
61.6	38.5	
(8)	(5)	(13)

Q. Total Monthly Debt Payments (V171)

≤ $100	>$100	N
51.6	48.4	
(16)	(15)	(31)

Note: a. Absolute numbers are in parentheses.

EXHIBIT B-17

OWNERS' ANNUAL EXPENDITURES FOR INSURANCE, MAINTENANCE, HEATING, AND UTILITIES, PITTSBURGH DELINQUENCY SURVEY
(percents)[a]

A. Annual Cost of Insurance (V172)

≤ $25	$26-50	$51-75	> $75	N
23.6	27.6	16.5	32.3	
(30)	(35)	(21)	(41)	(127)

B. Annual Cost of Repairs and Maintenance (V173)

≤ $100	$101-200	$201-500	> $500	N
39.5	25.4	21.9	13.2	
(45)	(29)	(25)	(15)	(114)

C. Annual Cost of Heating (V174)

≤ $100	$101-300	$301-400	> $400	N
25.4	32.3	21.5	20.8	
(33)	(42)	(28)	(27)	(130)

D. Annual Cost of Utilities, Excluding Sewer Taxes (V175)

≤ $100	$101-200	$201-300	> $300	N
28.9	28.9	21.1	21.1	
(37)	(37)	(27)	(27)	(128)

E. Total Annual Expenditures for Insurance, Maintenance, Heating, and Utilities (V176)

< $500	$500-1,000	> $1,000	N
34.7	36.7	28.6	
(51)	(54)	(42)	(147)

F. Change in Cost of Insurance in the Last Six Years (V177)

No Change	Increase < 10%	Increase 10-24%	Increase 25-49%	Increase 50-99%	Increase ≥ 100%	N
43.6	29.1	12.0	5.1	3.4	6.8	
(51)	(34)	(14)	(6)	(4)	(8)	(117)

G. Change in Cost of Repairs and Maintenance in the Last Six Years (V178)

No Change	Increase < 10%	Increase 10-24%	Increase 25-49%	Increase 50-99%	Increase ≥ 100%	N
29.5	17.1	23.8	15.2	7.6	6.7	
(31)	(18)	(25)	(16)	(8)	(7)	(105)

H. Change in Heating Costs in the Last Six Years (V179)

No Change	Increase < 10%	Increase 10-24%	Increase 25-49%	Increase 50-99%	Increase ≥ 100%	N
11.3	19.8	30.2	23.6	9.4	5.7	
(12)	(21)	(32)	(25)	(10)	(6)	(106)

I. Change in Utility Costs in the Last Six Years (V180)

No Change	Increase < 10%	Increase 10-24%	Increase 25-49%	Increase 50-99%	Increase ≥ 100%	N
17.3	15.4	28.8	20.2	11.5	6.7	
(18)	(16)	(30)	(21)	(12)	(7)	(104)

Notes: a. Absolute numbers are in parentheses.

EXHIBIT B-18

RENT LEVELS AND CASH FLOW FROM BUILDINGS, PITTSBURGH DELINQUENCY SURVEY
(percents)[a]

A. Average Monthly Rent Charged for One-Room Apartment (V254)

<$50	$50-99	$100-199	≥$200	N
0.0	50.0	50.0	0.0	
(0)	(1)	(1)	(0)	(2)

B. Average Monthly Rent Charged for Two-Room Apartment (V255)

<$50	$50-99	$100-199	≥$200	N
0.0	50.0	50.0	0.0	
(0)	(2)	(2)	(0)	(4)

C. Average Monthly Rent Charged for Three-Room Apartment (V256)

<$50	$50-99	$100-199	≥$200	N
41.7	41.7	16.7	0.0	
(5)	(5)	(2)	(0)	(12)

D. Average Monthly Rent Charged for Four-Room Apartment (V257)

<$50	$50-99	$100-199	≥$200	N
20.0	53.3	20.0	6.7	
(3)	(8)	(3)	(1)	(15)

E. Average Monthly Rent Charged for Five-Room Apartment (V258)

<$50	$50-99	$100-199	≥$200	N
7.7	69.2	15.4	7.7	
(1)	(9)	(2)	(1)	(13)

F. Average Monthly Rent Charged for Apartment With Six or More Rooms (V259)

<$50	$50-99	$100-199	≥$200	N
8.0	60.0	20.0	12.0	
(2)	(15)	(5)	(3)	(25)

G. Total Monthly Gross Income From Property (V264)

<$50	$50-99	$100-199	≥$200	N
5.5	47.3	25.5	21.8	
(3)	(26)	(14)	(12)	(55)

EXHIBIT B-18 (continued)

RENT LEVELS AND CASH FLOW FROM BUILDINGS, PITTSBURGH DELINQUENCY SURVEY
(percents)[a]

H. Are Apartments Furnished or Unfurnished? (V266)

All Furnished	All Unfurnished	Mixed	N
10.2	88.1	1.7	
(6)	(52)	(1)	(59)

I. What Utilities Are Included in Rents? (V267) (Up to Five Possible Answers)

Heat	Water	Electricity	Gas	Other	N
9.3	47.7	9.3	12.8	20.9	
(8)	(41)	(8)	(11)	(18)	(86)

J. Change in Gross Rental Income in the Past Six Years (V268)

Increase	Decrease	No Change	N
16.0	32.0	52.0	
(8)	(16)	(26)	(50)

K. Percent Change in Gross Income (V269)

No Change	<100%	≥100%	N
48.6	18.9	32.4	
(18)	(7)	(12)	(37)

M. Summarize the Change in the Level of Cash Flow (V270B)

Increasing	Stable	Decreasing	N
2.3	31.8	65.9	
(1)	(14)	(29)	(44)

N. Summarize the Level and Changes in Gross Income (V270C)

No Income— Vacant or Abandoned	No Income— Tenant Non-Payment	Stable Gross Income	Increase in Gross Income	Decrease in Gross Income	N
10.6	14.9	46.8	4.3	23.4	
(5)	(7)	(22)	(2)	(11)	(47)

O. Summarize the Level and Changes in Gross Costs (V270D)

No Costs— Vacant or Abandoned	Increase in Operating Costs	Increase in Taxes	Increase in Costs in General	N
35.0	10.0	10.0	45.0	
(7)	(2)	(2)	(9)	(20)

Note: a. Absolute numbers are in parentheses.

TENANT CHARACTERISTICS, PITTSBURGH DELINQUENCY SURVEY
(percents)[a]

A. Number of Tenant Households in Structure (V230)

One	Two	Three or More	N
57.6	23.7	18.6	
(34)	(14)	(11)	(59)

B. Number of White Tenant Households in Structure (V231)

None	One	Two or More	N
52.6	29.8	17.5	
(30)	(17)	(10)	(57)

C. Number of Black Tenant Households in Structure (V232)

None	One	Two or More	N
35.8	39.6	24.5	
(19)	(21)	(13)	(53)

D. Percent White of Tenant Households (V234)

0%	1-99%	100%	N
52.6	7.0	40.0	
(30)	(4)	(23)	(57)

E. Percent Black of Tenant Households (V235)

0%	1-99%	100%	N
35.2	7.4	57.4	
(19)	(4)	(31)	(54)

F. Number of Tenant Households Receiving Social Security (V237)

None	One or More	N
82.2	17.8	
(37)	(8)	(45)

G. Number of Tenant Households Receiving Welfare Assistance (V238)

None	One or More	N
58.0	42.0	
(29)	(21)	(50)

H. "Have the Characteristics of Your Tenants Changed in the Last Six Years?" (V239)

Yes	No	N
30.6	69.4	
(15)	(34)	(49)

I. Average Number of Children Per Tenant Household (V247)

None	One to Three	Four or More	N
37.0	42.6	20.4	
(20)	(23)	(11)	(54)

J. Average Length of Tenant Stay (V252)

<One Year	One-Two Years	>Two Years	N
14.3	26.8	58.9	
(8)	(15)	(33)	(56)

K. Change in the Average Length of Tenant Stay (V253)

Longer Average Stay	No Change	Shorter Average Stay	N
23.8	47.6	28.6	
(5)	(10)	(6)	(21)

Note: a. Absolute numbers are in parentheses.

EXHIBIT B-20

OWNERS' PROBLEMS WITH TENANTS,
PITTSBURGH DELINQUENCY SURVEY
(percents)[a]

A. "How Well Do You Get Along With Your Tenants?" (V271)

Very Poorly	Poorly	Neutral	Well	Very Well	No Direct Contact	N
6.6	9.8	9.8	13.1	52.5	8.2	
(4)	(6)	(6)	(8)	(32)	(5)	(61)

B. Important Problems With Tenants? (V272)

Yes	No	N
50.8	49.2	
(32)	(31)	(63)

C. Types of Problems With Tenants (V273)

Non-Payment of Rent	Destruction of Property	Lack of Concern for Upkeep	Lack of Cooperation	Noise and Disruption	Other	N
31.5	21.9	20.5	16.4	5.5	4.1	
(23)	(16)	(15)	(12)	(4)	(3)	(73)

D. Owner's Preference for Age of Tenants (V274B)

Young	Middle-Aged	Old	N
7.7	38.5	53.8	
(2)	(10)	(14)	(26)

E. Owner's Preference for Marital Status of Tenants (V274F)

Married	Single	N
89.5	10.5	
(17)	(2)	(19)

F. Age of Tenants Causing Greatest Problems (V275B)

Young	Middle-Aged	Old	N
46.7	40.0	13.3	
(7)	(6)	(2)	(15)

EXHIBIT B-20 (continued)

OWNERS' PROBLEMS WITH TENANTS,
PITTSBURGH DELINQUENCY SURVEY
(percents)[a]

G. Race of Tenants Causing Greatest Problems (V275C)

White	Black	N
44.4	55.6	
(4)	(5)	(9)

H. Owner Evicted Tenants Recently? (V277)

Yes	No	N
25.4	74.6	
(15)	(44)	(59)

I. Number of Tenants Evicted in the Past Year (V278)

One	More than One	N
75.0	25.0	
(9)	(3)	(12)

J. Reason for Tenant Eviction (V279)

Non-Payment of Rent	Destruction or Neglect of Property	Both Non-Payment and Destruction of Property	Lack of Cooperation	N
50.0	20.0	20.0	10.0	
(5)	(2)	(2)	(1)	(10)

K. Method of Locating Tenants (V280)

Newspaper Advertisements	Real Estate Brokers	Friends	Word of Mouth	Sign on Building	Through the City	N
25.0	25.0	6.3	35.9	4.7	3.1	
(16)	(16)	(4)	(23)	(3)	(2)	(64)

L. Difficulty in Finding Good Tenants Relative to Six Years Ago (V281)

Much More Difficult	Somewhat More Difficult	No Change	Somewhat Easier	Much Easier	N
41.9	16.3	25.6	14.0	2.3	
(18)	(7)	(11)	(6)	(1)	(43)

Note: a. Absolute numbers are in parentheses.

EXHIBIT B-21

VACANCY RATES IN RENTAL UNITS, PITTSBURGH DELINQUENCY SURVEY
(percents)[a]

A. Number of Presently Vacant Apartments in Building (V248)

None	One or More	N
72.5	27.5	
(37)	(14)	(51)

B. Change in Building Vacancy Rate in the Last Six Years (V249)

Much Lower	Lower	No Change	Higher	Much Higher	N
0.0	3.5	71.9	14.0	10.5	
(0)	(2)	(41)	(8)	(6)	(57)

C. Change in the Average Period of Vacancy (V250)

Much Lower	Lower	No Change	Higher	Much Higher	N
2.0	6.0	74.0	6.0	12.0	
(1)	(3)	(37)	(3)	(6)	(50)

D. Length of Vacancy Period for a Typical Apartment (V251)

<14 days	14-30 days	>30 days	N
26.7	26.7	46.7	
(8)	(8)	(14)	(30)

Note: a. Absolute numbers are in parentheses.

EXHIBIT B-22

OWNER'S EVALUATION OF PROPERTY RESALE POTENTIAL
PITTSBURGH DELINQUENCY SURVEY
(percents)[a]

A. "Could a Buyer Get a Mortgage on Your Parcel Today?" (V224)

No	Doubtful	Maybe	Difficult	Easy	N
12.9	12.2	14.4	20.9	39.6	
(18)	(17)	(20)	(29)	(55)	(139)

B. "Would You Have to Take Back a Mortgage in Order to Finance a Sale?" (V225)

Yes	No	N
34.9	65.1	
(51)	(95)	(146)

C. "Would You Be Willing to Take Back a Mortgage?" (V226)

Yes	No	N
29.1	70.9	
(43)	(105)	(148)

D. "Is Financing Easier or Harder to Get in the Neighborhood of the Property Than in the City as a Whole?" (V227)

Much Harder	Harder	Average	Easier	Much Easier	N
9.6	31.5	31.5	24.0	3.4	
(14)	(46)	(46)	(35)	(5)	(146)

E. "Have You Tried to Sell the Property Recently?" (V228)

Yes, Through Broker	Yes, Through Newspaper Advertising	Yes, By Word of Mouth	Yes, By Other Means	No	N
9.0	17.4	4.5	2.6	66.5	
(14)	(27)	(7)	(4)	(103)	(155)

F. "Did You Get Any Offers?" (V229)

Yes	No	N
51.3	48.7	
(20)	(19)	(39)

Note: a. Absolute numbers are in parentheses.

EXHIBIT B-23

OWNER'S EXPECTATION OF PUBLIC ACQUISITION OF PROPERTY, PITTSBURGH DELINQUENCY SURVEY
(percents)[a]

A. Is Property in an Area Scheduled for Public Acquisition? (V146)

No	Yes—Withing One Year	Yes—Within One to Five Years	Yes—Within Five to Ten Years	Yes—Eventually	Not Sure	N
69.9	6.8	2.7	2.1	12.3	6.2	
(102)	(10)	(4)	(3)	(18)	(9)	(146)

B. (If Yes), What Type of Public Programs Will Be Involved (V147)

Construction of Transportation Facilities	Residential Construction	Commercial Construction	N
52.4	42.9	4.8	
(11)	(9)	(1)	(21)

C. Owner Expects Public Acquisition of His Property (V148)

Yes	No	N
17.6	82.4	
(26)	(122)	(148)

D. Time in Which Owner Expects Property to be Acquired (V149)

One Year	Two Years	Three Years	Five Years	Seven Years	Eight Years	N
6.7	6.7	6.7	20.0	6.7	53.3	
(1)	(1)	(1)	(3)	(1)	(8)	(15)

E. Expected Price Relative To Price From Private Sale (V150)

Much Lower	Lower	Same	Higher	Much Higher	N
2.9	21.0	43.5	31.2	1.4	
(4)	(29)	(60)	(43)	(2)	(138)

F. Would Public Taking Pay for the Full Value of Improvements (V151)

Price Would Reflect Entire Cost of Improvements	Price Would Reflect Partial Cost of Improvements	Price Would Not Reflect Cost of Improvements	N
31.5	26.8	41.7	
(40)	(34)	(53)	(127)

G. Effect of the Prospect of Public Taking on Owner's Maintenance Program (V152)

Eliminate Maintenance	Emergency Repairs Only	Cut Maintenance Slightly	No Effect	Increase Maintenance	N
12.5	27.8	6.9	51.4	1.4	
(18)	(40)	(10)	(74)	(2)	(144)

Note: a. Absolute numbers are in parentheses.

EXHIBIT B-24

PROPERTY ASSESSMENT PROCEDURES,
PITTSBURGH DELINQUENCY SURVEY
(percents)[a]

A. "How Does the Assessment of Your Building Compare With Others in Your Neighborhood?"
(V218)

Very High	Somewhat High	About Right	Low	Very Low	N
1.4	11.4	69.3	13.6	4.3	
(2)	(16)	(97)	(19)	(6)	(140)

B. Owners' Complaints About Assessment of Building and Assessment Procedures in General (V219)

No Complaints	Neighborhood Reassessment	Inattention to Individual Structures	Reliance on External Features of Structures	General Assessment Inaccuracy	Miscellaneous	N
62.3	2.3	13.8	1.5	12.3	7.7	
(81)	(3)	(18)	(2)	(16)	(10)	(130)

C. Has Owner Ever Appealed Assessment? (V220)

Yes	No	N
5.3	94.7	
(8)	(143)	(151)

D. Results of Appeal of Assessment (V221)

No Change	Assessment Decreased < 10%	Assessment Decreased > 10%	N
66.7	33.3	0.0	
(6)	(3)	(0)	(9)

Note: a. Absolute numbers are in parentheses.

EXHIBIT B-25

ANNUAL TAX BILLS AND TAX PAYMENT BEHAVIOR, PITTSBURGH DELINQUENCY SURVEY
(percents)[a]

A. Annual Municipal Tax Bill (V290)

< $100	$100-199	≥ $200	N
33.1	37.1	29.8	
(41)	(46)	(37)	(124)

B. Annual School Tax Bill (V291)

< $100	$100-199	≥ $200	N
36.3	40.3	23.4	
(45)	(50)	(29)	(124)

C. Annual Sewer Tax Bill (V292)

< $30	$30-49	≥ $50	N
32.8	35.3	31.9	
(38)	(41)	(37)	(116)

D. Flat or Metered Water Bill (V293)

Flat	Metered	N
12.8	87.2	
(18)	(123)	(141)

E. Annual Water Bill (V294)

< $50	$50-99	≥ $100	N
31.2	38.4	30.4	
(39)	(48)	(38)	(125)

F. Usual Real Estate Tax Payment Date (V295A)

First of the Year	Quarterly	N
45.7	54.3	
(32)	(38)	(70)

G. Usual Timing of Real Estate Tax Payment (V295B)

Before Due	When Due	After Due	No Payment	N
27.4	0.0	53.6	19.0	
(23)	(0)	(45)	(16)	(84)

H. Usual Timing of Sewer Tax Payment (V296)

Before Due	When Due	After Due	No Payment	N
15.9	46.9	26.2	11.0	
(23)	(68)	(38)	(16)	(145)

I. Usual Timing of Water Bill Payment (V297)

Before Due	When Due	After Due	No Payment	N
16.0	46.5	26.4	11.1	
(23)	(67)	(38)	(16)	(144)

Note: a. Absolute numbers are in parentheses.

EXHIBIT B-26

DELINQUENCY BEHAVIOR AND ATTITUDES TOWARD TAX DELINQUENCY, PITTSBURGH DELINQUENCY SURVEY
(percents)[a]

A. Year First Stopped Paying Real Estate Taxes (V298)

Before 1965	1965- 1969	1970- 1972	1973- 1974	Denies Owing Taxes	Asserts Responsibility for Paying Lies Elsewhere	N
2.5	10.7	36.1	31.1	15.6	4.1	
(3)	(13)	(44)	(38)	(19)	(5)	(122)

B. Year First Stopped Paying Sewer Taxes (V299)

Before 1965	1965- 1969	1970- 1972	1973- 1974	Denies Owing Taxes	Asserts Responsibility for Paying Lies Elsewhere	N
4.3	10.6	35.1	26.6	19.1	4.3	
(4)	(10)	(33)	(25)	(18)	(4)	(94)

C. Year First Stopped Paying Water Bills (V300)

Before 1965	1965- 1969	1970- 1972	1973- 1974	Denies Owing Taxes	Asserts Responsibility for Paying Lies Elsewhere	N
4.4	10.9	36.3	24.2	19.8	4.4	
(4)	(10)	(33)	(22)	(18)	(4)	(91)

D. Amount Paid in Last Six Months (V301)

None	Paid Unknown Amount	<$100	$100-249	$250-499	≥$500	N
38.3	5.6	10.3	13.1	18.7	14.0	
(41)	(6)	(11)	(14)	(20)	(15)	(107)

E. Contacted by the City (V302) (Up to Three Possible Answers)

Yes — By Letter	Yes — By Telephone	Yes — Personal Visit	No	N
39.2	4.1	2.7	54.1	
(58)	(6)	(4)	(80)	(148)

F. Year First Contacted by City (V303)

Before 1970	1970	1971	1972	1973	1974	N
2.1	8.3	4.2	22.9	14.6	47.9	
(1)	(4)	(2)	(11)	(7)	(23)	(48)

G. Month and Year of City's Most Recent Contact (V304)

1973	Jan.-Mar. 1974	Apr.-June 1974	July-Sept. 1974	Unspecified Month-1974	N
6.0	34.0	36.0	8.0	16.0	
(3)	(17)	(18)	(4)	(8)	(50)

EXHIBIT B-26 (continued)

DELINQUENCY BEHAVIOR AND ATTITUDES TOWARD TAX DELINQUENCY, PITTSBURGH DELINQUENCY SURVEY
(percents)[a]

H. Is There a Lien on the Property? (V305)

Yes	No	N
30.2	69.8	
(32)	(74)	(106)

J. "Why Did You Initially Miss Your Tax Payments?" (V308)

Billing Inaccuracy	Denies Delinquency	Administrative Problems With Mortgage Holder	Lack of Money: Emergency Personal Expenditure
1.5	3.0	4.5	14.9
(2)	(4)	(6)	(20)

Lack of Money: Chronic Personal Expenditure	Lack of Money: Repairs on Building	Lack of Money: General Lack of Cash Flow from Building	Lack of Money: Tenant . Non-Payment of Rent
6.0	4.5	5.2	2.2
(8)	(6)	(7)	(3)

Lack of Money: General and Unspecified	Property of No Value: No Reason to Pay Taxes	Estate or Guardian Problems	General Conflict with City
20.9	10.4	7.5	2.2
(28)	(14)	(10)	(3)

Habitual Late Payment Related to Potential Interest Income	Bills Now Paid in Full	Misc.	N
3.7	3.0	10.4	
(5)	(4)	(14)	(134)

K. "Is This Still Your Reason (for Non-Payment of Tax Bills)?" (V309)

Yes	No	N
69.7	30.3	
(76)	(33)	(109)

L. "How Have Your Reasons Changed?" (V310)

Administrative Problems with Mortgage Holder	Lack of Money: Emergency Personal Expenditure	Lack of Money: General and Unspecified
3.6	3.6	3.6
(1)	(1)	(1)

Bills Now Paid in Full	Miscellaneous	N
78.6	10.7	
(22)	(3)	(28)

DELINQUENCY BEHAVIOR AND ATTITUDES TOWARD TAX DELINQUENCY, PITTSBURGH DELINQUENCY SURVEY
(percents)[a]

M. "What Are Your Plans Regarding These Tax Bills?" (V311)

Pay in Full	Minimum Payment	No Payment	As Much As Possible Whenever Possible	N
54.0	11.5	17.7	16.8	
(61)	(13)	(20)	(19)	(113)

N. "What Will You Have To Do To Keep Title for One More Year?" (V312)

Pay in Full	Minimum Payment	Nothing	No Desire to Keep Property	N
58.7	12.4	20.7	8.3	
(71)	(15)	(25)	(10)	(121)

O. "What Will You Have To Do To Keep Title for Another Three To Five Years?" (V313)

Pay in Full	Minimum Payment	Nothing	No Desire to Keep Property	N
54.7	14.0	24.4	7.0	
(47)	(12)	(21)	(6)	(86)

P. "What Will You Have To Do To Keep Title for More Than Five Years?" (V314)

Pay in Full	Minimum Payment	Nothing	No Desire to Keep Property	N
57.0	11.6	24.4	7.0	
(49)	(10)	(21)	(6)	(86)

Q. "Do You Think You Will Let the City Take Title to the Building?" (V315)

Yes	No	N
13.1	86.9	
(18)	(119)	(137)

R. "When Would You Expect This To Happen?" (V316)

1974	1975	1976	1977	1978	1980	N
9.1	54.5	9.1	9.1	9.1	9.1	
(1)	(6)	(1)	(1)	(1)	(1)	(11)

S. "Why Would You Let (City Take Title)?" (V317)

Property of No Value	Unwilling to Manage Property	Lack of Cash to Pay Taxes	N
50.0	31.3	18.8	
(8)	(5)	(3)	(16)

T. "What Could The City Do With the Building?" (V318)

Manage as Rental Property	Sell	Demolish and Redevelop	Demolish for Unspecified Purpose	Nothing	N
11.0	48.8	12.2	17.1	11.0	
(9)	(40)	(10)	(14)	(9)	(82)

Note: a. Absolute numbers are in parentheses.

EXHIBIT B-27

OWNERS' EVALUATIONS OF THE CITY'S ROLE IN TAX DELINQUENCY, PITTSBURGH DELINQUENCY SURVEY
(percents)[a]

A. "How Long Does It Usually Take from the Time an Owner Stops Paying Taxes to When the City Takes Title?" (V319)

< One Year	One Year	Two Years	Three Years	Four Years
1.1	5.4	16.1	44.1	12.9
(1)	(5)	(15)	(41)	(12)

	Five Years	Six Years	More Than Six Years	N
	16.1	3.2	1.1	
	(15)	(3)	(1)	(93)

B. "In the Past Six Years Has the City Changed Its Attitude Toward Property Owners Owing Taxes?" (V320)

Much Easier Today	Easier Today	No Change	Tougher Today	Much Tougher Today	N
0.0	5.7	57.1	32.4	4.8	
(0)	(6)	(60)	(34)	(5)	(105)

C. "Has This Had Any Effect on the Payment of Taxes?" (V321)

Yes	No	N
65.3	34.7	
(32)	(17)	(49)

D. "What Could the City Do To Improve Property Values in the Area?" (V322)
(Up to two possible answers per respondent)

	Percent	Number
Improve public education	0.7	(1)
Improve police protection	5.3	(8)
Improve street cleaning	3.9	(6)
Improve street lighting	0.7	(1)
Improve street conditions in general	21.1	(32)
Improve health services	0.7	(1)
Improve mortgage funding	3.3	(5)
Improve public transportation	3.9	(6)
Improve recreation facilities	3.9	(6)
Remove abandoned cars and other refuse	0.7	(1)
Other trash removal	4.6	(7)
Ameliorate problems caused by vacant properties	16.4	(25)
Miscellaneous	17.8	(27)
No improvements needed	2.6	(4)
City can't do anything	14.5	(22)
		(152) = N

EXHIBIT B-27 (continuation)

OWNERS' EVALUATIONS OF THE CITY'S ROLE IN TAX DELINQUENCY, PITTSBURGH DELINQUENCY SURVEY
(percents)[a]

E. "What Can the City Do To Improve the Neighborhood in General?" (V323)
(Up to two possible answers per respondent)

	Percent	*Number*
Improve public education	2.9	(4)
Improve police protection	11.7	(16)
Improve street cleaning	0.7	(1)
Improve street lighting	5.1	(7)
Improve street conditions in general	5.1	(7)
Improve health services	1.5	(2)
Improve mortgage funding	1.5	(2)
Improve public transportation	2.9	(4)
Improve recreation facilities	11.7	(16)
Remove abandoned cars and other refuse	0.7	(1)
Other trash removal	0.7	(1)
Ameliorate problems caused by vacant properties	9.5	(13)
Miscellaneous	23.4	(32)
No improvements needed	5.1	(7)
City can't do anything	17.5	(24)
		(137) = N

F. "What Can the City Do To Make the Tax System More Fair?" (V324)

	Percent	*Number*
City can't do anything	28.8	(30)
More flexible payment requirements	3.8	(4)
More accurate assessments	15.4	(16)
Assistance for older property owners	3.8	(4)
Housing investment tax rebate programs	3.8	(4)
Vary tax rates according to owner's income	4.8	(5)
Miscellaneous	13.5	(14)
No improvements needed	10.6	(11)
Reduce tax rates	15.4	(16)
		(104) = N

G. "What Can the City Do To Persuade Property Owners To Pay Taxes?" (V325)

	Percent	*Number*
City can't do anything	56.8	(46)
Stricter administration	16.0	(13)
Increase property values	0.0	(0)
Make home improvement money available	2.5	(2)
Miscellaneous	14.8	(12)
Provide public services commensurate with tax payments	9.9	(8)
		(81) = N

Note: a. Absolute numbers are in parentheses.